Free Soil in the Atlantic World

This book examines the principle that slaves who crossed particular territorial frontiers – from European medieval cities to the Atlantic nation states of the nineteenth century – achieved their freedom. Based upon legislation and judicial cases, each chapter considers the legal origins of Free Soil and the context in which it was invoked: medieval England, Toulouse and medieval France, early modern France and the Mediterranean, the Netherlands, eighteenth-century Portugal, nineteenth-century Angola, nineteenth-century Spain and Cuba, and the Brazilian–Paraguay borderlands. On the one hand, Free Soil policies were deployed by weaker polities to attract worker-settlers; however, by the eighteenth century, Free Soil was increasingly invoked by European imperial centres to distinguish colonial regimes based in slavery from the privileges and liberties associated with the metropole.

This book was originally published as a special issue of *Slavery & Abolition*.

Sue Peabody is Professor of History at Washington State University Vancouver, USA. Her interests lie in slavery and race in France and its colonies.

Keila Grinberg is an Associate Professor of History at Universidade Federal do Estado do Rio de Janeiro (UNIRIO), Brazil. She is an expert on slavery, gender and the law in Brazil.

Free Soil in the Atlantic World

Edited by
Sue Peabody and Keila Grinberg

Routledge
Taylor & Francis Group
LONDON AND NEW YORK

First published 2015 by Routledge

2 Park Square, Milton Park, Abingdon, Oxon, OX14 4RN
605 Third Avenue, New York, NY 10017

Routledge is an imprint of the Taylor & Francis Group, an informa business

First issued in paperback 2020

British Library Cataloguing in Publication Data
A catalogue record for this book is available from the British Library

ISBN 13: 978-1-138-82122-4 (hbk)
ISBN 13: 978-0-367-73947-8 (pbk)

Typeset in Minion
by RefineCatch Limited, Bungay, Suffolk

Publisher's Note
The publisher accepts responsibility for any inconsistencies that may have arisen during the conversion of this book from journal articles to book chapters, namely the possible inclusion of journal terminology.

Contents

Citation Information vii
Notes on Contributors ix

I: Introduction

1. Free Soil: The Generation and Circulation of an Atlantic Legal Principle 1
Sue Peabody and Keila Grinberg

II: Medieval Europe and Urban Liberties

2. An Alternative Genealogy of the Origins of French Free Soil: Medieval Toulouse 11
Sue Peabody

3. Urban Safe Havens for the Unfree in Medieval England: A Reconsideration 33
Stephen Alsford

III: The Northern Atlantic: New Perspectives on Free Soil

4. Access to the Netherlands of Enslaved and Free Black Africans: Exploring Legal and Social Historical Practices in the Sixteenth–Nineteenth Centuries 47
Dienke Hondius

5. Infidels at the Oar: A Mediterranean Exception to France's Free Soil Principle 67
Gillian Weiss

6. 'Lucky to be born in Pennsylvania': Free Soil, Fugitive Slaves and the Making of Pennsylvania's Anti-Slavery Borderland 83
Richard S. Newman

IV: Iberian Atlantic Iterations of Free Soil

7. Soil Free from Slaves: Slave Law in Late Eighteenth- and Early Nineteenth-Century Portugal 101
Cristina Nogueira Da Silva and Keila Grinberg

8. African Freedom Suits and Portuguese Vassal Status: Legal Mechanisms for Fighting Enslavement in Benguela, Angola, 1800–1830 117
Mariana P. Candido

9. Legislation on Free Soil in Nineteenth-Century Spain: The Case of the Slave Rufino and Its Consequences (1858–1879) 131
Aurelia Martín Casares and Margarita García Barranco

Index 147

Citation Information

The chapters in this book were originally published in *Slavery & Abolition*, volume 32, issue 3 (September 2011). When citing this material, please use the original page numbering for each article, as follows:

I: Introduction

Chapter 1
Free Soil: The Generation and Circulation of an Atlantic Legal Principle
Sue Peabody and Keila Grinberg
Slavery & Abolition, volume 32, issue 3 (September 2011) pp. 331–339

II: Medieval Europe and Urban Liberties

Chapter 2
An Alternative Genealogy of the Origins of French Free Soil: Medieval Toulouse
Sue Peabody
Slavery & Abolition, volume 32, issue 3 (September 2011) pp. 341–362

Chapter 3
Urban Safe Havens for the Unfree in Medieval England: A Reconsideration
Stephen Alsford
Slavery & Abolition, volume 32, issue 3 (September 2011) pp. 363–375

III: The Northern Atlantic: New Perspectives on Free Soil

Chapter 4
Access to the Netherlands of Enslaved and Free Black Africans: Exploring Legal and Social Historical Practices in the Sixteenth–Nineteenth Centuries
Dienke Hondius
Slavery & Abolition, volume 32, issue 3 (September 2011) pp. 377–395

Chapter 5
Infidels at the Oar: A Mediterranean Exception to France's Free Soil Principle
Gillian Weiss
Slavery & Abolition, volume 32, issue 3 (September 2011) pp. 397–412

Chapter 6
'Lucky to be born in Pennsylvania': Free Soil, Fugitive Slaves and the Making of Pennsylvania's Anti-Slavery Borderland
Richard S. Newman
Slavery & Abolition, volume 32, issue 3 (September 2011) pp. 413–430

IV: Iberian Atlantic Iterations of Free Soil

Chapter 7
Soil Free from Slaves: Slave Law in Late Eighteenth- and Early Nineteenth-Century Portugal
Cristina Nogueira Da Silva and Keila Grinberg
Slavery & Abolition, volume 32, issue 3 (September 2011) pp. 431–446

Chapter 8
African Freedom Suits and Portuguese Vassal Status: Legal Mechanisms for Fighting Enslavement in Benguela, Angola, 1800–1830
Mariana P. Candido
Slavery & Abolition, volume 32, issue 3 (September 2011) pp. 447–459

Chapter 9
Legislation on Free Soil in Nineteenth-Century Spain: The Case of the Slave Rufino and Its Consequences (1858–1879)
Aurelia Martín Casares and Margarita García Barranco
Slavery & Abolition, volume 32, issue 3 (September 2011) pp. 461–476

Please direct any queries you may have about the citations to
clsuk.permissions@cengage.com

Notes on Contributors

Stephen Alsford is an independent scholar based in Ottawa, Ontario, Canada.

Margarita García Barranco is in the Department of Social Anthropology at the University of Granada, Spain, and the Centre of Research into International and Atlantic History (CRHIA) at the University of Nantes, France.

Mariana P. Candido is Assistant Professor in the Department of History at the University of Kansas, USA.

Aurelia Martín Casares is Professor of Historic Anthropology at the University of Granada, Spain.

Keila Grinberg is Associate Professor in the Department of History at Universidade Federal do Estado do Rio de Janeiro (UNIRIO), Researcher of the National Council for Scientific and Technological Development (CNPq) and of the Foundation of Research of Rio de Janeiro (FAPERJ), Brazil.

Dienke Hondius is Assistant Professor in the Department of History at VU University Amsterdam, the Netherlands.

Richard S. Newman is Professor in the Department of History at Rochester Institute of Technology, New York, USA.

Cristina Nogueira Da Silva is Assistant Professor in the Faculty of Law at the Universidade Nova de Lisboa and Researcher at Cedis, The Research Center of the Law Faculty, financed by the Portuguese Foundation for Science, Lisbon, Portugal.

Sue Peabody is Professor of History at Washington State University, USA.

Gillian Weiss is Associate Professor in the Department of History at Case Western Reserve University, USA.

INTRODUCTION

Free Soil: The Generation and Circulation of an Atlantic Legal Principle

Sue Peabody and Keila Grinberg

Although each national regime in the Atlantic world developed its own unique legal tradition in regulating slavery and abolition, similar social conditions and the interactions throughout the hemisphere often led to similar legal 'solutions' to the tensions between slavery and freedom.[1] In particular, many societies in Europe, Africa and the Americas confronted the anomaly of enslaved people moving between societies or legal regimes where slavery was permitted by law and societies where slavery was rejected as alien to legal custom and tradition or as a result of the abolition movement. Considerable evidence suggests that local, popular traditions, dating back at least as far as the sixteenth century, freed people in bondage when they crossed particular state borders.[2] We call this custom, sometimes articulated in court decisions or positive legislation by various legislative bodies, the 'free soil principle'.[3]

This free soil principle was exploited by early English abolitionists in the celebrated Somerset case, decided in England in 1772. Somerset's legal team, headed by Granville Sharp, used the contradiction between colonial laws permitting slavery in America and an absence of positive law regulating slavery in England as the 'thin end of the wedge' to argue for a legal presumption that slaves entering England thereby became free.[4] Much ink has been spilled on whether Lord Mansfield's ambiguous legal decision in this case in fact freed all slaves then resident or subsequently arriving in England, but it is clear that the popular consensus held that it did.[5] The Somerset decision also lived on into nineteenth-century United States law, where it was frequently cited as a precedent and the free soil principle debated in northern and southern courts up to and after the infamous Dred Scott decision of 1857.[6]

But the notion that crossing particular territorial boundaries conferred freedom was neither original to English law nor was it limited to the Anglo-American common law tradition. Somerset's legal team drew on examples from earlier French and Dutch legal decisions to argue for a long-lived European free soil tradition.[7] More recently, many historians, beginning with Tannenbaum's celebrated study *Slave and Citizen* (1947), have presumed a fundamental distinction between Mediterranean legal codes, which, following Roman law, sanctioned and regulated slavery, and northern European jurisprudence, which rejected slavery as alien to its legal traditions.[8] Seymour Drescher's work, culminating in his magnificent synthesis, *Abolition: A History of Slavery and Antislavery* (2009), places this tension between slave states and free states, and the 'freedom principle', squarely at the centre of his narrative of the emergence and triumph of the Atlantic anti-slavery movement.[9]

However, the historical trajectory of the free soil principle was neither consistent nor always uniformly progressive in its effects. Contingent upon historical actors, free soil was formulated, advanced, contested and manipulated in specific and varied historical contexts. In the seventeenth and eighteenth centuries, free soil was often coupled with baptism as a prerequisite for formal or informal manumission. While the French *Code Noir* of 1685, requiring the Catholic baptism of *all* slaves held in French territory, effectively decoupled this linkage under French law, Equiano's narrative makes it clear that a popular tradition linking baptism and free soil persisted in England into the mid eighteenth century. And, while free soil was often asserted by serfs, slaves and municipal authorities, who sought to attain or maintain free status in many juridical contexts, the free soil principle was also resisted and undermined by masters and states, who found its liberating potential unsettling. In the early eighteenth century, for example, in both France and England, free soil was, at least temporarily, rejected in the informal Yorke–Talbot opinion of 1729 and the French royal ordinance of 1738 due to the influence of colonial interests in these respective states. Consequently, during the 1740s and 1750s, free soil was essentially suspended in France and England as a point of law. Only the Parlement of Paris's persistent challenges to royal 'despotism' and the nascent English anti-slavery movement, skilfully organised by Granville Sharp, would resurrect free soil in these jurisdictions for the late eighteenth and nineteenth centuries.[10]

Moreover, the willingness of certain monarchies – the French in 1716, 1738 and 1836, the Portuguese in 1761 and the Spanish in 1836 – to issue free soil legislation at key moments was due less to their enthusiasm for anti-slavery than to either an effort to distinguish metropolitan (European) legal spaces from those of the colonies or to concessions to their political opponents or allies.[11] In any event, due to the relatively few slaves permitted to travel to the United Kingdom or Europe, the recognition of the metropole as free soil never had the same radical liberational potential in Europe as in the Americas, where large numbers of enslaved people could demand their freedom through migration and legal decisions. In the Americas, slaves 'voted with their feet' by travelling to the free soil of Canada, Mexico, Haiti, Uruguay, Argentina and US border states (for example, Pennsylvania, Ohio, New York); the ratification of free soil in key court decisions further stimulated voluntary migration by slaves and free people of colour seeking state-affirmed free status.[12]

In this issue, we are presenting new perspectives on the judicial principle of free soil, from the Middle Ages to the mid nineteenth century. Together with other recent studies, we believe that it is possible to see how the principle of free soil – insisted upon by people resisting their bondage; recognised but also contested by masters and judicial and state powers to assert jurisdiction, authority and autonomy – contributed to state-building in a wide range of settings. The studies presented here are far from comprehensive, but many are suggestive of avenues for further research.

Medieval origins of the English 'free air' tradition are critically re-evaluated by Stephen Alsford in his essay, 'Urban Safe Havens for the Unfree in Medieval England: A Reconsideration'. The term 'free air', often touted in its German formulation, *Stadtluft macht frei* ('City air makes free'), was coined by nineteenth-century medievalists and subsequently popularised by sociologist Max Weber in his posthumously published study, *The City* (1958).[13] Alsford argues that the principle that residency for a year and a day in a medieval city released unfree people from bondage, far from being universal in England, was specific to particular urban settings. The heyday for English free air was the twelfth and early thirteenth centuries, and its presence may have been imported in imitation of Norman municipal charters, but it seems to have been in decline by the late thirteenth and early fourteenth centuries. Other recent studies of medieval 'free air' charters throughout Europe affirm Alsford's emphasis on its particular, local and temporary nature in a variety of urban settings.[14]

Sue Peabody's essay offers an 'alternative genealogy' for the origins of France's free soil principle, celebrated in French legal tracts since the late sixteenth century and the basis of hundreds of successful freedom suits in Paris. Eighteenth- and nineteenth-century French lawyers traced the free soil maxim back to a proclamation by the fourteenth-century King Louis X, but Peabody argues that the tradition actually originated outside of France in the independent city of Toulouse. There, it was initially rejected by the French monarchy, but finally accepted in the late fourteenth century during ongoing disputes over fugitive slaves fleeing from Catalonia. As such, free soil contributed to early French imperial and state-building processes as well as nationalist mythology.

In her forthcoming book, Gillian Weiss analyses the plight of Frenchmen held captive in North Africa before enslavement became synonymous with racialised blackness.[15] Here, she challenges the supposedly universal principle of free soil in early modern France by chronicling the fate of Muslim captives in the sixteenth and seventeenth centuries. French authorities had few qualms about the presence of so-called 'Turkish' slaves on French soil or condemned to galley service until the late seventeenth century, when the free soil principle invoked by black slaves from the Atlantic world began to be questioned with regard to the *turcs*.

Dienke Hondius examines the evidence for a Dutch free soil tradition from the sixteenth to the late eighteenth centuries, when a 1776 law explicitly recanted the principle of free soil for slaves entering the Netherlands. Hondius finds black people to be an important presence in the Netherlands throughout the early modern era, but emphasises that general emancipation came rather late to Dutch society, enacted in 1863 but with restrictions that were not lifted until a decade later.

The Iberian world experimented with free soil as well. Some historians date the earliest free soil urban charters to northern Spain in the ninth and tenth centuries, whence they supposedly passed through southern France (1107) and into Flanders, England and Germany (in the twelfth and thirteenth centuries).[16] Later, the Spanish Crown offered freedom to fugitive slaves to entice them to populate its frontier circum-Caribbean colonies in the eighteenth century.[17] Until recently, however, little scholarship has connected the 1761 Portuguese declaration of metropolitan free soil with wider Atlantic developments. Here, Cristina Nogueira da Silva and Keila Grinberg analyse the prime minister's provision declaring that all black slaves arriving in Portugal be free and subsequent developments regarding slaves' claims for freedom in Portugal and Brazil through the nineteenth century. They argue that, although the goal of the 1761 declaration was to deter the entrance of slaves with their masters into the kingdom of Portugal, many slaves arriving in Lisbon from Brazil and other areas of the Portuguese Empire successfully won their freedoms in the courts on the basis of this law.

In Portuguese West Africa, free people of colour, who had been participating as colonists of the Portuguese Empire for centuries, increasingly found themselves vulnerable to illegal enslavement in the early nineteenth century. Mariana Candido examines one such case and the arguments for freedom advanced by victims of enslavement in the Benguela highlands of Angola. Here, the principle of free soil is less significant than the traditional notion of vassalage, which was supported by claims to religious and linguistic ties to the Portuguese Empire.

In the nineteenth century, lawsuits and discussions involving free soil became more connected with the ending of slavery in the Americas, the state-building process and the debate over the control of freedmen in the recently independent states. Argentina, Uruguay and Peru offered freedom to Brazilian slaves who crossed their borders. At the same time, slaves won their freedom in Brazilian courts, alleging that, after crossing a border to a free country, they became citizens.[18]

The evolving situation of free soil in the United States was exceedingly complex, as each state produced its own legislation, which was further interpreted by its courts at multiple levels, and impacted by successive developments of federal legislation and Supreme Court rulings. In this issue, Richard Newman emphasises the agency of free blacks in advancing Pennsylvania as free soil in the early nineteenth century. This 'borderlands' state became the site of many critical legal contests over the status of African Americans who entered the state in the company of their putative masters or independently as fugitives, as well as those who had resided there free all their lives, only to be kidnapped for sale to masters in the South. Newman shows how the activism of African Americans in Pennsylvania produced a popular tradition of free soil, even while the courts began to retrench their support.

The self-liberation of the Haitian Revolution posed challenges to free soil doctrine throughout the Atlantic world. Would the emancipation of slaves in Saint-Domingue (1793) and the rest of the French Empire (1794) establish French colonies and the sovereign nation of Haiti as sites of free soil? Appeals courts in the United States recognised French and Haitian free soil only unevenly.[19] Emerging scholarship suggests that Alexandre Pétion, president of the southern Republic of Haiti, deliberately provoked both English and French governments to recognise Haiti as free soil, challenging these European nations to confront their respective limitations in imagining the sovereignty of a free black nation state.[20]

By the late 1820s and 1830s, pro-slavery forces in the Atlantic world rallied to challenge the free soil principle. The English Admiralty Court ruled that slaves who became free upon their arrival in England would lose that status if they returned voluntarily to jurisdictions that sanctioned slavery.[21] In Louisiana and Missouri, heirs to the French legal tradition, courts tended to uphold the principle of free soil until 1846, when Louisiana explicitly negated free soil by legislation, and 1850, when Missouri courts threw out 30 years of free soil precedents.[22] During these same decades, US lawyers and judges advanced the countervailing principle of comity – 'the courtesy or consideration that one jurisdiction gives by enforcing the laws of another, granted out of respect and deference rather than obligation' – as the price that free states must pay to retain southern slave states in the Union.[23]

After France abolished slavery throughout its empire in 1848, questions emerged regarding its colonies in Senegal and Algeria: could African slaves avail themselves of French free soil in these colonies? French administrators apparently feared the diplomatic consequences with African allies, especially Muslims whose legal tradition sanctioned slavery, and sought to minimise the recognition of free soil arguments there.[24]

In 1858, one year after the United States Supreme Court rejected free soil and erected a racial bar to citizenship in the Dred Scott decision, Queen Isabella was called upon to review Spain's 1836 free soil policy as it applied to a young boy, who had been brought to Spain but then sold again to masters in Puerto Rico and Cuba. In this issue, Aurelia Martín Casares and Margarita García Barranco examine the historical context of the case and the arguments offered for and against the boy's freedom, as well as the practical implementation of Spanish free soil.

In conclusion, we can see that the popular free soil principle was successively articulated in a variety of forms – as a vernacular custom; as positive law; as the implicit basis for judicial decisions – by a range of institutions and agents: the slaves themselves, lawyer activists, royal and republican legislators, and judges. Medieval urban charters and liberties sometimes offered freedom to residents, but this was by no means universal in all cities or uniform in its conditions. The transition from urban liberty to a national principle of free soil seems to have occurred along the French border with Spain in the fifteenth century and to have been consolidated in legal writings for France, England and the Netherlands in the late sixteenth century. By the late seventeenth century, as these nations embarked on colonial empires and staked a place in the transatlantic slave trade, the free soil tradition ran up against the potential profits to be seized.

In the eighteenth century, the Spanish Crown revived the idea of free soil for its original medieval purposes – as a means of enticing immigrants to settle the frontiers of its empire, thereby weakening its rivals. At the same time, northern Europeans started to back-pedal from their commitment to the free soil tradition, as anti-black racial policies sought to exclude people of African descent from the metropole. In 1774, one French colonial administrator proposed that all abandoned children born of biracial unions in the metropole be relocated to the South American colony of Guyane in order to create a more stable colonial population.[25] Eventually, eighteenth-century free soil legislation was accompanied by efforts to establish racial exclusion in the Netherlands (1776) and France (1777).

There is no doubt that the 1772 Somerset decision breathed new life into the free soil principle and inspired anti-slavery activists for decades to come – and, as these essays demonstrate, not only in the Anglo-American legal tradition. However, the limitations of free soil for anti-slavery activists eventually became apparent. Free soil law could only free those slaves who entered a jurisdiction that recognised the principle – usually a tiny minority of those held in slave colonies, states or nations. Freedom so established would not necessarily follow a former slave who sought return to friends and family still held in societies regulated by slave law. Within free soil jurisdictions, an immigration of pro-slavery citizens could easily overturn the free soil tradition by new legislation, as, for example, in Illinois.[26] Instead, the struggle to abolish slavery and extend the benefits of freedom to all would require not only general abolitionist legislation, but also constant challenges to the inequality of coercive labour regimes, often couched in racial terms. Vigilance, activism and prosecution – in courts of law and in daily life – continue the liberationist struggle into our own day.

Notes

[1] Sue Peabody and Keila Grinberg, eds., *Slavery, Freedom and the Law in the Atlantic World* (New York: St. Martin's Press, 2008); Josep M. Fradera, 'L'Esclavage et la logique constitutionnelle des empires', *Annales: Histoire, Sciences Sociales* 63, no. 3 (2008): 533–560.

[2] 'As for slaves and bondmen, we have none; naie, such is the privilege of our countrie by the especiall grace of God, and bountie of our princes, that if anie come hither from other realms, so soone as they set foot on land they become so free of condition as their masters, whereby all note of servile bondage is utterlie removed from them, wherein we resemble (not the Germans, who had slaves also, though such as in respect of the slaves of other countries might well be reputed free, but the old Indians and the Taprobanes, who supposed it a great injury to Nature to make or suffer them to be bond, whom she in hir wonted course doth product and bring forth free).' Raphael Holinshed, *The first and second volumes of Chronicles ... now newlie augmented and continued (with manifold matters of singular note and worthie memorie) to the yeare 1586* (London: Henry Denham, 1587), bk. 2, chap. 5, 163, Early English Books Online, ebbo.chadwyck.com (accessed 26 May 2010).

[3] Interestingly, the terms 'free soil' and 'free air' do not appear generally before the nineteenth century, though evidence of persistent legal traditions freeing slaves who cross territorial borders, previously studied as the 'freedom principle' by Sue Peabody and Seymour Drescher,

can be found. Seymour Drescher, *Abolition: A History of Slavery and Antislavery* (Cambridge: Cambridge University Press, 2009), ix–x, 23–24, 28, 35, 66–67, 93–97, 100–105, 134, 238, 398. For an earlier survey of the free soil principle, see also Sue Peabody, 'Slavery, Freedom, Statehood and the Law in the Atlantic World, 1700–1888', in *Democracy and Culture in the Transatlantic World: Third Interdisciplinary Conference, October 2004, The Maastricht Center for Transatlantic Studies, Maastricht, The Netherlands* (Växjö, Sweden: Växjö University, 2005). We offer the term 'free soil' in lieu of the more generic term 'freedom principle', but it should not be confused with the short-lived US antebellum political party by the same name. See Eric Foner, *Free Soil, Free Labor, Free Men: The Ideology of the Republican Party before the Civil War*, new ed. (New York: Oxford University Press, 1995), 81ff.

[4] For the most recent historiography on the Somerset case, see George Van Cleve, *A Slaveholders' Union: Slavery, Politics and the Constitution in the Early American Republic* (Chicago: University of Chicago Press, 2010), chap. 1; Justin Buckley Dyer, 'After the Revolution: Somerset and the Antislavery Tradition in Anglo-American Constitutional Development', *Journal of Politics* 71, no. 4 (2009): 1422–1434; 'Forum: *Somerset's Case* Revisited', *Law and History Review* 24, no. 3 (2006): 601–672, including: George Van Cleve, '*Somerset's Case* and Its Antecedents in Imperial Perspective'; Daniel J. Hulsebosch, 'Nothing but Liberty: *Somerset's Case* and the British Empire'; Ruth Paley, 'Imperial Politics and English Law: The Many Contexts of *Somerset*'; and George Van Cleve, 'Mansfield's Decision: Toward Human Freedom'. Our analysis here differs from Van Cleve's approach by considering the free soil tradition not only as a product of formal jurisprudence, but as the intersection of popular common traditions with more formal statist iterations.

[5] Drescher, *Abolition*, 101–104.

[6] The prominent pro-slavery Georgia jurist Thomas R.R. Cobb devoted several chapters of his 1858 *magnum opus* to the legal status of 'slaves escaping or carried into other states', thereby refuting the validity of free soil in US law in the wake of the 1857 US Supreme Court Dred Scott decision, in *An Inquiry into the Law of Negro Slavery in the United States of America* (Athens: University of Georgia Press, 1999), 117–225. The antebellum rejection of free soil was a major influence in the development of the principle of comity in US law. See Paul Finkelman, *An Imperfect Union: Slavery, Federalism, and Comity* (Chapel Hill: University of North Carolina Press, 1981); Edlie L. Wong, *Neither Fugitive nor Free: Atlantic Slavery, Freedom Suits, and the Legal Culture of Travel* (New York: New York University Press, 2009).

[7] The citations in the early nineteenth-century summary of the Somerset case are an invaluable point of entrée into continental free soil traditions: 'The Case of James Sommersett, a Negro, on a Habeas Corpus, King's Bench: 12 George III, A.D. 1771–72', in *A Complete Collection of State Trials*, vol. 20, *1771–1777*, by Thomas Bayly Howell (London: T.C. Hansard, 1814), columns 23–82.

[8] Frank Tannenbaum, *Slave and Citizen* (1947; Boston: Beacon Press, 1992). Charles Verlinden distinguishes between the Mediterranean cultures' proximity to Muslim slavery versus northern Europe's relative isolation from the Islamic world in *Esclavage dans l'Europe médiévale*, 2 vols. (Bruges: De Tempel, 1955–1977), 1: 18. Alan Watson also contrasts northern Europe's lack of a slave law tradition with that of the Roman world in *Slave Law in the Americas* (Athens: University of Georgia Press, 1989).

[9] Drescher, *Abolition*, 1, 23–24, 28, 35, 66–67, 93–96, 97, 100, 101–102, 104, 105, 134, 238, 398.

[10] Travis Glasson, '"Baptism doth not bestow Freedom": Missionary Anglicanism, Slavery, and the Yorke-Talbot Opinion, 1701–1730', *William and Mary Quarterly* 67, no. 2 (2010): 279–318; Olaudah Equiano, *The Interesting Narrative of the Life of Olaudah Equiano, or Gustavus Vassa, The African, Written by Himself: Authoritative Text, Contexts, Criticism*, ed. Werner Sollors, vol. 1 (New York: Norton, 2001), chaps. 4–5, 67–72; Sue Peabody, *'There Are No Slaves in France': The Political Culture of Race and Slavery in the Ancien Régime* (New York: Oxford University Press, 1996), 37–56.

[11] On the French decrees of 1716 and 1738, see Peabody, '*There Are No Slaves*'; for 1836, see Sue Peabody, 'Furcy, la question raciale et le "sol libre de France": une micro-histoire', *Annales: Histoire, Sciences Sociales* 6 (2009): 1305–1334. On the Portuguese proclamation of 1761, see Nogueira da Silva and Grinberg in this issue. On the Spanish court decisions, see Aurelia Martín Casares and Margarita García Barranco in this issue.

[12] Donald V. Macdougall, 'Habeas Corpus, Extradition and a Fugitive Slave in Canada', *Slavery & Abolition* 7, no. 2 (1986): 118–128; David M. Turley, '"Free Air" and Fugitive Slaves: British Abolitionists versus Government over American Fugitives, 1834–61', in *Anti-Slavery, Religion and Reform: Essays in Memory of Roger Anstey*, ed. Christine Bolt and Seymour Drescher (Folkestone: Dawson, 1980), 163–172; Robin W. Winks, *The Blacks in Canada: A History* (Montreal: McGill-Queen's University Press, 1997), 142–177; Sean Kelley, '"Mexico in His Head": Slavery and the Texas–Mexico Border, 1810–1860', *Journal of Social History* 37, no. 3 (2004): 709–723. On Uruguay, see Joseph P. Younger, '"Naturals of This Republic": Slave Law, Sovereignty and the Legal Politics of Citizenship in the Río de la Plata Borderlands, 1845–1864', *Law and History Review* 29 (forthcoming); Keila Grinberg and Rachel da Silveira Caé, 'Slavery, Frontier and Diplomatic Relations: Brazil–Uruguay, 1840–1860', in *The Politics of Second Slavery: Conflict and Crisis on the Nineteenth-Century Atlantic Slave Frontier*, ed. Dale Tomich, Rafael Marquese and Ricardo Salles (Albany: State University of New York Press, forthcoming). On Pennsylvania, see Richard Newman in this issue and Kirsten Sword, 'Remembering Dinah Nevil: Strategic Deceptions in Eighteenth-Century Antislavery', *Journal of American History* 97, no. 2 (2010): 315–343; Keith P. Griffler, *Frontline of Freedom: African Americans and the Forging of the Underground Railroad in the Ohio Valley* (Lexington: University Press of Kentucky, 2004); Stephen Middleton, 'Cincinnati and the Fight for the Law of Freedom in Ohio, 1830–1856', *Locus* 4, no. 1 (1991): 59–73; Thomas J. Davis, 'Napoleon v. Lemmon: Antebellum Black New Yorkers, Antislavery, and Law', *Afro-Americans in New York Life and History* 33, no. 1 (2009): 27–46.

[13] Max Weber, *The City*, trans. and ed. Don Martindale and Gertrud Neuwirth (Glencoe, IL: Free Press, 1958), 94.

[14] Ernst Werner, *Stadtluft macht frei: Früscholstik und bürgerliche Emanzipation in der ersten Hälfte des 12. Jahrhunderts*, Sitzungsberichte der Sächsischen Akademir der Wissenshaftern zu Leipzig, Philiologisch-Historische Klasse, vol. 118, bk. 5 (Berlin: Akademie-Verlag, 1976); Bern von Hans Strahm, 'Stadtluft macht frei', in 'Das Problem der Freiiheit in der Deutschen und Schweizerischen Geschichte', special issue, *Vorträge und Forschungen* 2 (1981): 103–121.

[15] Gillian Weiss, *Back from Barbary: Mediterranean Slavery and the Rise of France* (Stanford: Stanford University Press, forthcoming).

[16] David Nicholas, *The Growth of the Medieval City: From Late Antiquity to the Early Fourteenth Century* (London: Longman, 1997), 157.

[17] Linda M. Rupert, 'Marronage, Manumission and Maritime Trade in the Early Modern Caribbean', *Slavery & Abolition* 30, no. 3 (2009): 361–382; Jane Landers, 'Spanish Sanctuary: Fugitives in Florida, 1687–1790', *Florida Historical Quarterly* 62, no. 3 (1984): 296–313.

[18] Keila Grinberg, 'Slavery, Manumission and the Law in Nineteenth-Century Brazil: Reflections on the Law of 1831 and the "Principle of Liberty" on the Southern Frontier of the Brazilian Empire', in 'Slavery, Citizenship and the State in Classical Antiquity and the Modern Americas', special issue, *European Review of History/Revue Européenne d'Histoire* 16, *no.* 3 (2009): 401–411.

[19] Sue Peabody, '"Free upon Higher Ground": Saint-Domingue Slaves' Suits for Freedom in US Courts, 1792–1830', in *The World of the Haitian Revolution*, ed. David Patrick Geggus and Norman Fiering (Bloomington: Indiana University Press, 2009), 261–283.

[20] Ada Ferrer, 'Between Kings and Constitutions: Haiti and Free Soil in the Revolutionary Atlantic' (unpublished manuscript).

[21] David Brion Davis, *The Problem of Slavery in the Age of Revolution, 1770–1823* (New York: Oxford University Press, 1999), 499–500.

[22] Nevertheless, the New Orleans District Court continued to uphold the freedom of slaves who had travelled to free territory, especially France, prior to 1846. Judith Kelleher Shaeffer, *Becoming and Remaining Free: Manumission and Enslavement in New Orleans* (Baton Rouge: Louisiana State University Press, 2003), 16; Dennis K. Boman, 'The Dred Scott Case Reconsidered: The Legal and Political Context in Missouri', *American Journal of Legal History* 44, no. 4 (2000): 405–428.

[23] Finkelman, *Imperfect Union*, 4.

[24] Martin Klein, *Slavery and Colonial Rule in French West Africa* (Cambridge: Cambridge University Press, 1998), 28–29; Lawrence C. Jennings, *French Anti-Slavery: The Movement for the Abolition of Slavery in France, 1802–1848* (Cambridge: Cambridge University Press, 2000), 254–256.

[25] Alexandre Ferdinand de Bessner, Governor of Guyane, 'Mémoire sommaire sur la Colonie de Cayenne et la Guyane François', 1774, Centre des Archives d'Outremer, Aix-en-Provence, C14/42/192, cited in Barbara Traver, 'Populating El Dorado: The French Enlightenment and Colonization Schemes for Guyane' (PhD diss., Washington State University, forthcoming).

[26] James Simeone, *Democracy and Slavery in Frontier Illinois: The Bottomland Republic* (DeKalb: Northern Illinois University Press, 2000), 8.

An Alternative Genealogy of the Origins of French Free Soil: Medieval Toulouse

Sue Peabody

Since the fifteenth century, French lawyers and magistrates have upheld the principle that 'no one is a slave in France' [nul n'est esclave en France], extending freedom to many slaves who set foot on French soil. This article examines the medieval antecedents for France's Freedom Principle, arguing that Louis X's oft-cited 1315 ordinance did not free all slaves in France and was not the primary source of the French free soil tradition. Rather, municipal officers of the independent medieval domain of Toulouse were strong advocates of slaves' claims to freedom there by virtue of the city's liberties. In the late fourteenth and fifteenth centuries, as Toulouse entered the royal domain, this principle was first resisted, but ultimately adopted, by French judicial officers until its foreign roots were erased from legal memory.

In the eighteenth and nineteenth centuries, slaves from Africa, India and the Americas mounted hundreds of lawsuits for freedom in France, especially the judicial courts of Paris, on the grounds that: 'All persons in this kingdom are free; and as soon as a slave has set foot here, upon being baptised, [he] is freed.'[1] Lawyers representing these slaves traced the royal origins of this French legal maxim to four primary historical sources: (1) a historical tradition crediting the demise of ancient Roman slavery to the arrival of Christianity and the pious practice of freeing slaves, especially by testament; (2) a medieval ordinance by Louis X (1314–1316) equating the kingdom of France with the condition of freedom and authorising the freeing of serfs by 'good and suitable conditions'; (3) a sixteenth-century rivalry between the kings of France and Spain, which took the form of specific public manumissions of Spanish slaves; and (4) several legal decisions by late medieval and early modern Parlements (or sovereign high courts of appeal), the earliest being a decision before the *capitouls* of Toulouse in 1402.[2] For eighteenth-century lawyers, it was important to locate the origins of the French free soil tradition in royal sovereignty, since by early modern constitutional thinking, the king was the ultimate source of legitimate law; by the nineteenth century, some of this authority had been assumed by the French 'nation'.[3] But, in either case, the origins of French free soil were presumed to emerge from *within* the French kingdom.

In this essay, I explore some forgotten external origins to France's free soil tradition to argue that, when French kings first encountered the idea in thirteenth-century Toulouse, they summarily rejected the city's free soil principle. However, after Toulouse came into the royal domain, its municipal leaders resurrected and persistently defended the centuries-old free soil tradition, thereby ultimately prompting royal jurists to embrace free soil as indigenous to French law when the Toulouse tradition proved useful in ongoing rivalries between France and Aragon. The foreign origins of this free soil tradition would be fully erased in legal tracts of the late sixteenth and early seventeenth centuries, and free soil became 'French', thus setting the stage for seventeenth- and eighteenth-century freedom suits by slaves as France embarked upon its new Atlantic colonial ventures, increasingly dependent upon slave labour.

The historical search for 'origins', and, indeed, the continuity of a legal principle more generally, is always problematic, especially over a period of centuries. They presume a coherent object to be studied and its persistence through time. By tracing a legal tradition over the *longue durée*, we inevitably run into inconsistencies and mutations, reflective of wider changes in social relations and language. In the end, the reified object of study is not the same as the original because the extended historical and social conditions have also changed.

What follows in this essay is an alternative 'genealogy' of the French tradition of free soil. In some ways, it suffers from some of the same weaknesses as the lawyers' reconstructions of the principle's French origins – that is, it draws from evidence collected at disparate moments, arising from specific disputes, and from these constructs a linear narrative that may be spurious. Nevertheless, as genealogists tend to favour the more prominent lineages when reconstructing family origins, so too, I think, did eighteenth-century lawyers ignore the collateral origins of French free soil. This essay, as a kind of exercise in historical re-imagining, considers an alternative source for French free soil in the medieval municipal law of Toulouse as well as shedding light on the construction and centralisation of the French monarchy from competing medieval jurisdictions and polities.[4]

Medieval Toulouse

The earliest legal decision (as opposed to statute or historical incident) cited by eighteenth-century lawyers seeking to reconstruct France's historical tradition of free soil is a decision rendered in Toulouse in 1402.[5] Eighteenth-century lawyers drew their knowledge of Toulouse's 1402 case from the seventeenth-century published account by Germain de La Faille, who was king's advocate to the *siège présidial* (a legal court) of Castelnaudary from 1638 until 1655, when he was selected as syndic of Toulouse.[6] However, modern historians confirm documentation of the case from the Catalan point of view.[7] La Faille's summary of the case is fairly minimal:

> Four slaves escaped from Perpignan and took refuge in Toulouse. Their masters, having followed them to recover them, made [a] plea before the *capitouls* that they be returned to them. The syndic of this city intervened in this instance, holding that by a privilege of this city, any sort of slave was free as soon as he had set foot in the outskirts [*banlieu*] or wider jurisdiction of the city [*gardiage*].[8]

On the basis of Toulouse's free soil principle, the *capitouls* judged in favour of the slaves' freedom. Then, four years later, according to La Faille:

> in 1406, a similar case arose, but which drew more attention. A female slave, age twenty, and of an extraordinary beauty, also escaped from Perpignan; and taking refuge in this city, put herself under the protection of the *capitouls*. Her mistress, who complained that she had been stolen, sent a man to this city for the purpose of recovering her. This envoy, having requested her from the *capitouls* several times, finally requested from them a public certificate [*acte*] and, with great protestations, that they deliver her to him. The *capitouls* responded to him through an assessor [*assesseur*] that they had to be careful to do nothing against the privilege of this city; that the theft of this girl of which they were accused was nothing but a vain pretext; but that when this had occurred [before], there had never been a case when they had to return a slave seeking refuge in this city. This envoy was therefore constrained to return home, without having been able to accomplish anything.

But the affair did not end there, because the governor of Roussillon for (in the name of?) the king of Aragon wrote to the *capitouls* a long letter in an overt manner, by which, after having tried to refute this privilege, he asked them for this slave, mixing threats with pleas. He also wrote of it in the same way to the count of Foix, then governor of Languedoc. As all of these efforts met with failure for the Catalans, they turned to make an offer of 50,000 gold florins to this city to renounce the privilege in question – but this offer was rejected.[9]

The 1402 and 1406 cases discussed by La Faille brought Toulouse's free soil principle into conflict with slaveholders of Perpignan, a pattern that would continue well into the fifteenth century. In order to understand the basis of the *capitouls*' 1402 decision, it is necessary to backtrack to the earliest recorded legal decisions by that city's courts and, utilising the expertise of medieval historians, deconstruct the earliest formulations of Toulouse's free soil principle.

Toulouse, former seat of the Visigoth kingdom (409–508 CE) and the Carolingian realm of Aquitaine (768–877 CE), experienced a dramatic expansion from about 1050 through the 1100s.[10] Historians differ in their characterisations of the relationship between the count and the people of Toulouse during this time of growth. Philippe Wolff attributes the strong municipal liberties exacted by the city of Toulouse from their count over this period to their resistance against multiple invasions from the Aquitaine to the north and Catalonia to the south.[11] By contrast, John Hine Mundy characterises the relationship of count and subjects as 'tenuous' and weakening over the course of the twelfth century.[12] Instead, Mundy emphasises the rapid growth of Toulouse's patrician class in the early 1100s, whose wealth was based on the ownership of land and who created an 'egalitarian' ethos where the distinction between knight and burgher was blurred, as in the Italian city states.[13]

The truth probably lies somewhere in between. Situated beyond the direct authority of both the French and Catalonian kingdoms, the city of Toulouse and its surrounding territory, the Toulousain, were under the direct rule of the count of Toulouse from the tenth through the late thirteenth centuries. However, when Count Raymond IV absented Toulouse to join the First Crusade to the Holy Land in 1098, and again in 1114, neighbouring Duke Guillaume IX of Aquitaine seized the opportunity to enforce the collection of a grain tax upon the people of Toulouse. Guillaume IX's hold on Toulouse was brief; in 1118, he took his army to Spain. Toulouse rose up against Guillaume's rule and forcibly supported the return of Count Raymond's heir, Alphonse-Jourdain. Guillaume's successors, Henry II and the indomitable Eleanor of Aquitaine, would try unsuccessfully to subdue Toulouse again in 1159, 1162 and 1164. However, the French King Louis VII successfully drove them off during the first attack and the count and citizens of Toulouse held their own in the two latter invasions. In 1179 and 1181, Alphonse II of Aragon attacked from the south, but was successfully repelled by Raymond V, the new count of Toulouse.[14] From 1182 until 1194, the English–Aquitaine enemy from the north sought to reimpose its authority on Toulouse.[15] Clearly, the nearly constant state of battle against would-be invaders forged the residents of Toulouse into warrior-citizens, merging the identities of knight and burgher. Their successes empowered them to demand special privileges or liberties from the count during the twelfth century.

Sometime in the midst of this turbulent period, before 1141, Count Alphonse-Jourdain set aside a portion of the city of Toulouse as a protected area, known as a *salvetat*, along the banks of the Garonne river. The boundaries of Toulouse's *salvetat* were demarcated with crosses. Persons residing within this area received legal and military protection as well as special privileges, such as trading rights and exemption from tolls. The aim of the *salvetat* was to attract new settlers. A second *salvetat*, known as the *gardiage*, was established sometime between 1189 and 1195.[16]

The emergence of Toulouse's consular court is one example of the concessions wrested by citizens from their count. Prior to 1189, civil suits could be tried in any of a number of ecclesiastical, seigniorial or mediatory courts.[17] In 1189, the city revolted against the count, ultimately extracting many new kinds of political authority for their leaders. For example, the consuls won the right to legislate independently of the count and to judge crimes such as murder, destruction of property, brawling and sedition (precisely those crimes likely to have been committed during the uprising). The consular court judged its first known case in 1193. By 1226, the consuls of Toulouse had extended their power to judge crimes committed outside the city walls. By the mid thirteenth century, they held a practical monopoly of judicial authority, eclipsing both the count and the vicarial tribunal, though no constitutional document spelled out that right.[18]

From 1202 until 1204, the city of Toulouse summoned its growing powers and waged war on nobles and villages in the Toulousain. Toulouse defeated the town of Verfeil, some 20 kilometres east of Toulouse across the Girou river, forcing Aton Izarn, a member of its lordly family, to sign a peace treaty in June 1203.[19]

The following year, Aton and his brother Arnaud became petitioners in the first known judicial case to explicitly invoke Toulouse's customary tradition of free soil.[20] This 1203 case merits special attention because numerous historians cite it as the first known example of Toulouse's protection of residents against claims of ownership by foreign masters. The judges' decision in favour of the freedom of two bondsmen contains the first surviving explicit formulation of the free soil principle as applied to Toulouse. Even so, to modern eyes, the protective free soil of Toulouse looks quite different from the national principle of free soil invoked centuries later by French lawyers.

The free soil of Toulouse: a case study (1203)

In the spring of 1203, Arnaud Izarn stood before the 24 consuls of Toulouse to reclaim two serfs, Pierre and his brother, Guillaume.[21] We may presume that Arnaud's lordly status was conveyed in fine dress and haughty manner. Pierre likely presented a more humble manner; a tanner of deer hides (*cervunerius*), he was probably dressed like an artisan or peasant and spoke more roughly. While Arnaud sought to establish his family's proprietorship over the two men, Pierre and Guillaume argued for their free status as residents of Toulouse. All parties involved – the masters, the putative serfs and the magistrates – acknowledged a long-standing tradition of Toulouse that freed serfs from their foreign seigneurs and prohibited the alienation of citizens of Toulouse through sale: 'such is the custom in the city of Toulouse that anyone from Toulouse cannot buy any person living in Toulouse nor acquire [such a person] in any way from anyone outside of Toulouse'.[22]

As this is the first documented articulation of the notion of something like free soil in Toulouse, it is worth spending a moment to examine its essential features. This principle essentially prohibits citizens of Toulouse from becoming masters or owners of other citizens of Toulouse through market exchange. It does not sever the feudal relationship between citizens of Toulouse and their count (who does not need to purchase citizens or their descendents to acquire dominion over them). Nor does it liberate serfs or slaves belonging to current residents of Toulouse. However, by prohibiting the sale of residents to foreign masters, it protects residents of any status from being sold by their current masters to a foreign lord. Anyone moving to the city would be protected from seizure by a resident of Toulouse (though it is not clear that it would protect a foreign lord from coming to claim his bondsman before the municipal court).

How did this principle, thus articulated, apply to the case of Arnaud and Aton versus Pierre and Guillaume? According to Arnaud, now a resident of Toulouse for at least a year, he and his brother, Aton Izarn, had purchased the two men and their father, Pierre Jean, from their former masters in Verfeil sometime in the distant past. According to Arnaud, Pierre and Guillaume, 'by their own request . . . agreement and choice, and . . . by their own free will and without any force occurring, had approved of and granted the ownership [*dominium*] and homage [*hominium*] and their fidelity' to the Izarn brothers.[23]

Pierre and Guillaume countered that they had never approved or granted the *dominium* or *hominium*, or promised their fidelity to Arnaud or his brother. Indeed, although they seemed to accept that 'acquisition or purchase' from their former masters had occurred, they insisted that 'they had not been present at it nor approved of it'. Even if such a transaction had occurred, they insisted, it should not be considered valid because Pierre and Guillaume were 'from the city of Toulouse', in that they had

> stayed and remained [*stabant et steterant*] in the city of Toulouse for twenty years or so, and, when they were able to, had performed the military duty and followed the customs and paid taxes [*fecerant exercitus huius ville et consuedtudines et husus*], of that city just like other inhabitants of Toulouse, according to their position and ability, in good faith.[24]

Arnaud countered that Pierre and Guillaume were lying. The two men had done none of the duties towards the city that they claimed – in fact, 'they were from Verfeil and ... spent the summer there and came and went as they pleased until they learned of their subjection [*domination*]' to the Izarn brothers. Furthermore, when the sale took place, Arnaud was not 'of Toulouse', and hence had not 'given to the commons ... done military service ... or the other duties [*husus*] of Toulouse', though since that time he had 'acquired homes and other honours [in the city] ... and had placed himself before the magistrates of Toulouse'. Hence, the Izarn claims to Pierre and Guillaume preceded his residency in Toulouse, and thus were legitimate. Now, however, Arnaud claimed to be a citizen (and hence able to seek justice from the consuls). In order to support his current status of being 'of Toulouse', Arnaud produced 'an authentic document, done in the hand of the public clerk [*tabellio*]' to that effect.[25]

Pierre and Guillaume replied that they did not believe that Arnaud was not 'of Toulouse' when he acquired them, but that in any case, regardless of his residency status, the 'acquisition' should not be allowed to stand because they, themselves, were residents. At the end of this initial hearing, the magistrates called for a trial so that each side could produce witnesses to support their respective claims.

Before we proceed to the trial and judgment, it is worth pausing to examine the issues at stake. First, there is the fuzzy status of the 'serfs'. Ambiguities abound. Though Pierre and Guillaume were both sons of the same father, Pierre Jean, they somehow came under the dominion of two separate masters, Pierre Saquetus and Furnerius.[26] How did two brothers come to be subordinate to different masters and what had become of the father? Second, all parties seem to accept without question the legal capacity of the original masters to alienate Pierre and Guillaume through sale: 'Arnaud ... and Aton ... had acquired and *purchased* [*emerant*] ... Pierre Jean and his ... sons' (my emphasis). To modern ears, the buying and selling of men sounds like chattel slavery, not serfdom. The relationship of ownership is also implied in the expression *dominium*. Yet, the remaining characteristics of their bondage, the 'homage' (*hominium*) and 'fidelity' (*fidelitatum*), and the insistence on the men's capacity to accept or reject this relationship, clearly indicate something other than chattel slavery – a form of fealty. Both master and serf (if we want to use this term) had to agree that the relationship was fundamentally consensual (though fidelity, once promised, implicitly may not be broken). Finally, there is the question of whether the status of serf was inherited. Arnaud insisted that the father, Pierre Jean, had been transferred together with his sons, which suggests that the father's servile status was passed directly to his children. No one raised the question of whether the father had agreed to the 'purchase' of his family or mentioned his present whereabouts; perhaps he had died in the time since the initial sale, or perhaps he was loyally serving his master – whoever that was – in Verfeil.

The ambiguity of Pierre and Guillaume's servile status is consistent with historians' characterisation of medieval feudal law, where local customs ruled and varied tremendously. According to Susan Reynolds, 'the boundary between free and unfree, *liberi* and *servi*, shifted according to the economic and legal context in which the words were used'.[27] As one thirteenth-century legal scholar put it: 'Diverse are the duties owed to different seigneurs, according to the peculiarity of servile conditions or locales ... Therefore, should you have to deal with such things in some country, first ask those who know its customs'.[28] Although Pierre and Guillaume were clearly 'local boys' of the greater Toulouse region (as opposed to slaves imported from the wider world beyond), the physical proximity of Toulouse to Mediterranean slave-trading routes meant that slaves transported via long-distance trade were probably not unknown in thirteenth-century Toulouse. But the words for 'slave' and 'serf' had not yet differentiated in Latin or French.[29] In the documentation for this case, the nouns 'slave' and 'serf' (*servus* and *servii*) do not appear at all, though the verb *servire* ('to serve' or 'to be the slave of') describes Pierre and Guillaume's putative relationship to the Izarn brothers.[30] We can deduce that this relationship of 'service' consisted of the mutually agreed-upon terms. The obligation to serve was understood to be freely accepted by the serf/slave, and consisting of 'proprietorship' (*dominium*), 'homage' (*hominium*) and 'fidelity' (*fidelitatum*). Based upon more general studies of French serfdom, we must assume that *hominium* included an economic duty to pay taxes, such as the annual head tax (*chevage*), a tax on marriage outside the domain (*formariage*) and an inheritance tax (*mainmorte*).[31]

As Pierre and Guillaume's trial proceeded, the consuls followed typical judicial procedure of the time, acting as both prosecutors and magistrates, gathering evidence, questioning witnesses and deliberating on the judgment. No one seems to have questioned the general capacity of a master to buy or sell his 'serfs' under local law (indeed, as framed in the custom, such transactions were anticipated and considered normal), or the fact of the sale itself; instead the consuls quickly focused on the question of what we might call citizenship. The case boiled down to two questions: (1) whether the masters, Arnaud and Aton Izarn, were 'of Toulouse', and (2) whether the putative serfs, Pierre and Guillaume, were 'of Toulouse'.

As the question of municipal citizenship is the critical one for the judges, it is worth examining how it was understood by the people involved. First, the word 'citizen' does not appear in the original documentation. The literal translation from the original Latin is 'being of (or "from") Toulouse'. No prior written customary law survives from this period that would categorically define municipal citizenship of Toulouse. However, once again, all parties in the lawsuit agree on the general factors that constitute citizenship, even if they dispute whether the specific parties enjoyed that status. To be 'of Toulouse', a man must 'stay and remain' (*stabant et steterant*) in the city for an unspecified period of time; perform the military duty; 'follow the customs and pay taxes' (*fecerant exercitus huius ville et consuedtudines et husus*). There is no requirement that the citizen be born in the city.

It is interesting that Toulouse's custom did not specify a term of residency, such as the 'year and a day' commonly required in so many medieval cities.[32] The policy seems to have been a more liberal one, perhaps born out of the need to attract able bodies to a city that was so often under attack by foreign enemies. Arnaud tried to undermine Pierre and Guillaume's claims to citizenship by arguing that they spent the summers in Verfeil, 'coming and going as they pleased', as though year-round residency should be a requirement of citizenship.

For Arnaud, being 'of Toulouse' meant owning property there. He had 'acquired homes and other honours' there.[33] Arnaud took pains to insist that when he and his brother purchased Pierre and Guillaume from their former masters, neither master was 'of Toulouse'; he had not 'given to the commons ... done military service ... or the other duties [*husus*] of Toulouse'. But, Arnaud insisted, 'he had placed himself before the magistrates of Toulouse in order that they should recognise him as being of Toulouse, which they had done', as authorised in the 'authentic document'.[34]

On 4 April 1203, the consuls of Toulouse ruled in favour of Pierre and Guillaume on the basis of the many witnesses who could testify to their citizenship, while 'Arnaud proved nothing with witnesses from the city'. The magistrates proclaimed Pierre and Guillaume 'free from ... Arnaud for all time', so that no one 'could make any petition based on *hominium* or *dominium* against [them] ... their progeny, born or yet-to-be born' on the basis of the original sales by Pierre Saquetus and Furnius.[35] Essentially, the citizenship status of the masters, Arnaud and Aton, was irrelevant. Pierre and Guillaume had fulfilled the requirements of Toulousain citizenship prior to the transaction between the former owners and the new claimants, supplying witnesses to that effect, and therefore would not belong to the Izarn brothers.[36]

The careful reader will have noticed the limited scope of Toulouse's customary law and the consequent narrow impact of the consuls' 1203 decision: Pierre and Guillaume, freed from all claims by the Izarn brothers (on the basis of the putative sale), were nevertheless not entirely free men. They belonged to Pierre Saquetus and Furnerius. However, since Pierre and Guillaume were now officially 'of Toulouse', any claims that their owners might have to their homage and customary taxes would presumably need to be claimed and enforced within the tribunal of the masters' jurisdiction. Unfortunately, we have no knowledge of whether any subsequent litigation occurred (though the fact that a copy of the original documentation was transcribed and witnessed in Toulouse in 1237 suggests that the matter was still relevant to a future generation).

The French Crown and Toulouse's free soil

Toulouse's free soil principle evolved over the thirteenth century in direct opposition to the French Crown. Through most of the first 50 years, the kings of France waged war, directly or indirectly, with Toulouse under the mantle of the Albigensian Crusade against the Cathar heresy. On 10 May 1226, the recently excommunicated Count Raymond VII of Toulouse, facing an invasion by French forces, presided over an assembly of the 24 consuls of Toulouse and at least 30 signing witnesses in the beautiful brick and stone Basilica of Saint-Sernin du Taur in the city centre. The purpose of the ceremony was to authorise a dramatic expansion of the *salvetat*, or protected area of Toulouse. At the assembly, the consuls reminded the count of an ancient tradition, whereby 'any person established in this territory may not be claimed by foreign seigneurs but neither the men of the count, nor the citizens and burghers of Toulouse have the right to invoke this privilege against their masters'.[37]

In functional terms, this law would serve the count well, loosening the bonds of serfs belonging to his regional rivals while inducing them to come to live in and fight to protect his realm. The count gave his permission to the consuls to expand this territory of asylum to encompass the existing administrative boundaries around Toulouse by about a league, with a maximum radius of about eight miles from the centre of the city.[38]

In the following years, the citizens of Toulouse took pains to set their municipal archives in order and to assure the preservation of their *droits, privileges et franchises* ('rights, privileges and freedoms'). In 1227, they established four public notaries charged with maintaining the registers of the judicial decisions of the consular court. Over time, however, this produced an unmanageable and contradictory body of common law decisions (which were eventually discarded and are no longer extant). Meanwhile, several men intimately involved in the daily practice of municipal law took it upon themselves to compile their own personal collections of court decisions.[39]

By the 1229 Treaty of Meaux (also called the Treaty of Paris), Count Raymond VII was forced to do penance in Paris for having protected the Cathars from the Inquisition, and to offer his daughter, Jeanne of Toulouse, in marriage to Alphonse of Poitiers, brother of King Louis IX of France. The marriage took place in 1237 (coincidentally, the same year that the 1203 case was transcribed). This was the beginning of Toulouse's submission to the French Crown. Raymond VII eventually died in 1249 without a male heir and the county of Toulouse passed to Alphonse and Jeanne. Alphonse ruled from Paris, but took an exceptionally detailed interest in the governance of his southern realms.

Under Alphonse's rule, the municipal leaders of Toulouse expressed their desire to see the *coutumes de Toulouse*, or customary law of Toulouse, written down in 1268 – a request to which their count agreed (though any documents resulting directly from this act have since been lost). In 1270, Alphonse and Jeanne, still childless, accompanied Louis IX upon his ill-fated 1270 crusade to Tunis; husband and wife died within days of each other during their return in 1271. As a result of their death, the county of Toulouse passed directly into the royal domain.[40]

In 1273, Alphonse's nephew, King Philippe III (1245–1285), agreed in principle to accept Toulouse's liberties and customs. According to the foremost expert on the customs of Toulouse, Henri Gilles, a written collection must have existed in 1275, though it is no longer extant. In the summer of 1283, the city consuls presented Philippe III with a comprehensive list of 160 *coutumes* when he passed through the city.[41] Included among the liberties put forward by the consuls of Toulouse was the right of asylum articulated in the consular court decision of 1203 and affirmed by Count Raymond VII in 1226 (subsequently enumerated as Article 155b). The 1283 articulation of Toulouse's free soil principle reads:

> [I]t is the use and custom of Toulouse that men [*hominess*] coming to Toulouse to take up residence, and living there no matter where they're from, although they may have lords [*dominos*], they can and ought to be able to remain free from their lords and to carry out their business [*facęre negotia sua*, probably meaning 'trade'] without petition and the impediment or contradiction of their lords. The said lords shall not nor ought not to force in any matter [*fortiare*] those men so living in Toulouse or in the suburbs [*barriis*, i.e. along or near the city walls], by the lord's reason or whim.[42]

Like the consuls' 1203 articulation of the free soil of Toulouse, the 1283 version does not use the words 'slave' or 'serf'. However, the freedoms specified in the two articulations are rather different. In 1203, residents of Toulouse could not be 'bought or acquired'. The liberty specified in the customary law of 1283 is more expansive: men of Toulouse may operate in contradiction to the will of their former lord. Nor is there the exemption for subjects of the count of Toulouse spelled out in the 1226 expansion of the boundaries of the *salvetat* (perhaps because the title of count of Toulouse had been absorbed by the king). Article 155b of the customs of Toulouse, by virtue of its generality, is the most extensive articulation of the freedom of Toulouse yet.

Philippe III reviewed the consuls' 160 articles and consented to the majority, but objected to 20 of them, including Article 155b. However, in accordance with the king's wishes, two copies of the *coutumes* were made – one for the Chateau-Narbonnais, the seat of the royal *sénéchausée* (the royal administrative jurisdiction); the other for the consuls. In making their copy, the consuls retained the 20 provisions struck down by the king, though marking them as rejected. Soon after reviewing the customs of Toulouse, Philippe died during a campaign on 12 October 1285 and was succeeded by Philippe IV ('the Fair').[43]

Philippe III did not offer a rationale for rejecting the 20 problematic articles. Perhaps he anticipated that the provision might promote conflict with other lords within his kingdom by authorising subjects' flight and claims to freedom in Toulouse, or with foreign monarchs, such as the kings of Aragon or Catalonia. Certainly, Toulousain free soil as articulated in 1283 created a vague and potentially limitless challenge to seigneurial authority, on which feudalism depended.

Whatever the rationale, especially for the future of the idea of free soil, Philippe III's rejection of Article 155b makes it clear that the principle of free soil was not, at least as articulated in the customary law of Toulouse, a core element of the law of the French kingdom in 1283. That is, if Philippe III considered the French kingdom as free soil, freeing all residents from enslavement or subjection to foreign lords, it seems unlikely that he would have objected to its articulation as one of the customary laws of Toulouse.

Borderland conflicts: France and Aragon

Beginning in the late thirteenth through to the fourteenth century, medieval cities in northern Europe experienced a series of crises, leading to a decline in populations, increased immigration and, in many cases, more restrictive citizenship policies. First, the European climate began to worsen in the late 1200s, prompting a series of famines and disease, including the catastrophic crisis of 1315–1316 (in which perhaps 10 per cent of the population of northern Europe perished), followed by the Hundred Years War (1337–1453) and the bubonic plague of 1347–1349, with subsequent outbreaks in 1357–1358, 1361–1363, 1373–1374, 1382–1383 and 1400. While the demographic and economic crises facing European cities stimulated massive migration to cities, many cities' beleaguered survivors seem to have resisted the full integration of newcomers by increasing the requirements for citizenship status, such as charging entry fees, requiring master status or guild membership in a given trade, prolonged residency requirements or marriage to a daughter of a citizen.

It is in this context that Louis X's royal letters patent of 3 July 1315 – cited, but rarely quoted accurately or completely by eighteenth- and nineteenth-century lawyers as evidence of France's free soil principle – must be situated. Philip IV's son had only recently ascended to the throne and many French cities had formed leagues to protest against increased royal taxation to fund the French war against Flanders as well as royal administrative control.[44] According to the carefully annotated 1723 critical edition of the *Ordonnances des roys de France*, Louis Le Hutin's emancipation decree reads:

> As, according to the law of nature, everyone must be born free [*franc*]. And by usages or customs, which since ancient times have been introduced and kept here in our Kingdom, and by circumstance for the crime [*mesfaits*?] of their ancestors, many of the persons of our common people, have ended up in the bonds of servitude and diverse conditions, which greatly displeases us. We, considering that our Kingdom is called and named the Kingdom of the Francs, and wishing that the thing be in truth in accordance with its name, have ordained and do ordain, that throughout our kingdom, as much as it can belong to us and our successors, such servitudes will be restored to freedoms, and to those who, by origin or antiquity, or newly by marriage, or by residence in places of serf condition, have ended up or might end up in the bondage of servitude, freedom will be given at good and suitable conditions.[45]

The decree goes on to exempt common people who have been subject to specific forms of serfdom (*formariage* and *mainmorte*) from harassment by 'Collectors, Sergeants and other Officials' and exhorts other lords to follow the royal example. As I have noted elsewhere, Louis X's declaration is clearly aimed at serfs, rather than slaves, and it provides for emancipation to be granted *at good and suitable conditions*, which might permit seigneurs to demand emancipation fees.[46] However, we might consider whether Louis was not using general emancipation in much the same way as later political and military leaders would – to attract the loyalty of subalterns away from rival leaders during a time of revolt or political instability.

By the late fourteenth and fifteenth centuries, the notion that 'town air makes free' was rarely admitted by most European cities, and serfs were actively discouraged from moving there. Yet local conditions prompted some exceptions. Bordeaux, Ghent and Reims had more lenient policies, encouraging immigration. The lingering impact of climatic change and disease on European cities meant that many saw decline in their population in the fifteenth century. In France, Toulouse had the lowest replacement rate of heirs per deceased person – a 1:1 ratio – due to high infant mortality rates.[47] Perhaps this demographic crisis kept alive the tradition of freedom for immigrants to Toulouse.

In 1373, a Greek slave, Anthony Soldani, fled from his master in Perpignan to Toulouse.[48] Perpignan, a city near the Mediterranean coast and former capital of the kingdom of Majorca, had been successively claimed by the kings of France and Aragon since the mid thirteenth century.[49] Slavery does not appear there in positive law or notarial records of the eleventh or twelfth centuries; however, following the Majorcan conquest of the region in 1229, several notarial records mention slaves. By the mid fourteenth century, slaves are a common feature in Perpignan.[50] When French royal officers attempted to confiscate the escaped Greek slave in 1373, Toulouse's municipal leaders, the *capitouls*, challenged the Crown for having violated Toulouse's free soil privilege (Article 155b). As a result of their challenge, Louis d'Anjou, the lieutenant of the French king for Languedoc, reaffirmed the free soil principle of Toulouse.[51] Toulouse's free soil principle, formerly rejected by Philippe III, was now accepted by French royal policy as a valid custom of Toulouse.

Toulouse's willingness to uphold the free soil tradition, now backed by French royal authority, stimulated many slaves to attempt a similar escape from Perpignan in the principality of Catalonia, within the kingdom of Aragon, in the first half of the fifteenth century. At this time, the flourishing Catalonia region of north-eastern Spain held a significant slave population of about 4400 slaves in a general population of about 50,000 (9 per cent).[52] The problem of fugitive slaves became a matter of serious concern for officials. In 1413, the General Deputation of Catalonia issued provisions to regulate slaves and to curb their escape.[53] Based upon a treaty of extradition between Aragon and France, the seneschal of Carcassonne was required to appoint an officer to send the town crier twice a year, at the expense of the Catalonia Generality, to announce that anyone holding escaped slaves from Catalonia or who knew where they were hidden, must capture and transport them to royal authorities in the region, who would repay them 10 Aragon florins for their troubles. The seneschal would send a similar message to the Catalonian governor of Roussillon and the local authorities in Perpignan.[54]

Perhaps hearing of the success of previous fugitives achieving freedom in Toulouse, more slaves from Perpignan travelled the route to Toulouse, rising some 1300 metres over about 200 kilometres (approximately 130 miles) and passing over limestone hills at the base of the Pyrenees. Keeping the snow-capped peaks to the left, a fugitive slave would pass through valleys and gorges, forests, meadows and pastures, perhaps skirting villages and stealing from orchards, or begging for food along the way.[55] The vast majority of the slaves escaping from Catalonia were of Moorish origin, though some were Turks, Bulgarians and Russians.[56] Some disguised themselves as pilgrims, travelling to the holy sites of the region, to escape along the roads.[57]

As we have seen, in 1402 and 1406, the *capitouls* of Toulouse successfully resolved Catalonian attempts to recover several slaves escaping from Perpignan. In the succeeding decades, a new judicial court, the Parlement of Toulouse, emerged. Documentation of the earliest years must be scant; the foremost historian of its first century, André Viala, speaks only generally of the 'diverse vicissitudes' and weak royal administration that caused it to be established.[58] As only the second 'Parlement' or sovereign tribunal in France, the Parlement of Toulouse undertook its first business in 1420 and acted as the court of appeal for the region of Languedoc.[59]

Soon after the new court was established, the flood of slaves escaping from Perpignan to Toulouse drew the ire of the king of Aragon. In 1427, he sent a messenger to the Parlement of Toulouse with letters patent from the governor of Roussillon and Cerdagne, who demanded compensation for a white female slave and prisoner (*serva et captiva*) and for other fugitive slaves in general. The Parlement of Toulouse summoned the judge of Béziers (midway between Carcassonne and Montpellier), who had arrested the escaped slave. After learning from the Aragonese envoy that the fugitive slaves would be severely beaten upon return, the Parlement consulted the bishop of Agde, who recommended that the slaves be returned to their masters. Finally, on 30 April 1427, the Parlement of Toulouse decided that the slave should be returned to the Aragonese authorities. Perhaps the Parlement of Toulouse did not invoke its free soil principle because the slave in question had not reached the *salvetat* of Toulouse itself.[60]

During the trial, the *procureur du roi* ('royal prosecutor') had raised some interesting new arguments. In opposing the Aragonese claim to the slaves, he asserted that they achieved their freedom as soon as they left their masters. Only *after* becoming free had they entered the French kingdom, where they were subsequently captured. Had they escaped by sea, 'which was something in common', then the Catalans would have legal claim to them. But the fact that they travelled overland meant that they were free before entering French territory and the French were under no obligation to return them. Consequently, according to the king's attorney, 'the slaves in question belonged to the king of France'.[61]

The king's attorney's arguments and the Parlement of Toulouse's decision make it clear that free soil was not envisaged in 1427 as a French (national or royal) prerogative. Not only was the free soil argument not advanced by the *procureur du roi* in this case (nowhere does he claim that the slaves are free by setting foot on French soil), his assertion of royal ownership makes it clear that nothing prevented the king or others from owning slaves in France.[62] The following year, 1428, the Parlement of Toulouse was united with that of Poitiers, only to be re-established as a commission in 1437.[63]

During treaty negotiations between France and Aragon, the Spanish king's emissaries complained vociferously against Toulouse's free soil privilege.[64] In 1437, the French King Charles VII agreed to the establishment of a commission in Montpellier that would review contested claims regarding escaped slaves between Aragonese subjects and the city of Toulouse.[65] This is further evidence that the free soil privilege was seen as peculiar to Toulouse, rather than a privilege of the French kingdom in the early fifteenth century.

A key development in the transformation of Toulouse's municipal tradition of free soil to a national principle of the French kingdom occurred in the 1440s. On 28 September 1440, Jean Solacii, the syndic of the *capitouls* of Toulouse, came before the Montpellier commission. As in 1373, 1402 and 1406, the *capitouls* were accused of harbouring fugitive slaves. Solacii gave an eloquent defence of Toulouse's free soil principle:

> ceded to the city by its counts, then confirmed by the kings and ... enjoyed ... since then by the effect of an ancient custom, whose origins were lost in time, [the free soil principle] is one of the most beautiful titles of the glorious *cité*. If [Toulouse] had not used it, her tribulations, in particular the English wars, would have depopulated her much more. [The city] is reproached for claiming and appropriating the fugitives' belongings, but this is a pure lie; it prohibits her residents from doing them any harm. Who would doubt that liberty is naturally favourable and desirable for every living being? For one who reasons correctly, servitude was introduced in effect by violence and fear, contrary to the first natural law.[66]

Solacii's 1440 speech is striking for its invocation of natural law ('liberty is naturally favourable and desirable for every living being') and the insistence that slavery is effected by violence and coercion. More importantly, for our concern, Solacii deliberately sought to link Toulouse's free soil principle to the beneficence of the French Crown:

> The king of France is called 'glorious and very Christian'; he is venerated even amongst the infidels and the barbarians, his fame resides in the freedom of all the inhabitants of his kingdom. Also, to hold that the monarch cannot concede the privilege under discussion is to contradict the royal majesty; it is an injury, for the vengeance of which all his faithful subjects must stand up, arm themselves of the laws and of the law.[67]

In this way, Solacii explicitly linked the privilege of Toulouse for the first time with the protection of the French kingdom. In addition to defending Toulouse's free soil privilege, Solacii challenged the authority of the Montpellier commission to regulate the actions of the *capitouls* and demanded a removal of the case to the Parlement of Paris.[68]

Finding against the *capitouls*' petition for removal, the commissioners deferred their judgment until September 1441, ultimately rejecting the Toulousain privilege on 24 January 1442.[69] Later in the summer of that year, on 30 July 1442, the commissioners concluded an accord between France and Aragon, which was ratified by Charles VII in September.[70]

In 1443, the king re-established the Parlement of Toulouse as a sovereign court, over the vociferous protestations of the Parlement of Paris, and it met for the first time on 4 June 1444.[71] It is confusing that, given the evident jockeying for sovereignty and judicial independence, the Toulouse *capitouls* pursued their appeal of the Montpellier's commission to the Parlement of Paris in September of the same year. Nevertheless, the Paris *procureur du roi* supported the Toulousain privilege. On 19 September, the Parlement of Paris declared the Aragonese commissioners 'in default' (*défaillant*). In 1445, the Parlement of Paris agreed to register the 1442 accord between France and Aragon, but rejected the part concerning the slaves, which violated the free soil privilege of Toulouse.[72]

Soon, another city in south-western France claimed the same privilege. In 1446, a 'black' slave (also characterised by the nineteenth-century historian who summarised the case as a 'Moor') named Antoine Simon, fleeing his master in Barcelona, was arrested and imprisoned in the chateau of Pamiers.[73] Antoine based his claim to freedom on 'the liberties accorded by the Abbé Maurin', articulated in the city of Pamiers' 1228 charter. Merchants testifying on Antoine's behalf cited several precedents of Greek slaves rendered free by the town's liberties. One syndic, arguing for Antoine's freedom, asserted that 'slaves could live in Pamiers *francs et libres*, and that as soon as the holy baptism had delivered him from servitude ... he was [a] good Catholic', and that he had been seized 'despite the privileges of the city, according to which no resident could be troubled, bought or sold by any temporal or ecclesiastical lord'. The Pamiers appeals court, contrary to demands by the governor of Catalonia and the queen of Aragon, recognised Antoine's freedom and declared him a 'new citizen' of Pamiers.[74] Several years later, in 1451, a Tartar slave fled his Catalonian master by crossing the Pyrenees via Andorra, arriving safely in Toulouse, where he was declared free.[75]

By the late fifteenth century, the kingdom of France was cited as the source of an enduring freedom among would-be fugitive slaves in Valencia. In 1462, a Valencian attorney appointed an agent to seek and recover two fugitive black slaves who had tried, unsuccessfully, to reach France's free soil and were now apparently headed in the direction of Castile, whence they would try to achieve freedom by sea (presumably the Atlantic). The lawyer accused one of the slaves of leading a fugitive slave conspiracy. Another late fifteenth-century case concerned a slave who reached France via Navarre, then returned to his wife or mistress in Valencia, with the expectation that the free status achieved in France would follow him back home. In 1495, another black slave testified that other slaves had persuaded him to escape with them to France, where 'four days later they would all be free'; they too apparently believed that his free status was permanent and would allow him to return to Valencia.[76]

Sixteenth-century French adoption of the free soil tradition

The French free soil tradition was further consolidated in the second half of the sixteenth century, shaped defensively as a contrast to the centralising and expanding Hapsburg Empire, and especially the Spanish and Portuguese conquests in America, which established and accelerated the transatlantic slave trade. Spanish and Portuguese theologians wrestled with the morality of enslaving Indians and Africans, thereby helping to establish distinctive legal and social categories as the foundations of modern race.[77] According to one historian, it was France's persistent support of the liberating power of its soil that prompted the Spanish Hapsburg Emperor Charles V to prohibit the exportation of slaves from his territories to France under penalty of a lifetime sentence to the galleys in 1553.[78] But it was not only the Iberians who trafficked in slavery. In 1571, the Parlement of Guyenne in Bordeaux underscored the free soil principle as a national tenet, freeing a shipment of slaves proffered there by a Norman merchant on the grounds that 'France, the mother of liberty, does not permit any slaves'.[79]

In 1576, the most prominent early modern French political theorist, Jean Bodin, cited the free soil principle as a fundamental law of the French nation, though he hints at important ties to the customs of Toulouse, where he studied law. In the first edition of his *Les Six Livres de la République*, Bodin cites two instances when the Parlement of Toulouse opposed the serfdom and the enslavement of people who had taken residence in their city. The first concerned a 1558 decision regarding the:

> Lord of Rocheblanche in Gascony, [who] claimed to have not only the right of mortmain over his subjects, but also that they were held to care for his vineyards, to work his lands, reap his meadows, cut and winnow his wheat, build his house, pay his ransom, and the customary seigneurial tax [*taille és quatre cas*] in this Kingdom, as well as being able to bring them back with a halter [*cheuestre*] if they left his land without his consent.

According to Bodin, the Parlement of Toulouse denied Rocheblanche's claim to be able to seize serfs who left his land without permission as 'contrary to the law of liberty'. Secondly, Bodin recalled that when he was a law student in Toulouse, from around 1550 until about 1555, he had witnessed a similar decision by the municipal court of Toulouse:

> I remember being in Toulouse that a Genoese passing there was constrained to free a slave that he had purchased in Spain, seeing that the *Capitouls* wanted to declare him free [*franc et libre*] as much by the general custom of the kingdom as by the special privilege the Emperor Theodosius the Great had given them, as they said, that any slave setting foot in Toulouse was free [*franc*].

Bodin clearly respected Toulouse's free soil tradition, but rejected its supposed Roman origins as a myth:

> [Such] a thing ... is nevertheless not plausible, as Narbonne, true colony of the Romans, and the most ancient that was in France, Lectore, Nysmes, Vienne, Lyon, Arles, Romans and several others, which were also colonies, nor Rome itself, which was the seat of the empire, had this privilege.

Rather, Bodin articulated the free soil principle in specifically *national* terms: '[E]ven the slave of a foreigner is free [*franc et libre*] as soon as he sets foot in France'.[80] He warned that Spanish and Portuguese expansion of slavery and the slave trade threatened to erode a tacit line erected between European countries that eschewed slavery and the world beyond Europe.[81] Clearly, Bodin was an important source of the characterisation of the local Toulouse tradition as a national principle of France.

By the time that Antoine Loisel published his *Institutes coutumières*, a generation later in 1608, the principle of French free soil had been adopted as the third fundamental maxim of French law regulating persons, following only: 'Titre 1: Qui veut le Roy, si veut la loy' ('As the King wishes, so wishes the law') and 'Titre 2: Au Roy seul apartienent [*sic*] de prendre tribute sur les personnes' ('Only the King may demand tribute of the people').[82] Of course, Loisel's celebration of French free soil would soon crash into France's overseas ambitions, with the establishment of colonies in the Americas and the Indian Ocean that, over the course of the seventeenth and eighteenth centuries, increasingly came to depend on slave labour. The French Crown's efforts to balance its essential mythology as a nation of free soil and competing interests, such as wealthy colonists who wished to bring their enslaved servants to the metropole and the royal use of galley slaves, would require some complicated rationalisation and legal compromises.[83]

The full transformation of free soil from a purely municipal liberty, rejected by royal authority, to an essential maxim of French law took place between the thirteenth and sixteenth centuries. Toulouse's magistrates defined, expanded and aggressively defended the principle of free soil in the medieval period, probably initially to attract and retain loyal citizen-soldiers, but ultimately as an essential expression of civic independence and autonomy. In the first half of the fifteenth century, as increasing numbers of fugitive slaves from Catalonia fled to Toulouse, the French Crown reversed its policy, ultimately defending the city's free soil tradition against the rival Aragon Crown. By the late sixteenth century, free soil came to be seen and defended as an inviolable foundation of French national law, thus setting the stage for conflict and contradictions as France entered the Atlantic slave economy.

Acknowledgements

Research for this essay was conducted under a Sabbatical Fellowship by the American Philosophical Society and an early version was presented to the Working Group on Slavery and the Law at the Gilder Lehrman Center for the Study of Slavery, Resistance and Abolition, Yale University, organised by Paul Finkelman. It represents a long journey from my 'comfort zone' of the eighteenth and nineteenth centuries. I have depended on the kindness of strangers for their suggestions and insights, especially Susanne Roberts and John Ott. I am also indebted to Chris Piuma for his thoughtful translations and conversations about the medieval Latin. Many thanks to Robin Blackburn, Seymour Drescher, Brett Rushforth, Alyssa Sepinwall, Nathalie Dessens and Chris Hodson for their astute comments on earlier drafts.

Notes

[1] 'Toutes personnes sont franches en ce roïaume; et sitost qu'un esclave a atteint les marches d'icelui, se faisant baptizer, est affranchi.' Antoine Loisel, *Institutes coutumières* (Paris: Abel l'Angelier, 1608), 1.

[2] Sue Peabody, '*There Are No Slaves in France': The Political Culture of Race and Slavery in the Ancien Régime* (New York: Oxford University Press, 1996), chap. 2.

[3] Sue Peabody, 'Furcy, la question raciale et le ≪sol libre dr France≫: une micro-histoire,' *Annales: Histoire, Sciences Sociales* 64 no. 6 (2009):1305–1334.

[4] On the emergence of the French monarchy, see Georges Duby, *France in the Middle Ages, 987–1460: From Hugh Capet to Joan of Arc*, trans. Juliet Vale (Oxford: Blackwell, 1991); Jean Dunbabin, *France in the Making, 843–1180*, 2nd ed. (New York: Oxford University Press, 2000); Elizabeth M. Hallam, *Capetian France 987–1328* (London: Longman, 1980); J.A. Everard, *Brittany and the Angevins: Province and Empire, 1158–1203* (Cambridge: Cambridge University Press, 2000).

[5] Peabody, '*There Are No Slaves*', 12. The first lawyer's reference to this case that I have found appeared in the 1783 edition of Antoine Loisel's *Institutes coutumières* (Paris: Nyon l'Ainé), 12, citing La Faille's *Histoire de Toulouse.*

[6] Alexander Chalmers, ed., *General Biographical Dictionary*, vol. 14 (London: J. Nichols, 1812–1817), 53.

[7] Auguste Brutails, 'Étude sur l'esclavage en Roussillon du XIIIe au XVIIe siècle', *Nouvelle revue historique de droit français et étranger* 10 (1886): 399.

[8] Germain de La Faille, *Annales de la ville de Toulouse depuis la réunion de la comté de Toulouse à la couronne, avec un abrégé de l'ancienne histoire de cette ville et un recueil de divers titres et actes pour servir de preuves ou d'éclaircissement à ces Annales...* (Toulouse: G.-L. Colomiez, 1687–1701), 156. On the establishment of the *gardiage*, see John Hine Mundy, *Liberty and Political Power in Toulouse, 1050–1230* (New York: Columbia University Press, 1954), 5–7, 27, 127.

[9] Faille, *Annales de la ville*, 203–204.

[10] Mundy, *Liberty and Political Power*, 8.

[11] Philippe Wolff and M. Durliat, *Histoire de Toulouse*, ed. Philippe Wolff, Univers de la France et des pays francophones, Histoire des Villes (Toulouse: Privat, 1974), 94–97.

[12] Mundy, *Liberty and Political Power*, 50.

[13] Ibid., 44.

[14] Wolff and Durliat, *Histoire de Toulouse*, 96.

[15] Mundy, *Liberty and Political Power*, 59.

[16] Ibid., 5–7, 27, 127.

[17] Ibid., 137–144.

[18] Ibid., 95, 97–99.

[19] Ibid., 134.

[20] Henri Gilles, *Les Coutumes de Toulouse (1286) et leur premier commentaire (1296)* (Toulouse: Recueil de l'Académie de Législation, 1969), 147n2. Mundy also discusses this case in *Liberty and Political Power*, 132–134. Following these historians, I have rendered the participants' Latin names into modern French spellings.

[21] The sole documentation for the case is a copy of the original, made by a notary in 1237, 34 years after the events it describes. It is not clear why the scribe, Pierre de Beceto, duplicated the document held by Pierre Sancius (a witness called in the original trial). Perhaps a subsequent trial needed the evidence of the prior decision. 'Jugement des consuls prononçant la liberté de deux serfs de Verfeil établis à Toulouse, April 4, 1203', in *La Commune de Toulouse et les sources de son histoire (1120–1249)*, ed. R. Limouzin-Lamothe (Toulouse: Didier, 1932), 475–478. The original document is in Latin. I commissioned a translation into English by Chris Piuma, then of Portland State University, now of the University of Toronto, and we reviewed together the meaning of critical phrases. Needless to say, any errors in interpretation are my own. The case is summarised in E. Roschach, *Inventaire des archives communales antérieures à 1790, tome I, Série AA, nos 1 à 60* (Toulouse, 1891), http://www.archives.marie-toulouse.fr/index.php?id=103&L=0&tx_amtinventaire_pi1[mode]=2 (accessed 7 July 2011), summarising the records for the Archives Municipales de Toulouse, AA 2, No. 84.

[22] 'Et est talis consuetude in hac villa Tolose quode aliquis de Tolosa non potest aliquem hominem statem in Tolosa emere, nec ullo modo adquirere ab aliquo extra Tolosam.'

[23] 'Jugement des consuls', 476.

[24] Ibid.

[25] Ibid., 476–477.

[26] The document refers to the purchase of Pierre and Guillaume 'de Petro Saqueto et de Furnerio' – that is, 'from Peter Saquetus and from Furnerius' – four times. This phrase suggests that the two brothers were previously in the service of two different masters, Peter Saquetus and Furnerius. Furnerius was a common family name in the region. See, for example, John Hine Mundy, *Studies in the Ecclesiastical and Social History of Toulouse in the Age of the Cathars* (Burlington, VT: Ashgate, 2006), 73n132; Jean Duvernoyf, ed., 'Régistre de l'inquisition de Toulouse (1273–1280)', 109, http://jean.duvernoy.free.fr/text/pdf/Parnaclatin.pdf (accessed 29 March 2008). It is not clear who owned the father, Pierre Jean.

[27] Susan Reynolds, *Kingdoms and Communities in Western Europe, 900–1300* (Oxford: Clarendon Press, 1997), 223.

[28] Jacques d'Ableiges, *grand coutumier*, quoted in Marc Bloch, *Slavery and Serfdom in the Middle Ages: Selected Essays by Marc Bloch*, trans. William R. Beer (Berkeley: University of California Press, 1975), 36.

[29] Bloch, *Slavery and Serfdom*, 24, 28. The word *servus* was also used in Italy to mean 'slave' well into the thirteenth century, though the word *sclavus* had also entered the language to mean 'slave' in the eleventh century. See Steven A. Epstein, *Speaking of Slavery: Color, Ethnicity, and Human Bondage in Italy* (Ithaca, NY: Cornell University Press, 2001), 18–19.

[30] 'For that reason, Arnaldus Ysarnus wished Petrus de Viridifolio and his brother Willelmus to serve [*servire*] them willingly through their *hominium* and *dominium*.' It could be rendered either as 'to serve' or 'to be a slave'.

[31] Bloch, *Slavery and Serfdom*, 37–47.

[32] Reynolds, *Kingdoms and Communities*, 114; David Nicholas, *The Growth of the Medieval City: From Late Antiquity to the Early Fourteenth Century (A History of Urban Society in Europe)* (London: Longman, 1997), 157.

[33] Latin translator Chris Piuma suggests that the 'other honours' (*alios honores*) might refer to holding some public office in the city – perhaps these were available for purchase.

[34] 'Jugement des consuls', 477.

[35] Ibid. In the judgment, the brother Aton Izarn has dropped out of the picture.

[36] Mundy, *Liberty and Political Power*, 133–134.

[37] 'Aucune personne établie dans ce territoire ne peut être réclamée par des seigneurs étrangers; mais ni les hommes du comte, ni ceux des citoyens et bourgeois de Toulouse n'ont droit d'invoquer le privilège à l'encontre de leurs maîtres' (Roschach, *Inventaire des archives communales*).

[38] Mundy, *Liberty and Political Power*, 125.

[39] Gilles, *Coutumes de Toulouse*, 16–17.

[40] William Chester Jordan, 'Alphonse of Poitiers', in *Medieval France: An Encyclopedia*, ed. William W. Kibler (London: Routledge, 1995), 27.

[41] Gilles, *Coutumes de Toulouse*, 15–18; Adolphe Tardif, *Le Droit privé au XIIIe siècle: d'après les coutumes de Toulouse et de Montpellier* (Paris: Alphonse Picard, 1886), 6–7.

[42] 'Item, est usus et consuetudo Tholose quod homines venientes in Tholosa causa habitandi et ibi habitantes undecunque venerint, quamvis habeant dominos, possunt et debent ibi stare liberi a dominis suis et facęre negotia sua sine petitione et impedimento et contradictione dominorum suorum et quod dicti domini non possunt nec debent ipsos homines sic in Tholosa habitantes vel in barriis in aliquo fortiare ratione seu occasione dominii.' From Gilles, *Coutumes de Toulouse*, 147; Adolphe Tardif, *Coutumes de Toulouse publiées d'après les manuscrits 9187 et 9993 fond latin de la Bibliothèque nationale* (Paris: Alphonse Picard, 1884), 77; Tardif, *Droit privé*, 21. Many thanks to John Ott for this translation (private communication, 23 January 2008).

[43] Tardif, *Coutumes de Toulouse*, ix–xxi; Gilles, *Coutumes de Toulouse*, 18–19.

[44] Hallam, *Capetian France*, 282, 304–306.

[45] 'Comme, selon le droit de nature, chacun doit naître franc. Et par aucuns Usages ou Coustumes, qui de grant ancienneté ont esté entroduites & gardées jusques cy en nostre Royaume, & par aventure, pour le messet de leurs predecesseurs, moult de personnes de nostre commun peuple, soient encheues en lien de servitudes & diverse conditions, qui moult nous desplait. Nous considerants que notre Royaume est dit, et nommé le royaume des Francs, et voullants que la chose en vérité soit accordant au nom, & que la condition des gents amende de nous en la venue de nostre nouvel gouvernement. Par deliberation de nostre grant Conseil avons ordené et ordenons, que généralement, par tout notre Royaume, de tant comme ile peut appartenir à nous, & à nos sucesseurs, telles servitutes seront ramenées a franchises, & a tous ceux qui de ourine, ou ancienneté, ou de nouvel par mariage, ou par residence de lieus de serve condition, sont encheües, ou pourroient eschoir ou lien de servitudes, franchise soit donnée o bonnes & convenables conditions.' Eusèbe de Laurière, Emmanuel Pastoret, Denis François Secousse and Louis Guillaume de Vilevault, *Ordonnances des roys de France de la troisième race, recueillies par ordre chronologique*, vol. 1 (Paris: Imprimerie Royale, 1723), 583. The preface to this work reviews earlier compendia of royal legislation. This edition seems to be quite erudite and trustworthy, but I have not consulted earlier editions.

[46] Peabody, '*There Are No Slaves*', 28.

[47] David Nicholas, *The Later Medieval City, 1300–1500* (London and New York: Longman, 1997), 14, 50, 59–60, 62.

[48] Philippe Wolff, *Commerces et marchands de Toulouse (vers 1350 – vers 1450)* (Paris: Plon, 1954), 155n252, citing Archives Municipales de Toulouse, AA 45, No. 79. Roschach's *Inventaire des archives communales* summarises the case as follows: 'Mandement du Louis de France, duc d'Anjou au sénéchal et au viguier de Toulouse portant vidimus de deux extraits du Livre Blanc du roi, collationnés par le viguier Bernard de Gresinhano le 10 mars 1373: [including] un article de la coutume relatif à l'affranchissement des serfs étrangers réfugiés à Toulouse. Les officiers royaux sont accusés de porter atteinte à ce privilège, notamment dans l'affaire du grec Antoine Soldani, quoique le procureur de son maître Guillem-Roger Suau, marchand de Perpignan, consentît qu'il fût livré aux capitouls. Les privilèges doivent être vérifiés et la coutume maintenue'.

[49] From 1344 until 1462, Perpignan lost its status as capital as it was absorbed into the kingdom of Aragon, where it enjoyed more than a century of peace. Residents of medieval Perpignan had traded and held slaves at least since the mid thirteenth century. Rebecca Lynn Winer, *Women, Wealth and Community in Perpignan, c.1250–1300: Christians, Jews and Enslaved Muslims in a Medieval Mediterranean Town* (Aldershot: Ashgate, 2006), 134–138; Guy Romestan, 'Femmes esclaves à Perpignan aux XIVe et XVe siècles', in *La Femme dans l'histoire et la société méridionales (IXe–XIXe s.): actes du 66e congrès de la Fédération historique du Languedoc méditerranéen et du Roussillon organisé a Narbonne les 15 et 16 octobre 1994...* (Montpellier: Fédération Historique du Languedoc Méditerranéen et du Roussillon, 1995), 187–218.

[50] After 1500, there are numerous references to slaves fleeing their owners to reach French free soil. Brutails, 'Étude sur l'esclavage', 392–393.

[51] Wolff, *Commerces et marchands*, 155n252.

[52] Charles Verlinden, *L'Esclavage dans l'Europe médiévale*, vol. 1 (Bruges: De Tempel, 1955), 432.

[53] All masters were required to register their slaves (including name, age and value) to local authorities within 15 days of their acquisition. Escaped slaves were to be reported immediately to authorities in Barcelona. If the escaped slaves were arrested within two months, they would be returned to their masters after a brutal beating (100 blows for 10 days' flight, 20 blows on naked flesh for 20 days, 30 blows for 30 days, etc.); after two months, the master had to pay an indemnity. Verlinden, *L'Esclavage dans l'Europe médiévale*, 499–500.

[54] Bienvenido Oliver y Esteller, *Cortes de los antiguos reinos de Aragón y de Valencia y principado de Cataluña*, vol. 9 (Madrid, 1907), 287–295, 347–351, 461–462; Verlinden, *L'Esclavage dans l'Europe médiévale*, 498–501.

[55] Alan Mattingly, *The Cathar Way: A Walker's Guide to the Sentier Cathare* (Milnthorpe, UK: Cicerone, 2006), 13.

[56] Not all of these were headed for French territory. Verlinden, *L'Esclavage dans l'Europe médiévale*, 504.

[57] Verlinden, *L'Esclavage dans l'Europe médiévale*, 506.

[58] André Viala, *Le Parlement de Toulouse et l'administration royale laïque, 1420–1525 environ*, vol. 1 (Albi, France: Reliure des Orphelins, 1953), 43–50.

[59] Viala, *Parlement de Toulouse*, 53–54. The first French Parlement was that of Paris, founded out of the king's council in the early fourteenth century.

[60] This summary of the case comes from Verlinden, *L'Esclavage dans l'Europe médiévale*, 815–816, who, in turn, is summarising Viala, *Parlement de Toulouse*, 566–567. Viala erroneously mentions the case as occurring in 1527. Both describe the slave as 'de race blanche'.

[61] Viala, *Parlement de Toulouse*, 567.

[62] Viala cites the customary foundation of Toulouse's free soil principle as Title V, Article 1: 'If anyone declared to wish to enter Toulouse and become a citizen and if another master of his body prevented him on the road, branded him or hanged him, the consuls and the community of Toulouse must reclaim him, guard him and if he was captured, retake him and all his belongings as if he had been a citizen of Toulouse'. He continues: 'By an arbitrary extension of the technical sense, but humanely rich in signification, the *capitouls* used this very limited text to claim that absolutely anyone could acquire freedom from everyone'. Viala seems completely unaware of the *capitouls*' thirteenth- and fourteenth-century evocations of the free soil principle (Article 155b), beginning only with the 1402 case discussed by La Faille. Viala, *Parlement de Toulouse*, 568–569.

[63] Félix Aubert, *Histoire du Parlement de Paris de l'origine à François Ier 1250–1515*, vol. 2 (Paris: Alphonse Picard, 1894), 268.

[64] Wolff, *Commerces et marchands*, 155n254.

[65] Germain de La Faille gives the date as 1417 (*Annales de la ville*, 204), but modern historians place the establishment of the commission in 1437. A copy of the letter of Charles VII of 31 January 1438 can be found in the Archives Municipales de Toulouse, FF 39, f. 11v. See Viala, *Parlement de Toulouse*, 569–570; Verlinden *L'Esclavage dans l'Europe médiévale*, 816, who quotes Viala pretty much verbatim on this and in his account of the cases of the 1440s.

[66] This is my translation of Viala's summary of Solacii's speech. Viala, *Parlement de Toulouse*, 571.

[67] Ibid.

[68] Ibid., 570.

[69] Ibid., 571–572; La Faille, *Annales de la ville*, 203.

[70] Viala, *Parlement de Toulouse*, 572.

[71] Aubert, *Histoire du Parlement*, 268.

[72] Viala, *Parlement de Toulouse*, 572; Verlinden, *L'Esclavage dans l'Europe médiévale*, 816–817.

[73] J. de Lahondès, 'Un process d'esclave au quinzième siècle', *Mémoires de la Société Archéologique du Midi de la France* 13 (1885): 334–343; Verlinden, *L'Esclavage dans l'Europe médiévale*, 817–818; Viala, *Parlement de Toulouse*, 573–574.

[74] Lahondès, 'Process d'esclave', 340.

[75] J. Miret y Sans, 'La esclavitud en Cataluña en los ultimos tiempos de la edad media', *Revue Hispanique* 41 (1917): 54.

[76] All of these cases are discussed by Debra Blumenthal in *Enemies and Familiars: Slavery and Mastery in Fifteenth-Century Valencia* (Ithaca, NY: Cornell University Press, 2009), 235–236. She notes that Muslim fugitives were more likely to try to achieve freedom by returning to areas of Islamic rule.

[77] David Brion Davis, *The Problem of Slavery in Western Culture* (New York: Oxford University Press, 1966), 165–196.

[78] Brutails, 'Étude sur l'esclavage', 412. Eighteenth-century lawyers would draw upon similar examples from the late sixteenth century to support the notion that French soil conferred freedom to all slaves who achieved its shores.

[79] Peabody, *'There Are No Slaves'*, 29–30. Brett Rushforth offers a fuller account of this famous case and explores sixteenth-century theorists of slavery, including Jean Bodin and Hugo Grotius, in his forthcoming study, *Bonds of Alliance: Indigenous and Atlantic Slaveries in New France* (Chapel Hill: University of North Carolina Press for the Omohundro Institute of Early American History and Culture), chap. 2.

[80] Jean Bodin, *Les Six Livres de la République* (Lyon: Jean de Tournes, 1579), 43.

[81] Seymour Drescher's very important synthetic study explores the historical development of this distinction between Europe as a land without slavery and slavery elsewhere. Seymour Drescher, *Abolition: A History of Slavery and Antislavery* (Cambridge: Cambridge University Press, 2009), 24 and *passim.*

[82] Loisel, *Institutes coutumières*, 1. Unlike a modern constitution, these maxims – their organisation and even their specific wording – changed with editions published by legal scholars. The 1846 edition, for example, lists the free soil maxim as number 24, sixth in the chapter on the status of persons. Antoine Loisel, *Institutes coutumières d'Antoine Loysel...*, ed. André Marie Jean-Jacques Dupin and Edouard Laboulaye, new ed. (Paris: Videcoq Père et Fils, 1846), 38. Dupin, as *procureur général* to the Cour de Cassation, supported the freedom of a nineteenth-century litigant, Furcy, in his free soil lawsuit, which was ultimately successful upon appeal to the Cour Royal de Paris in 1843. Sue Peabody, 'Furcy, la question raciale et le "sol libre de France": une micro-histoire', *Annales: Histoire, Sciences Sociales* 6 (2009): 1305–1334.

[83] In addition to the works cited in notes 2 and 3, as well as Gillian Weiss' article in the present volume, see André Zysberg, *Les Galériens; vies et destines de 60,000 forçats sur les galères de France, 1680–1748* (Paris: Éditions de Seuil, 1987); Pierre H. Boulle, *Race et esclavage dans la France de l'Ancien Régime* (Paris: Perrin, 2007).

Urban Safe Havens for the Unfree in Medieval England: A Reconsideration[1]

Stephen Alsford

Through historiographical error, the belief persists that 'town air makes free' was a principle applicable throughout medieval England. However, it was not in force in all towns, nor advantageous to all hoping to escape servitude. This avenue to emancipation was introduced for pragmatic, not philosophical, reasons, and to benefit the free rather than the servile sector of society. Caught up in larger trends, it became a nuisance to the intended beneficiaries.

In discussing how a man might refute an accusation that he was of servile status, the textbook on legal procedure known to us as *Glanvill*, written around 1188, states that: 'If any villein resides undisturbed for a year and a day in any privileged town, to the point that he is accepted into its community (that is, guild), he is thereby freed from villeinage'.[2] A generation later, this was reiterated in the equally influential legal treatise known as *Bracton*, which identified as one of the grounds for disproving servility: 'because resident in any privileged city or town, or on royal demesne, for a year and a day without being laid claim to'.[3] Such statements continue to appear in the work of jurists down to the time of Sir Edward Coke. They became, in the nineteenth century, a basis for historians – drawn to a study of English urban history in part by changes wrought by the Municipal Corporation Act of 1835 and in part by a desire to demonstrate the early roots of democratic freedoms – to represent the 'town air makes free' privilege as of universal applicability in medieval England.[4] This belief, reinforced by widespread expressions of the privilege in other northern European countries and by the discovery of grants of it in seigneurial charters to a number of towns in England, as well as to English colonies in Wales and Ireland, found its way unquestioningly into classic and authoritative studies.[5] Reservations have occasionally been expressed in passing.[6] However, many historians continue to accept the universality of the privilege, without enquiring more closely.[7]

Although the evidence is fragmentary and much of the dating uncertain or imprecise, it mitigates against the notion that 'town air makes free' was universal, whether geographically, chronologically or in terms of the entire servile sector of the population. This article will suggest how and why the privilege arose in England, spread, then fell from favour, and will identify limitations on its applicability. It seems doubtful that the privilege was intended by its grantors, or perceived by municipal authorities, as a sweeping measure to make English towns in general a sort of secular sanctuary, so that any escapee serf who merely crossed onto urban soil could thereby expect emancipation to follow after a grace period; on the other hand, it was in the interest of servile beneficiaries to attempt to have it interpreted thus. The absence of detailed attention or definition in legal documents left room for ambiguity and uncertainty. We should think of it more as a measure to address particular needs at a particular period – a measure that eventually outlived its usefulness to those free by birth, but persisted because it became embedded in common law and in the hard-won chartered franchises that towns resisted surrendering, while remaining useful to those seeking to sunder the shackles of the near slavery that serfdom had become for many.

There is no trace of a 'town air makes free' principle in the laws of the Anglo-Saxon or Danish kings of England. However, in the *Leges Henrici Primi*, a compilation during Henry I's reign (1100–1135) of those laws of his predecessors still considered valid, we can perceive some of the foundations for subsequent receptivity to such a principle. These include the king's duty to act as legal protector of those not powerful enough to look after their own interests and the sanctuary-like status accorded by the king to the 'burhs' (an ancestor of boroughs). As well, we can detect precursors of the law of villeinage that was in gestation – for example, any serf who left his lord without permission could be obliged to return and, should the fugitive be protected by some other power, the king would intervene to see justice done. A roughly contemporary compilation of laws purported to have been issued by William the Conqueror does refer to the 'free air' principle, but it represents one of the undatable additions made to a later edition to pretend ancient precedent for what were more recent innovations – particularly those of the administration of Henry II, trying to re-establish the rule of law following the Anarchy (1135–1154).[8]

For the English origins of the principle, we must look less to the Crown than to some of the Norman nobility whose support of the Conqueror brought them new estates in England, the king being the greatest of those landlords and serf owners. The new overlords sought to enhance the profitability of their estates in a variety of ways. One was to link servile dependency more closely to tenancy of land, so that the persons of serfs (along with the labour obligations they owed) became little more than appurtenances that could be alienated with the land, and lordly demands on them in various forms of services and payments could be increased at will. At the same time, uninterested in the fine degrees of freedom and unfreedom that existed in Anglo-Saxon society, Norman lords were inclined to treat as servile tenants who considered themselves free. Although conditions varied in different parts of the country, for many villeins conditions were worsening between the twelfth and fourteenth centuries.[9] The prospect of purchasing manumission was slim when anything serfs owned or earned belonged, in theory, to their lords, and those able to accumulate modest wealth in lands or goods faced its dissipation as they provided modest estates for their offspring.

Greener pastures might be seen in freeholdings on nearby villages, on the estates of less oppressive lords or in towns, where the range of employment opportunities was widening as the economy expanded. Personal status – free or servile – became defined in part by the right of a tenant to depart from a manor. Mobility was hard for lords to control, short-term absences (such as when taking produce to market) occurring with some regularity and longer-term relocations (for a variety of reasons) not uncommon; it was usually not far afield, but some headed for nearby towns.[10] Long absences were regulated to some degree through a required fee (*chevage*) to live off-estate, paid periodically, which the courts accepted as evidence of servile status; but it could be a fine line between licensed departee and fugitive – *Bracton* specifically identifying itinerant merchants and labourers looking for work as individuals likely to make the transition.[11] Failure to monitor absences, pursue fugitives in a timely manner or enforce *chevage* was, under the law of villeinage, considered a neglect of custodial responsibility tantamount to an acknowledgement that a departee was of free status. By obtaining a writ of naifty from the king, a lord could call on the support of royal officials to secure the return of an alleged fugitive serf. But if the latter then claimed to be free, the question of status had first to be resolved by the king's court.[12] The time, trouble and expense of a process to repossess a serf probably allowed many to flee with impunity, particularly if some form of protection was available at their destination.

A second tactic for revenue enhancement was to establish on one's estates (which were geographically fragmented) one or more towns, either as new foundations or upgrades to existing villages, as well as to foster the growth and competitiveness of existing urban settlements through investment in or encouragement of commerce. This was a speculative and entrepreneurial activity involving factors such as strategically advantageous location, investment in infrastructure, a certain amount of luck, and reliance on industrious and ambitious settlers to develop the manufacturing and marketing potentialities of a town. New towns were not guaranteed to thrive; many did not. But at least some of the families of England's new ruling class could bring to the task experience as seigneurs of towns in Normandy.

A key challenge was to provide a critical mass of settlers with the right skills and aptitudes. In a few instances, this was attempted by emancipating an entire village population of serfs, or a portion thereof, but more usually the aim was to attract newcomers from further afield. This was effected by endowing townsmen with privileges that accorded greater freedom, in terms of personal status, of action and self-determination, and of exemption from demotivating feudal burdens. In a famous study, Mary Bateson showed how one minor town in Normandy – Breteuil – could become the model for a set of such privileges – including the concession of emancipation to serfs who dwelt in a town for a year and a day – obtained by perhaps two dozen English towns in direct imitation of Breteuil (some explicitly, some by inference), or indirectly by imitating one or other of the first wave of imitators. Subsequent generations of this type of mother–daughter relationship help explain the dissemination of the 'free air' privilege to other towns in England and its colonies, and we cannot rule out the possibility of copying from other French or possibly Flemish urban exemplars, through the agency of men who came to England in the wake of the Conqueror.[13] The danger of it encouraging fugitivism – probably a risk more to neighbouring lords rather than the town founder – was outweighed by new sources of income such as market tolls, rents and perquisites of local judicial administration, as well as providing controllable venues for regional distribution of produce from agrarian components of the estates.

If it seems likely that the 'free air' privilege first appeared in England as the result of Norman importation, the first datable instances appear almost a century after the Conquest. Seigneurial charters are often hard to date precisely, and it is recognised that privileges may well have been put in place earlier than their formalisation in written instruments; some of the earliest charters only confirmed prior grants for which no record has survived. Among the first documented instances are royal grants to Lincoln and Nottingham (probably 1157).[14] However, imprecision of terminology leaves it uncertain whether emancipation of serfs was the underlying intention. What might be an even earlier expression of 'free air' appears in a custumal (collection of local legal customs) of Newcastle upon Tyne, which reads as though it were derived from a seigneurial charter; here serfs are clearly the beneficiaries of the clause stating that:

> If a villein comes to reside in the borough and lives there for a year and a day as if a burgess, he may stay in the borough forever, unless he or his lord had previously announced that he would reside only for a set term.[15]

Unfortunately, custumals are even harder to date than charters, and the Newcastle document's self-attribution to a grant of King Henry I is unverifiable, other evidence suggesting compilation during Henry II's reign. So, too, is a 'free air' chapter in Northampton's custumal, tentatively dated to 1190.[16]

Perhaps we should look at the Welsh Marches rather than England for the earliest introduction of the 'free air' privilege. After securing England, the Conqueror set some of his most trusted supporters to protecting (partly by subjugation) the sparsely populated region on either side of the England–Wales border from incursion or uprising. English towns there were bolstered with new fortifications and by fostering commerce-based settlements around castles; dependable supporters were introduced in the form of French settlers. On the Welsh side, the efficacious town–fortification combinations were established in an area of little previous urbanisation; one example being Pembroke, another of the earliest surviving documented grants of the 'free air' privilege (in the early part of Henry II's reign). Prominent among the executors of this programme were William Fitz-Osbern, Earl of Hereford and lord of Breteuil, and his kinsman Roger de Montgomery, Earl of Shrewsbury and founder of Pembroke; Bateson fingered such men as agents of the transfer of Bretollian privileges to English and Welsh towns, with their descendants and/or successors as Marcher lords spreading those privileges further afield. As a frontier settlement of proven resilience in the face of adversity, Breteuil may have seemed a good model for towns near the Welsh and Scottish borders, and in newly conquered territories in Ireland. Given the need to attract men capable of supporting local garrisons in a variety of ways, including defending the walls, a 'free air' clause would have had particular utility.[17]

As a magnet for migrants, hub for travellers and distribution centre for news, London must soon have got wind of advantages being granted to provincial towns. None of the capital's surviving royal charters contains mention of the 'free air' privilege, but this was no impediment to leading citizens always seeking to bolster the city's jurisdictional powers. In 1428, in defending two long-time residents against an accusation of servility, city authorities asserted that it had been the custom since before the Conquest that any slave who resided in the city for a year and a day without being reclaimed by his master could remain without challenge, and that William I had granted the same to the city by charter. It was a not uncommon ploy to allege ancient origins for privileges, and we can give no credence to London's claim. The reference to the charter grant seems to be to a set of laws purportedly granted to the city, of which one edition (*c.*1210) includes a 'free air' clause, but historians consider it an invention of that era. They feel a statement of the privilege in a thirteenth-century city compilation looks more authentic; some of its contents are believed to date from the reign of Stephen (1135–1154), and 'free air' may conceivably have been among concessions wrung from him in return for London's support in his contest for the throne.[18]

Following the end of that civil war, propagation of the 'free air' privilege was furthered by Henry II as he tried to re-establish the authority and the revenue base of the monarchy. Like other lords, the king wished to see his rural estates and the towns over which he had lordship amply peopled with workers, tenants, taxpayers and potential army conscripts. It was in the king's interest to treat serfs, as regards their implication in public duties and obligations, as if on equal footing to free men. Henry's administration pursued the formulation of common law (*Bracton* and *Glanvill* being expressions of that process) and its widespread application through royal courts, which served as a court of appeal for free men. Since court revenues increased as judicial business grew, it served the king to intervene in legal disputes in which a defendant resisted seigneurial authority by claiming to be free. Many of the same administrators engaged in these legal reforms were also trying to expand the definition of which territories comprised royal demesne, off whose revenues the king was expected to live. From the 1160s, royal demesne and royal towns began to be treated comparably in regard to direct taxation, and it must have been after this and between the time of *Glanvill* and *Bracton* that 'free air' was extended from 'privileged boroughs' (those with explicit grants of the privilege) to the royal demesne – that is, around the 1220s or 1230s. Although it is not clear whether royal boroughs were strictly part of the royal demesne, this generalisation of the privilege may have brought under the 'free air' umbrella other urban or urbanising settlements, which now did not need to seek explicit grants of it in charters; grants do, indeed, begin to decline in numbers after this time, as did the craze for town-founding.[19]

Despite the gradual spread of the privilege, for quite a few English cities and towns there is no evidence that it was ever in force; *Bracton* and *Glanvill* were conscious that it was not universal. Loss of written records may explain some gaps, yet in others where surviving archives are rich, there is no reference to town air making free. Such is the case at Ipswich and Norwich, and, indeed, peaceful East Anglia as a whole provides almost no evidence of the privilege – the exception being Dunwich, which could be considered a coastal frontier town. Other examples of absence include Chester and Gloucester, not quite so close to the Welsh frontier as Hereford and Shrewsbury; also Leicester, which was slow in loosening the feudal grip of its earl. Although London usurped the privilege, its emulators, Winchester and Oxford, show no signs of having claimed it. Perhaps we should understand 'free air' as a tool to address specific perceived situations, such as frontier protection and/or population displacement during troubled times; Roger de Montgomery's estates were distributed among a dozen shires, but the 'free air' privilege appeared only in his towns around the Welsh border. Because some Norman lords saw benefit from importing it does not mean it appeared attractive to their peers and, strictly speaking, they had no authority to offer emancipation to each other's serfs. That the privilege continued to spread throughout the thirteenth century (with only scattered instances in the next) was as much due to the copycat character of charter grants as anything else.

The patchwork distribution of the privilege could cause uncertainty in the courts. Around the time of *Bracton*, Andover's bailiffs were unsure what to do when William of Amesbury, an itinerant merchant who had married a woman of their town, was laid claim to within a year of his marriage; circumstances were muddied by the fact that the alleged serf had previously resided in the town of Wilton, which might have given him freedom. The bailiffs sought clarification from the king on how the law might apply, but this was pre-empted by an out-of-court agreement between claimant and accused. And, in 1227, Nicholas Baker of Wycombe, an unchartered seigneurial town, tried to inherit his father's land through an assize of *mort d'ancestor*, assuming his residence in Wycombe gave him the free status to enable such an action. A jury rejected his claim to the property on the grounds that his servile father had no right to heirs, but avoided pronouncing definitively on whether Nicholas himself had any claim to be free.[20]

The applicability of 'town air makes free' was limited not only geographically, but in other ways. The grant of the privilege to Nottingham specified that it applied only during peacetime, doubtless intending to exclude serfs who had taken refuge there for an extended period during the recent civil war. Newcastle excluded serfs who might try to parlay temporary visits, licensed by their lords, into permanent asylum. Exclusions – explicit or implicit – in several minor towns applied to serfs of the town's lord who were already resident at the time of the grants.[21]

A more common constraint built into 'free air' grants was the expectation that fugitives to towns not simply remain there for the year and day, but become permanent members of the community, as indicated in requirements that they enter the town guild (if there were one) or be contributory to communal financial obligations alongside the other burgesses. Although, in the century or so on either side of the Conquest, burgess status may have been defined primarily by residence, it subsequently began to become more restrictive, as formal admission into the community, involving payment of a more than nominal fee, was added to the requirement of building a house. Obviously, escapee serfs with no resources were disadvantaged here and may have been considered undesirables. The privilege's appeal to urban authorities was that new recruits would bear their share of communal financial obligations and help develop economic infrastructure, in return for privileged access to the chartered advantages of citizens.

Fugitives with resources, be it fiscal or personal, were also favoured in that the process of defending oneself against a writ of naifty could entail some expense and documentation of a claim to have been an urban resident for the legal term. In 1313, 18 men were claimed as serfs or their offspring belonging to a manor near Norwich; its new lord had evidently compiled from manorial archives a list of long-time fugitives. Four of the accused asserted freedom as citizens of Norwich, a royal borough: one – wealthy trader William de Colton – declared he had been at scot and lot and paying taxes for 60 years unchallenged, and a second for 30 years, while the last pair, brothers, stated they and their ancestors had been born in the city. Since Norwich had no charter grant of 'town air', they asked the court's cognisance of a charter of William the Conqueror stating the principle – doubtless the same held up by London authorities as evidence of that city's claim to the privilege. The court apparently found this suspect or insufficient, as three then produced deeds proving they or a parent had owned borough property since the previous reign, and Colton also provided documentation of a favourable inquisition *ad quod damnum* for some of his property; on this basis they were judged free. The fourth's case was postponed for jury inquest.[22]

But if it could be difficult for some townsmen to prove free status, it was also challenging to reclaim escaped serfs. Lords lacked the resources to prevent flights from their widespread estates and the law required a prompt effort to pursue, followed by success in discovery and laying of claim before local authorities within the year. If the accused asserted free status, the matter was transferred into the king's court, pending which the accused could not be detained and might disappear again, while the lord had to produce concrete evidence of servility, often in the form of the kin of the accused to testify (if they could be persuaded to cooperate) to status. Particularly when an accused was ensconced in a town whose authorities wished to defend its chartered liberties, reclamation or even pursuit might be considered more time and trouble than it was worth by lords whose estates were sufficiently furnished with labourers, in the pre-plague period when the population was growing. There was perhaps greater concern about loss of capable or prospering tenants. In 1306, the London mercer Simon de Paris, who had risen to the city offices of alderman and sheriff, was seized as a serf on a return trip to his native village; his defence of citizenship won him exoneration and damages.[23] However, the scarcity of lawsuits on such matters may reflect acceptance of a certain amount of fugitivism and/or a preference for out-of-court settlements.

Although some expressions of the 'free air' privilege have it applicable to any serf, the exclusions I have noted suggest the privilege may have created more problems than it solved. From the late thirteenth century, we can see signs of a decline in its promulgation or enforcement, as lords lost interest in town-founding and borough authorities exerted more control over recruitment to citizenship. There was no longer the need to stimulate urban growth proactively. Even though the disruptive effects of the Black Death (1349, with later recurrences) created a renewed need for fresh blood, as well as employment opportunities, the wealthy class that dominated municipal administration had no wish for a large influx of fortune-hunting serfs who, if disappointed, might expand the number of local beggars or criminals. Nor had they any wish to antagonise local landlords (consumers of urban products and services, and men with whom the landed urban elite were increasingly feeling a certain community) by siphoning off agricultural labourers at a time of manpower shortage. The 'free air' privilege might now be seen as providing a route to citizenship counter to the restrictive urban policy of purchasing membership; in 1288, William de Colton of Norwich had been accused of enjoying a citizen's advantages without having formally taken out citizenship. The same year saw the Earl of Cornwall's attorneys register, in London's court, a claim of naifty to eight men recently fled from a neighbouring shire, asking that those fugitives not be admitted as citizens.[24] Although the city authorities' response is not recorded, it is more likely they complied than protected men in whom they had no vested interest (unlike the case in 1428, mentioned above, in which a civic liberty was clearly at stake).

The urban elite's developing sense of privileged status and dignity found expression in prohibitions against those tainted with servility. In its chapter dealing with citizenship admissions, Norwich's custumal (reflecting late thirteenth-century conditions) specified that the status of applicants should be investigated by examining them and, if necessary, others who knew them, and that a servile applicant could not be accepted without written permission from his lord. Similarly, a Lynn ordinance (1386) prohibited any burgess from taking on an apprentice born unfree, all candidates being subject to questioning by the mayor; if it was later found that a candidate had lied, his term as apprentice was not to qualify him for citizenship. The merchant guild at Lynn likewise refused admission to serfs and required expulsion of any member found to be servile. At London, in 1305, several butchers were stripped of citizenship when found to be holding land in villeinage. Embarrassments such as this and the Paris case may have prompted two ordinances of 1387: one prohibiting anyone from becoming an apprentice, or proceeding thence to citizenship, without first swearing he was no serf; the other disfranchising any man born to a servile father who, later in life, was nominated for election to high office and failed to declare his ineligibility. Another indicator of fading interest in 'free air' is that the only reference to it in Colchester's records comes in the context of a late fourteenth-century glossary of antiquated legal terms, while a further relic is in a list (*c.*1430) of citizenship privileges at Canterbury, which concedes only that children born to resident serfs would be free.[25]

What must already have been an aggravation for manorial lords, in terms of encouraging departures outside of *chevage* licences, was exacerbated by the Black Death, which disrupted seigneurial control, depleted the rural labour force and opened up new or higher-paid employment opportunities in urban areas. Lords used their collective power base – Parliament – to try to solve the problem through legislation limiting mobility and restricting wages. While avoiding a direct attack on the free soil principle, which would have challenged the royal prerogative, they sought to hobble it by eliminating procedural tricks exploited by fugitive serfs. This had begun pre-plague with a complaint to Parliament that fugitives were suing their lords in distant courts so that, when the defendant countered that he could not be sued by his own villein, the plaintiff could claim to be free and obtain support through an inquest of locals who did not know his true origins. In 1348, the king granted that such inquests be taken near a plaintiff's birthplace. The year 1373 saw a similar complaint that serfs went to London to use its court to initiate fraudulent suits of debt or contract against their lords, so that simply being permitted to initiate a legal process (something not allowed to the unfree) would itself imply the plaintiffs were free men. On this occasion, the king was unwilling to change common law, perhaps for fear it might work against those truly free. A statute of 1352 allowed that a claim to free status could no longer prevent an alleged serf from being detained until trial. In 1377, the concern expressed was that serfs were obtaining copies of portions of the Domesday Book for the manors where they were villeins, to prove the locations royal demesne and that they were subject to 'free air'. The previous year had seen a general complaint about lazy scoundrels who hid in towns to have an easier life, and the following one saw another about rural labourers seeking other employment in urban areas. Fears fed by the Peasants' Revolt (1381) gave fresh opportunity, and into the 1390s objections were raised about towns shielding fugitive serfs. In 1385, the old complaint about town courts being used to launch suits against lords resurfaced and it was legislated that a lord responding to such a suit could not be used by the plaintiff as evidence of free status. But nothing stemmed the tide of escapes. In the fifteenth century, protests about serfs' efforts to win freedom became infrequent as landlords adjusted to changed circumstances and serfdom withered away, replaced by less oppressive landlord–tenant relationships.[26]

A few lords seem to have capitalised on altering circumstances by identifying serfs who had prospered after escaping to towns, and trying to extort manumission payments from them. Simon de Paris and William de Colton may represent early examples. Other cases would have left little evidence because they were settled privately, but we have one particularly well-documented instance. In 1346, one of Norwich's wealthiest citizens, Richard Spynk, together with his brother and business partner William, obtained judicial commissions on complaints that men of the Bishop of Ely were conducting an intimidation campaign against them: stealing their livestock, lying in wait to ambush them when they came out of the city, and threatening them with violence and imprisonment. The case came before Parliament (1348), where the bishop argued that the Spynks had been born his villeins and had only brought the charges to engineer a claim to free status. The bishop wanted an inquest into their status held near their native village. Spynk responded that the bishop could pack a jury there and asked for the benefit of the doubt on his right to pursue his case as a free man. But with the reaction against fugitive serfs already setting in, his plea fell on deaf ears. The bishop's request was granted and the charges against him quashed. Spynk, apparently reluctant to try claiming the 'town air' privilege (thereby admitting he had become a citizen under false pretences), preferred to reach a financial settlement with the bishop. Other extortionate initiatives of this impecunious bishop suggest his intent was not to regain one-time serfs, but to make money out of them.[27]

Possibly this high-profile case influenced Laurence de Reppes, a fairly well-to-do burgess of Lynn prominent enough to have been elected to the town council, when in 1353 he purchased manumission for himself and his offspring from Alan Reyner of Roughton (a village near Repps). Whether this was precautionary or a response to a claim laid by Reyner, we do not know; Lynn lacked the 'town air' privilege, leaving Reppes vulnerable. A couple of fifteenth-century cases may also fall into this genre. In its early years, John Bishop of Newport complained that an armed group had dragged him from his bed, plundered his house and held him prisoner for several days; the party accused claimed that Bishop was his villein, but the outcome of the case is not known. In 1447, the Duke of Gloucester laid claim to John Whithorne, a prosperous gentleman with property in Salisbury, and imprisoned him for several years; only after the duke's death did the king restore Whithorne's property and declare him never to have been a villein.[28]

Richard Spynk's plea to Parliament had made call to the principle *in favorem libertatis* ('in favour of liberty'), an assumption that a party to litigation was of free status, manifested in royal protection accorded before 1352 to an alleged serf, until his status had been judicially determined. But this was a relatively recent import from Roman law. English common law was not born with an inherent assumption that men were free unless proven otherwise; its purpose was to lay out the rights of free men, define the circumstances under which those rights could be claimed and guide the courts in upholding them. But the consequent emergence within it of a law of villeinage, in order to determine who was unfree, provided some procedural loopholes that escapees could exploit.[29] One late thirteenth-century legal treatise might describe servitude as repugnant.[30] But on the whole, the law saw nothing morally wrong with servitude, as distinct from outright slavery – the slave trade in Christians having been banned by the English Church in 1102, although it remained tolerable in the case of non-Christians. That some men and women were bound in service to others was viewed as part of the natural order.

The Norman lords' extension of personal freedom through the 'town air makes free' privilege, imported from their French dominions, was intended to foster urban development, to create new, diversified revenue streams and to help consolidate their military hold in insecure border regions. For existing townsmen, the expected benefit was a boost to the local labour force and tax base; migrants from the countryside were needed in a competitive economic environment characterised by the proliferation of markets and excessive town-founding, in which winners would emerge and losers sink into relative obscurity. These were the two parties to the negotiation of terms of charters, which are our principal source of evidence of the 'town air' privilege in England and its colonies. To what extent that privilege was requested by the recipients of charters and to what extent it was an initiative of the grantors is hard to say, but it became lumped in with other liberties to which towns aspired in their ongoing effort to dissociate themselves from feudal lordship. As the Crown sought to reassert its influence following the Anarchy of the mid twelfth century, it too came to appreciate how a free soil principle could further its own needs to build a fiscal and human support base, and to establish a standardised system of justice applicable to all free men.

If the heyday of the 'town air' privilege in England appears to have been the late twelfth and early thirteenth centuries, as it spread from town to town and into those parts of the countryside of which the king was the immediate lord, it outlived its usefulness to feudal lords and towns alike. It remained useful to the serfs, whose benefit, however, may never have been a consideration of any consequence to the framers of the privilege. It would be a mistake to think of towns as champions of free status simply because of the equation of burgess status and freedom; they were self-interested and protectionist, prepared to defend their own, but not necessarily welcoming to outsiders, except those who arrived with some wealth or, by dint of hard work or talent, proved themselves capable of shouldering their share of a citizen's burdens and contributing to the prosperity of the community. I have found no evidence that the privilege had any philosophical underpinnings, such as the establishment of safe havens for fugitives from a heinous bondage.

Such indications as we have from the late thirteenth and fourteenth centuries suggest a reaction against the 'town air' principle. Its spread continued, but in an automatic fashion rather than through any enduring enthusiasm for it. Many towns never bothered to add it to their list of chartered privileges. For them, it had little value as an incentive to attract new settlers; what they wanted was men who had already prospered in lesser locations and wished to move up to greener pastures, not poor peasants who might become a burden on the community or merely stay long enough to effect escape from their bonds. Both rural and urban ruling elites acted to limit the applicability of what had become an inconvenience.

Despite the limitations on that privilege, for at least a fortunate few, escape from manorial servitude into certain towns – places where personal freedom had become the rule rather than the exception – could bring about emancipation, if they could avoid detection long enough to establish themselves. A measure originally intended to work to the profit of feudal lords eventually proved to be against their interests. Although its importance has been exaggerated by some historians, the designation of certain territories as free soil contributed to the decline of serfdom in late medieval England.

Notes

[1] A more detailed examination of the evidence can be found in an earlier draft of this article, posted to the Florilegium Urbanum Web site at http://users.trytel.com/~tristan/towns/florilegium/community/cmmemb01.html.

[2] D.G. Hall, ed., *The Treatise on the Laws and Customs of the Realm of England Commonly Called Glanvill* (London: Thomas Nelson, 1965), 58 (my translation).

[3] Samuel Thorne, ed., *Bracton on the Laws and Customs of England* (4 volumes) (Cambridge, MA: Harvard University Press, 1968–1977), 3: 85 (my translation).

[4] Notably, Henry Alworth Merewether and Archibald John Stephens, *The History of the Boroughs and Municipal Corporations of the United Kingdom*, vol. 1 (London: Stevens and Son, 1835), 350.

[5] Charles Gross, *The Gild Merchant* (Oxford: Clarendon Press, 1890), 1: 30; William Stubbs, *The Constitutional History of England in Its Origin and Development*, 6th ed., vol. 1 (Oxford: Clarendon Press, 1903), 452; Paul Vinogradoff, *Villainage in England* (Oxford: Oxford University Press, 1892), 86; Adolphus Ballard, *The English Borough in the Twelfth Century* (Cambridge: Cambridge University Press, 1914), 5; Frederic Pollock and Frederic William Maitland, *The History of English Law Before the Time of Edward I*, 2nd ed., vol. 1 (Cambridge: Cambridge University Press, 1898), 648–649.

[6] Gross, *Gild Merchant*, 1: 30; Alice Green, *Town Life in the Fifteenth Century*, vol. 1 (New York: Macmillan, 1894), 174; A.H. Thomas, ed., *Calendar of Plea and Memoranda Rolls of the City of London*, vol. 2 (Cambridge: Cambridge University Press, 1929), xxiv; Richard Holt, 'Society and Population 600–1300', in *The Cambridge Urban History of Britain*, vol. 1, *600–1540*, ed. David M. Palliser (Cambridge: Cambridge University Press, 2000), 86.

[7] For instance, Maurice Beresford, *New Towns of the Middle Ages: Town Plantation in England, Wales and Gascony* (London: Butterworth, 1967), 191; Sandra Raban, *England under Edward I and Edward II* (Oxford: Blackwell, 2000), 45.

[8] L.J. Downer, ed., *Leges Henrici Primi* (Oxford: Clarendon Press, 1972), 108–109, 153, 215, 257; H.G. Richardson and G.O. Sayles, *Law and Legislation from Aethelbert to Magna Carta* (Edinburgh: Edinburgh University Press, 1966), 41–49; Pollock and Maitland, *History of English Law*, 649.

[9] It is risky to generalise. Detailed discussion can be found in works such as: David Pelteret, *Slavery in Early Mediaeval England* (Woodbridge: Boydell, 1995); Marc Bloch, *Slavery and Serfdom in the Middle Ages: Selected Essays* (Berkeley: University of California Press, 1975); and R.H. Hilton, *The Decline of Serfdom in Medieval England*, 2nd ed. (London: Macmillan, 1983); along with classic treatments such as in 'Essay 1' of F.W. Maitland, *Domesday Book and Beyond* (Cambridge: Cambridge University Press, 1907).

[10] J.A. Raftis, *Tenure and Mobility: Studies in the Social History of the Mediaeval English Village* (Toronto: Pontifical Institute of Mediaeval Studies, 1964), 129; J.A. Raftis, *Peasant Economic Development within the English Manorial System* (Montreal: McGill-Queen's University Press, 1996), 99, 103; Christopher Dyer, *Making a Living in the Middle Ages* (New Haven, CT: Yale University Press, 2002), 194; *Calendar of Inquisitions Miscellaneous*, vol. 9 (London: Her Majesty's Stationery Office, 1916), 34.

[11] Thorne, *Bracton*, 2: 36.

[12] The development of the law in response to such complications is dealt with by Paul Hyams, *King, Lords and Peasants in Medieval England: The Common Law of Villeinage in the Twelfth and Thirteenth Centuries* (Oxford: Clarendon Press, 1980).

[13] Mary Bateson, 'The Laws of Breteuil', *English Historical Review* 15, no. 57 (1900): 73–78, 302–318, 496–523, 754–757; 16, no. 61 (1901): 92–110, 332–345. The mother–daughter principle had already been charted by Gross, *Gild Merchant*, 1: 245–257, and would be elucidated in the systematic study of Adolphus Ballard, ed., *British Borough Charters 1042–1216* (Cambridge: Cambridge University Press, 1913).

[14] Ballard, *British Borough Charters*, 104.

[15] Charles Johnson, 'The Oldest Version of the Customs of Newcastle Upon Tyne', *Archaeologia Aeliana* 4th ser. 1 (1925): 170 (my translation).

[16] Ballard, *British Borough Charters*, 104; Mary Bateson, ed., *Borough Customs*, vol. 1 (Selden Society, vol. 18, 1904), xli–xlii; Christopher Markham, ed., *The Records of the Borough of Northampton*, vol. 1 (Northampton Corporation, 1898), 220.

[17] Lynn H. Nelson, *The Normans in South Wales, 1070–1171* (Austin: University of Texas Press, 1965), 29–30, 166–170; Bateson, 'Laws of Breteuil', 308, 335–336; David M. Palliser, *Towns and Local Communities in Medieval and Early Modern England* (Aldershot: Ashgate, 2006), VIII–185; Holt, 'Society and Population', 99; Ralph A. Griffiths, 'Wales and the Marches', in *The Cambridge Urban History of Britain*, vol. 1, *600–1540*, ed. David M. Palliser (Cambridge: Cambridge University Press, 2000), 681–683, 695–696.

[18] Reginald R. Sharpe, ed., *Calendar of Letter-Books ... of the City of London. Letter-Book K* (London, 1911), 80, 90–91 (hereafter *Letter-Book*); Robert S. Hoyt, *The Royal Demesne in English Constitutional History: 1066–1272* (Ithaca, NY: Cornell University Press, 1950), 188; Mary Bateson, 'A London Municipal Collection in the Reign of John', *English Historical Review* 17, no. 67 (1902): 714; Martin Weinbaum, *London unter Eduard I. und II.*, vol. 2 (Stuttgart: W. Kohlhammer, 1933), 70; Derek Keene, 'Text, Visualisation and Politics: London 1150–1250', *Transactions of the Royal Historical Society* 18 (2008): 83.

[19] Hoyt, *Royal Demesne*, *passim*; B.P. Wolffe, *The Royal Demesne in English History* (London: Allen and Unwin, 1971), *passim*; G.O. Sayles, *The Medieval Foundations of England* (New York: A.S. Barnes, 1950), 328–329; Hyams, *King, Lords and Peasants*, *passim*.

[20] Hyams, *King, Lords and Peasants*, 66; A.E. Bland, P.A. Brown and R.H. Tawney, eds., *English Economic History: Select Documents* (London: G. Bell and Sons, 1914), 125.

[21] Adolphus Ballard and James Tait, eds., *British Borough Charters 1216–1307* (Cambridge: Cambridge University Press, 1923), 137, 141, 144; Martin Weinbaum, ed., *British Borough Charters 1307–1660* (Cambridge: Cambridge University Press, 1943), 95.

[22] William Hudson, ed., *Leet Jurisdiction in the City of Norwich* (Selden Society, vol. 5, 1892), lxxxvii–lxxxviii; William Hudson, 'Notes about Norwich before the Close of the Thirteenth Century', *Norfolk Archaeology* 12 (1895): 79–82.

[23] Thomas, *Calendar of Plea*, xxv.

[24] Sharpe, *Letter-Book A*, 170.

[25] William Hudson and J.C. Tingey, eds., *Records of the City of Norwich* (2 volumes) (Norwich: Jarrold and Sons, 1906–1910), 1: 177–179; Holcombe Ingleby, ed., *The Red Register of King's Lynn*, vol. 2 (King's Lynn: Thew and Son, 1922), 26; Gross, *Gild Merchant*, 2: 164; Sharpe, *Letter-Book A*, 170; Sharpe, *Letter-Book C*, 148; Sharpe, *Letter-Book H*, 309–310; Thomas Riley, ed., *Munimenta Gildhallae Londoniensis*, vol. 1, *Liber Albus* (London, 1859), 33–34, 452; Thomas, *Calendar of Plea*, xxv–xxvi; W. Gurney Benham, ed., *The Oath Book or Red Parchment Book of Colchester* (Colchester, 1907), 13; A.R. Myers, ed., *English Historical Documents, 1327–1485* (London: Spottiswoode, 1969), 570.

[26] Philip Schofield, *Peasant and Community in Medieval England, 1200–1600* (New York: Palgrave Macmillan, 2003), 111–112; Joan Thirsk et al., *The Agrarian History of England and Wales, 1348–1500* (Cambridge: Cambridge University Press, 1991), 767; Raftis, *Tenure and Mobility*, 143; Hilton, *Decline of Serfdom*, 29–36; Merewether and Stephens, *History of the Boroughs*, 624–625, 669, 688, 770; Hyams, *King, Lords and Peasants*, 207; Palliser, *Towns and Local Communities*, VIII–185.

[27] Hudson and Tingey, *City of Norwich*, 2: 216–225; John Aberth, *Criminal Churchmen in the Age of Edward III: The Case of Bishop Thomas de Lisle* (University Park: Pennsylvania State University Press, 1996), 95–115, 239–240; Hilton, *Decline of Serfdom*, 29–30, 51–53; Hyams, *King, Lords and Peasants*, 206.

[28] *Calendar of Close Rolls 1349–1354* (London: Her Majesty's Stationery Office, 1906), 609; Bland, Brown and Tawney, *English Economic History*, 98–101.

[29] Hyams, *King, Lords and Peasants*, xxi, 123, 160, 203–205.

[30] H.G. Richardson and G.O. Sayles, eds., *Fleta*, vol. 2 (Selden Society, vol. 72, 1953), 172.

Access to the Netherlands of Enslaved and Free Black Africans: Exploring Legal and Social Historical Practices in the Sixteenth–Nineteenth Centuries

Dienke Hondius

Dutch merchant and maritime history includes a black presence from the sixteenth century onwards. As a country that self-identifies as freedom-loving, the Dutch involvement in the slave trade and slavery creates a problem of justification within the Netherlands. This article explores the development of legal history as well as individual case histories. Slaves could obtain freedom from their owners as a result of an owner's individual decision, by marriage, by baptism, by remaining in the Netherlands long enough, or when their enslaved parents were freed. The Dutch authorities attempted to keep the involvement in slavery out of sight in the Netherlands. The small presence of blacks in the country was the result of a highly selective process of enabling and restricting access. The Netherlands remained 'white' for centuries, in spite of its colonial empire, but not entirely. This article presents the long absence of visibly black communities in Europe as the result of practical restrictions as well as conscious legal exclusion.

> Either by way of a contract, or enforced by violence, may the liberation be pursued and obtained of these imprisoned Christians, groaning under the joke of the Turks in miserable slavery.[1]

> Although the English and Dutch colonists did regard the first Africans as slaves and not as indentured servants, they had not yet defined slavery as lifelong, inheritable servitude but only as indefinite service, which might explain their opportunities for expanded rights, including freedom, social acceptance, and mobility . . . The Christian background of many Atlantic Creoles may have been the key that made these opportunities more attainable.[2]

Whereas migration is a world historical phenomenon, a visibly multiracial Europe is a recent phenomenon, provoking new academic research in the field of immigration law.

This article explores how legal historical questions emerged centuries ago in the Dutch colonial empire and at home. Mixed relationships received, as always, mixed reactions, but there was no general outcry and no general attempt to prohibit or outlaw mixed relationships in the early phases of expansion and exploration. With the argument that mixed marriages could help to 'stabilise' the newly occupied territories, Dutch colonisers and merchant companies even promoted intermarriage during the early modern period.[3] Moreover, the Dutch experience and regulation of immigration and interracial marriages did not operate in a national vacuum. Similar experiments took place in all the European imperial regimes, with the most important parallels occurring in France and England.

As Orlando Patterson has argued, the European idea of freedom was shaped in the confrontation with slavery, creating deep ambivalence, and this is accurate for the Dutch situation as well.[4] Although the terms 'enslaved' and 'free' are used across the centuries, the historical terminology of enslavement and serfdom is complicated and layered. While modernity considers individual freedom as a right, early modern Europeans saw their lives primarily as characterised by variations in privilege. In an almost individual, private decision, one person would grant a privilege to another person, or refuse or withdraw a privilege, thus creating a social hierarchy based on dependency. The person to whom no privilege whatsoever was granted may not formally have been enslaved, but in practice had a status far removed from freedom. One clear dividing line was that of the enslaved who could be sold and traded at will by their owners, versus serfs who could not be sold.[5] Another issue was whether serfdom was temporary or indefinite, permanent, or whether it was also hereditary.

In the early modern Atlantic world, the terminology of the legal status of Africans became entangled with the terminology of colour. In Portuguese, Spanish, English and Dutch – the European languages most directly connected to the history of enslavement – the terminology is remarkably similar: the Portuguese were the first to coin the terms, and other Europeans easily integrated them into their own languages. For example, as Linda Heywood and John Thornton point out, the terms 'negroes', *negar* and *neger* were borrowed directly from the Portuguese, and had no meaning in Dutch or English until the middle of the sixteenth century, when speakers of both languages began visiting those areas in Africa frequented by the Portuguese – no meaning other than 'black', that is. But 'at some point during the sixteenth century the term negro took on a second meaning of "slave" when referring to people that might even be independent of skin color'.[6] In the Netherlands, black Africans were named by direct indications of their dark colour: *swarten* and *swartinnen*, and *negros*. As long as they were regarded as remarkable, their presence as blacks was noted in various sources, enabling us to reconstruct some of their histories today.[7]

When the black presence became less remarkable, the relevance of 'race' and visible difference seems to have disappeared from view in the sources, because it was simply not mentioned. This is one of the paradoxes in the study of black Europeans.[8] Legal sources vary as to whether or not blackness as such is mentioned. Sometimes there is no indication at all of the African origin of persons in a court case: their names are European, Christian, and their place of birth or region of origin is not named.

Nevertheless, there are cases from which we know that the defendants apparently were considered black – for instance, in court cases around mixed-marriage laws in the seventeenth and eighteenth centuries in the Netherlands, as well as in England and France.

Slaves in the Netherlands

Forms of human bondage, servitude and slavery were found across medieval Europe. In the international historiography of modern Europe, this was forgotten after the enslavement of black Africans became the dominant phenomenon.[9] Steven A. Epstein has shown the continuities and connections between premodern and modern slavery in Europe, both in language and in numbers. Slavery and slaves were present in 'the world that Columbus grew up in'.[10] European expansion created a convenient division of events in history between 'here', in the Old World, and 'there', across the sea. The idea was that there was no slavery in the Netherlands: slavery came to appear as something outside Europe, far away. The study of history becomes split as well, between those who study and write about national issues in Europe, and others who focus on colonial or 'non-Western' history. The history of slavery and the slave trade thus becomes situated outside Europe, as an element of African, Caribbean or American history, and this continues throughout the twentieth century and during decolonisation. The extent to which the political and legal processes of slavery – decision making, overseeing and financing – remained situated within European cities becomes generally unnoticed and remains under-researched until today. Most historians of the slave trade and slavery limit their remarks about slavery in Europe to the Middle Ages, then move on to the transatlantic slave trade and plantation slavery, never to look back at Europe.

Very recently, the field of Atlantic history and the concept of a Black Atlantic, in particular, have begun to reconnect these split histories. Nell Irvin Painter shows inspiring and highly relevant new research possibilities in her book on the long history of the concept of 'white people' within and outside Europe.[11] Seymour Drescher assumed in 1994 that Dutch slave owners in the seventeenth century 'understood that when they brought slaves to the Netherlands, they implicitly manumitted them', but he is right in noting a lack of research in Dutch colonial archives that could support this thesis.[12] In 2004, Drescher summarised the new insights as a deep trend in European history, located particularly in the north-west: 'Conceptually as well as legally, the operative distinction in northwestern Europe between slavery and freedom was geographical and racial, and it remained so.'[13] How it did so is explained by Arend Huussen in an intriguing reconstruction of Dutch parliamentary debates at the end of the eighteenth century about a new constitution. After days of debating, the Assembly decided 'that the constitution would make no mention of the institution of slavery at all'.[14] A committee of learned jurists in charge of drafting the national codes of law accepted this line: 'they chose not to mention the institution of slavery in the civil or other codes'. Huussen calls this 'an agreed silence on slavery', a highly relevant term that is also suited to describe a much longer period of Dutch history.[15]

Recent research shows that in the late seventeenth and eighteenth centuries, there were black African slaves present in the Netherlands. Their presence as slaves was controversial and their legal status created uncertainty. The first captain who brought a group of black African slaves to the city of Middelburg in Zeeland in 1596 was told that they could not stay there as enslaved; the local authorities announced their liberation. However, this did not happen: instead, when the Dutch captain Pieter van der Hagen requested permission to take the ship, with its crew and the 'Moors', to Portugal and the West Indies, the national States General first refused, then allowed the captain to 'do as he pleased', which was to take the slaves to the West Indies.[16]

The first black Africans came from Spain or Portugal to the Netherlands, England and Germany, in the context of north European contact and competition with south European merchants. Some, but by no means the majority, of the slaveholders were part of the Sephardic diaspora that facilitated trade and colonisation in the Portuguese Atlantic. This migration was not massive or even a clear group phenomenon, as far as we know. By the early seventeenth century, quite a few black Africans had found their way to the city of Amsterdam.[17] Dozens of black Africans, enslaved and free, were buried at Beth Haim, the Portuguese Jewish cemetery of Amsterdam in the town of Ouderkerk aan de Amstel.[18] They were named and described by their skin colour as *swarten* and *swartinnen*, *negros* and *negerinnen*, and their legal status was often uncertain. Ad hoc decisions characterised emerging legislation, as in the case of four Portuguese merchants in Amsterdam – Izak Brazilai, Antonio Mendes, Rodrigo Alvares Drago and Antonio Henriques Alvin – who left statements with Amsterdam notaries in February 1626. Having survived piracy and the takeover of their ship by Dutch privateers, they arrived in the city with several black African men and women. In October 1625, Drago and Alvin came to Europe – first to Portugal, then to the Netherlands. Arriving in Vlissingen, some went south to Rouen in France, others to Amsterdam:[19]

> from Pernambuco [Brazil] to Viana [do Castelo, northern Portugal] with the ship *De Engel Rafael* of skipper Gaspar Maciel Entaon, this ship was seized by a certain Captain Jacob who took them to Vlissingen. There they and the rest of the crew were released, each with one Spanish *pistole* in money. The others of the crew went to Rouen; he and Alvin went to Amsterdam with three negroes and five negresses that belonged to Alvin. All declare that Alvin remained in Amsterdam with the eight negroes for about three months and that he was free to go where he pleased and that he could leave with them whenever he wanted.[20]

The last sentence is important, as this makes clear that the status of these African men and women as property of the Portuguese merchants had not changed during their stay in Amsterdam. It is likely that the four Portuguese merchants had gone to the notary in order to have this confirmed in writing.[21] Although indications of skin colour and servant status can be found, the Portuguese word for 'slave', *escravo/escrava*, vanished from the burial records after 1617. Why the word for slave would be avoided has not been ascertained, but there could be a connection with the Dutch and Amsterdam authorities' wish that slavery and slaves would be absent from Dutch soil, possibly to avoid controversy about the ambivalent status of slaves. This ambivalence is also clear in a case from 1656.

Juliana's idea of freedom in the Netherlands

The Amsterdam City Archives contain information about the case in 1656 of a Portuguese merchant, Eliau Burgos, who came from Pernambuco and settled in Amsterdam with his slave Juliana. Notary records indicate that Burgos wanted to force Juliana to stay with him against her will and to travel with him to Barbados. Several witnesses declared that they had known Juliana as a slave of Burgos in Brazil, where she lived with him. For example, two Portuguese witnesses who had made their way to Amsterdam following the Portuguese conquest of Recife declared that they knew Burgos 'as well as Juliana *negerinne* and they know that Juliana was the slave of Burgos in Recife'. After Recife became Portuguese, Burgos would have been able to sell Juliana for 500–600 guilders, but 'he did not do so because Juliana prayed to him very strongly for his mercy'. Juliana promised Burgos that she would serve him for the rest of his life and that she would stay with him. Then Burgos decided to bring Juliana from Brazil to Amsterdam 'at high cost'. In another statement, Burgos confirms this account, but declares that since their arrival in Amsterdam, Juliana understands that she could be free, and she has walked away from him. The idea came to her, according to Burgos, 'through the raking up of others who made her believe that she was here free and not obliged to serve him'.[22] He wished to go to Barbados and to take Juliana with him, but

> Juliana did not wish to do this as if it were her business; so that he promised her that he would let her go free after she would have served him there for three years. So he, because the slaves here are free and he, seeing that he would not get Juliana from here to Barbados, promised her and had an act [notary's act or agreement] made up: he was forced to have the promise confirmed in an act, to have Juliana experience this and to have the act pass [confirmed] in her interest, with the notary Benedict Baddel and several witnesses. Since he had this act passed, compelled by necessity and forced by Juliana, he now wishes to declare this statement null and void with the notary. Since he stills maintains the full rights because of his purchase.[23]

Burgos now wished to have this confirmed in writing by the notary, so that he could leave Amsterdam and take Juliana to Barbados. He had bought her in 1643 for 525 guilders when she was then 10 or 11 years old. The statements in Amsterdam were made in 1656 when Juliana would have been 23 or 24 years old.[24] We do not know what, if any, action was taken on the basis of these statements.

Obtaining freedom in Amsterdam

The explicit documented presence of black Jews, slaves and servants in the Amsterdam Portuguese cemetery records of the early seventeenth century stands in contrast to their absence from the same records in the eighteenth century. For the beginning of the eighteenth century, very few specific references to black people can be found. Neither is there an indication of a separate area for black Africans in this cemetery. The designations 'black', 'slave' or 'servant' noted their separate and inferior status and justified their being buried apart. As far as we know, these rules were not formally changed. One explanation could be that this had become customary practice, but this is a subject for further research.

Amsterdam notary archives document the presence of black men and women frequently, showing that there were both individuals and groups of free black women and men.[25] These black Africans lived in Amsterdam as free people, away from their former masters or owners. How had they obtained freedom? We know that they sometimes received benefits from the Jewish poor service, the Imposta, and that their funerals were paid for. In the period from 1629–1634, benefits were paid by the Imposta to the *mulata* Sara d'Algarve, to Francisqua, Judich and Angelica, to the *mulat* of Espinoza and to a *Moreno*. The Imposta's accounts included an intriguing sum of 12 guilders and 10 *stuivers* 'per a soltar o preto' ('to buy freedom for the black man'). Would the Jewish poor service spend money on buying slaves their freedom from Jewish owners? Hagoort found no manumission letters or forms, though these may be found elsewhere in Europe. She explained this absence of paperwork by pointing out that slavery did not officially exist, so no official emancipation or liberation was possible, and everything remained informal.[26] Perhaps a simple cash transaction was made to free an enslaved African living in Amsterdam. This could have been paid for by slaves themselves who had gained some money, or by their owners, as part of their regular payments to support the poor service.[27] Jonathan Schorsch has found one formal manumission in a notarial deed of 1659. It concerned the manumission of 'a black woman slave who was to accompany [David Nassy's] daughter from Amsterdam to Cayenne, then in Dutch hands'.[28] It is likely that liberation in this case was enabled by one owner's individual decision.

Eighteenth-century challenges to slavery

Historians of French and British law regarding black immigration and interracial marriages note that the eighteenth century was a crucial period of transition. In France, a long-standing legal tradition held that slaves were free upon arrival in the metropole. French colonial expansion, including slavery, tested that tradition. According to the French *Code Noir* of 1685, slaves were defined as *meubles*: movable, inheritable, sellable property that could be used to repay debts. *Meubles* could follow their owner when he or she moved. Over the course of the eighteenth century, many slaves challenged their enslavement in the French Admiralty courts of the metropole. Eventually, the French royal government deliberately replaced earlier legislation, which used *esclave* and the ambiguous *nègre*, with exclusions based on racial terms like *noirs*, *mulâtres* and *gens de couleur*.[29] In England, a similar resolution – to distinguish the law of slavery, applicable in the colonies, from the law of the metropole – emerged in the landmark 1772 freedom suit of Somerset.[30] A first indication that a similar mechanism was at work in the seventeenth-century Netherlands is the disappearance of the Portuguese word for slave.[31] The absence or masking of the terminology of slavery makes the relations between slaves and masters an individual, private affair. In the early eighteenth century, slaves could try to find their freedom by contacting diplomats, comparable to refugees seeking asylum today, but indeed, one by one, on an individual basis. For example, a Polish slave who was held in the Russian embassy to the Netherlands sought protection from his Russian master in the house of the Polish ambassador. When the Dutch arrived, they removed the man and returned him to the Russians.[32]

The English legal author Bankton cited a freedom suit in the Netherlands, similar to Somerset and numerous French cases based on the free soil principle, where some Spanish slaves had made their escape, claimed their liberty and, by a solemn decision, were declared free. Without citing evidence, he claims that the same law was also at work in Germany.[33] According to Bankton, the common basis for this practice in Europe was a reference to the Bible and the Mosaic Law:

> Thou shalt not deliver unto his master the servant which is escaped from his master unto thee. He shall dwell with thee, even among you, in that place which he shall chuse in one of thy gates, where it liketh him best, thou shalt not oppress him.[34]

However, not all slaves arriving in European metropoles were escaping; many, like Somerset, accompanied their masters there, but resisted their forced return to the colonies.

The American legal historian Daniel Hulsebosch places the Somerset case and similar decisions in a wider context. Their common aim and function was 'to keep slavery in the empire while keeping it out of England'. In the Dutch case in 1596, local authorities in Zeeland decided to liberate a large group of African men, women and children who had unexpectedly arrived in the Dutch city of Middelburg. This ruling was an active effort to keep the immediate, visible consequences of the Atlantic slave trade out of Zeeland. However, the national government overruled the decision by allowing the captain to do with the Africans as he saw fit – that is, elsewhere, anywhere, but not in Zeeland. This was a national decision but, significantly, the action was left to the Dutch captain. The line that was drawn here was a local, geographical one: there could be no visible slavery in Europe. The racial aspect also remains implicit. I regard Hulsebosch's analysis of the Somerset case as applicable to the case in Zeeland in 1596: 'The primary argument here, was to keep slavery an ocean away. The judges agreed with that argument.'[35]

By liberating the group of Africans, the Zeeland authorities sent a double message to the wider community. To the individual shipowner and captain, and the wider community of maritime commerce, the message was: 'You made a mistake. Don't try selling slaves here in Zeeland'. To the general population, the message could be interpreted as a stand against slavery itself: there was to be no slavery in Zeeland, and baptised slaves would have to be treated as employees and further raised as Christians.

In retrospect, we can see that both layers of this message were effective. It served first of all as a geographic boundary: it kept the visible realities of the slave trade away from the Netherlands. The story lived on in local tradition as an example of the freedom-loving nature of the people of Zeeland, a tradition in evidence 15 years earlier in 1581. As the Leiden historian Johanna Kardux reminds us, in the 1581 *Akte van Verlatinge*, the Dutch declared their independence from Spain, conceiving of the foundation of their nation as a rejection of slavery, and thus justifying the right to revolt.[36]

Even earlier, the Dutch had embraced the opportunity to oppose Spanish 'barbarism' against the American Indians and compared their situation as 'slaves' of the Spanish Empire.[37] At the same time, Dutch merchants were actively exploring the possibilities of international trade and conquest, in fierce competition with Portugal and Spain.

This simultaneity was not considered problematic as a distinction was made between what happened 'here', in Europe, and 'there', across the sea. The crucial separation of what could be done 'here', in Europe, and 'there', elsewhere, was helpful in further ignoring the role that port cities of Zeeland were ready to play in the triangular transatlantic trade of slaves from Africa to the West Indies and North America. After the Dutch West Indies Trade Company lost its monopoly in 1730, Middelburg became the centre of the Dutch slave trade. Ships fitted out in Zeeland carried about 30 per cent of the Dutch slave trade between 1601 and 1803, transporting a total of 180,000 slaves; business opportunity won out for several centuries.[38]

Immigration restrictions for slaves in the eighteenth-century Netherlands

In the last quarter of the eighteenth century, the inhuman status of enslaved Africans and the system of individual privileges for favourites was interrupted when several European nations, including France and Portugal, designed new rules regarding the access of slaves to the metropole. This included the establishment in France of depots where blacks reaching European soil were incarcerated until they could be returned to the colonies.[39] In the Dutch West Indian colonies, local authorities coined laws to manage the enslaved population. They were published in so-called *Plakkaatboeken*.[40] Among the first rules was the permission to travel. Slaves could travel with their masters, provided that he requested a passport in time for the slave. In Curaçao in 1638, marriage with *wilde vrouwen* ('local indigenous women') or *zwartinnen* ('black women') was only allowed when the women had a Christian education, were christened and became members of the Christian community. The same rule was formulated and confirmed unchanged in 1739.[41] In 1742, all *negers en mulatten* ('negroes and mulattoes') going on any ship had to prove that they were free, following disorder among the free and the enslaved on ships.[42] A man could marry when he was 14 years old and a woman when she was 12 years old, provided their parents give their consent. The age for witnesses was a minimum of 18 years old. These rules appear to have been similarly inspired as those in the East Indies, aimed at stabilising the colony by encouraging marriages. The double standard regarding mixed marriages is clear: the white rulers facilitated marriages between white men and black women, but prohibited marriages between white women and black men. As in Asia, further restrictions were made regarding the possibility of travelling to Europe.

Emy Maduro has published several individual histories of enslaved women and men travelling to Europe from the Dutch Caribbean island of Curaçao. She argues that individual blacks who came to the Netherlands until the first decade of the eighteenth century were often allowed to stay, but groups were returned to the Caribbean to continue their lives enslaved. Things began to change mid-century when, for instance, a judge in Amsterdam ruled for the first time in 1736 that a fugitive slave from

Curaçao now living in Amsterdam could remain free. However, when the female owner appealed the same case with the high court, the Hoge Raad van Holland en Zeeland, this overruled the Amsterdam court, arguing that in these cases – there had been another similar case two years earlier, also regarding a slave from Curaçao – the slaves had to be returned to Curaçao, because 'for the slave not the law of the Republic, but the law of Curaçao where the slave belonged, had to be applied'.[43] This decision anticipated by two years a similar royal declaration in France, which required that all slaves brought to the metropole in violation of certain conditions be confiscated and resold in the colonies to the king's profit.[44] In 1766, a group of 22 'slaves and mulattoes' who travelled to the Dutch island of Texel, north of Amsterdam, by way of Cadiz, Spain, was ordered to return to Curaçao by the West India Company in Amsterdam.

Maduro's pioneering study indicates that there is no complete picture available of the numbers of enslaved or free blacks travelling to Europe because a significant percentage of them were never registered and travelled without permission or passport. In the Curaçao archives, she found that no more than 20 passports were issued to slaves and *domestiquen* ('domestics') to travel to the Netherlands between 1765 and 1790, and about 40 to slaves and domestics travelling elsewhere in the Caribbean and to New York.[45] In 1755, the local law confirmed that slaves could only sail away from the Dutch Caribbean islands if they had a passport and a permission letter from their master; a fine of 100 *pezos* would have to be paid by the shipper if this condition was not met.[46] This rule was soon considered too lenient. In 1772, the States General of the Dutch republic liberated a Surinamese enslaved woman and her daughters, leading the colonial Surinam authorities, the Amsterdam-based Sociëteit van Suriname, to believe that 'slaves through or with the consent of their masters brought into Europe thus obtain complete freedom'.[47] For the Sociëteit van Suriname, this verdict was received as a dangerous precedent. It sent out a warning to the governor of Suriname, Jan Nepveu.[48] Very soon thereafter, new rules regarding permission to travel and passports were made more restrictive. In December 1773, a new rule in Suriname stated that

> from now on no passports will be handed out to slaves who will travel to the fatherland, unless they are registered at least six weeks in advance in the form of a certificate on their ticket or separate declaration, according to the wish of the masters.[49]

The law of 1776: arriving in the Netherlands does not imply freedom

The new law, 'Regarding the Freedom of Negro and other Slaves, who are brought or sent over from the Colonies of the State to these Lands' (*Placaat*), was confirmed by the States General on 23 May 1776. It said that slaves arriving in the Netherlands would *not* become free persons, with two exceptions: (1) when the enslaved had already been officially liberated by their masters, the masters would thereby lose any authority over their former slaves (should these freed men or women return to the colony, they would be recognised as free persons there as well); (2) when the period of a maximum of six months' stay in the Netherlands had passed without the master requesting and obtaining permission from the local authorities to prolong this with another maximum of six months. In the latter case, the enslaved would be considered free, and they could not be forcibly returned to the colony.[50] Emy Maduro argues that this law was created solely for Suriname, as it was not published in the Antillean colonies. The law was known in Curaçao, however, and particularly the period of six months' maximum stay can be found in several court cases after 1776 until as late as 1852.

In the early nineteenth century, the Curaçao permission to travel for slaves was regulated, but mostly within the Caribbean. In 1830, a standard form had to be filled in to obtain permission for enslaved domestics to travel away from Curaçao, in particular to Saint Thomas, Venezuela, Puerto Rico and Suriname. A clear geographical limit was set for travel, both for domestic slaves and for enslaved men working as crew on ships: these ships, according to the official publication in the *Publicatieblad* of 1830, were allowed to travel 'no further than between the tropics [*keerkringen*], with the exception of the African seas and coasts'.[51] Subsequently, the legal travel of enslaved women and men to Europe became exceptional. One motivation for the restrictive policy was the fear that people who came to the Netherlands as slaves and who returned as free men or women to the colony would cost the colony money. The Surinamese governor Jan Nepveu ordered a compulsory registration of freed men and women, and an obligation to provide their own livelihood.

France first instituted a ban on racial intermarriage in 1778. George Fredrickson writes that 'the ban was not enforced and disappeared with the Revolution'.[52] The interracial ban was resurrected under Napoleon, but only as it applied to black men (but not mulattoes) with white women. This prohibition of racial intermarriage was also exported as part of French international rule during the period of French rule in the Netherlands from 1811 onwards. In 1814 and 1815, cases show that, in practice, the French prohibition was not carried through in the Netherlands, and mixed couples were able to marry after the High Court of Justice had delivered its judgement.[53]

How many enslaved men, women and children travelled between the Dutch Caribbean and the Netherlands is the subject of ongoing research. Two quantitative studies of ship records show roughly between 450 and 750 black slaves, free blacks, including a few dozen Surinamese indigenous people, and 'mulatto girls' travelling between Suriname and the Netherlands in a period of roughly 50 years during the eighteenth century.[54] In the first decades of the nineteenth century, the emancipation and humanisation of the enslaved Africans was approached step by step.

Slowly towards abolition: the humanity and rights of black people

In the Netherlands, as in the Americas, the idea that slaves were 'not ready' for emancipation can be found as a standard statement until the very day the laws were changed.[55] Even in 1863, the Dutch authorities resisted full emancipation for another decade, during which the formally freed men and women were, as a group, placed under supervision. Only on 1 July 1873 did this period come to an end.[56]

A study of the development of local legislation shows how this slow process evolved during the nineteenth century.

In 1816, a new set of rules was confirmed in Suriname, following the end of the temporary rule of the British there. Many of the new rules reinstated the pre-1795 legislation.[57] As late as 1825, the full humanity of slaves was still rejected in law, as when the head of Suriname's tax office wrote to the governor of Suriname that slaves could not share

> in those rights, which assume the legal personality [*regterlijke personaliteit*] of the one to enjoy them, [because] such a personality cannot be assigned to any being which is considered a thing, an object [*eenig wezen, hetwelk voor eene zaak gehouden wordt*].[58]

In 1828, a special envoy of the King of the Netherlands, 'commissaris generaal' Jan van den Bosch published a new set of rules for Surinam, which, for the first time, established the legal personality of slaves. While the new regulations accorded equal rights to free people of colour, it designated slaves as minors:

> The slaves will be, considering their daily treatment, regarded to stand in relation to their owners as underage [*onmondigen*] to their curators or guardians [*voogden*], who retain fatherly disciplinary jurisdiction [*vaderlijke tucht*] over them, but against whose abuse all public authorities are obliged to guard, and to watch, that the law, designed in their interest, is strictly upheld; thus from now on the unjust principle that in Legal affairs slaves can only be regarded as objects and not as persons, is permanently abolished.[59]

The crucial moment of the legal recognition of slaves as human beings coincided with the announcement of their new status as underage children. In the same move, all their rights were apparently placed in the hands of their owners, who now became their curators or guardians. The enforcement of this new *Reglement* was actively hindered, as Dutch historian Susan Legêne shows: four years later, a group of Surinam planters revoked the measure, using the opportunity of a change in local authority.[60] Moreover, the protection of the enslaved was also revoked. The idea of slaves as minors would return soon, however.[61] New rules for the registration of slaves were announced, presented as part of the legislation against the slave trade, and aimed at collecting more tax from the owners of slaves. Detailed legislation shows to what extent one dividing line defined the social structure in the colony: every single government service was calculated in separate prices and tariffs for three categories: *blanken* ('white'), *vrylieden* ('freeman') and *en slaven* ('slave'). Fees for slaves were always and everywhere lower, in order to signify that they were considered to be worth less. This division in three categories was applied uniformly for all fees and taxes, such as costs of medical treatments, burial, the questioning of suspects, the inspection of corpses and the work of midwives. The costs of slaves were further calculated according to their age: 'Slaves from eight to fourteen are given half, and the younger ones are given one third of the food rations. Should the children be fed from the Master's own table, they will be given nothing else.'[62]

Permission to travel and citizenship rights of freedmen

The idea and practice of manumission had grown, but quickly freedmen leaving the colony became a concern for the authorities. In 1816, the restored Dutch colonial government in Suriname announced that manumission did not mean that former slaves were free to go where they wished: freedmen had no right to travel outside the colony until one year and one day after they had received their freedom letter, and had formally requested dispensation from the prohibition to travel. Only in very special cases could there be an exception to this rule – for instance, when 'one would wish to take the service of one or the other very trusted freed or yet to be freed servant away outside the Colony', an exception would be considered by the court.[63] The governor also continued to decide whether and which civil servants and officers were allowed to enjoy leave, within the country as well as overseas, well into the twentieth century.[64]

In 1831, a new law defining the citizen rights (*burgerregt*) of the Dutch West Indian colonies' people stipulated that those who held citizenship were entitled to enjoy 'all the privileges' of citizens in the colony. Children had the same status as citizens as their parents, but citizenship rights were bound by the duty to personally live in the colony.[65] The 1831 regulation designated the following categories with these citizenship rights: all colonial property holders; all freeborn persons who had been living in the colony since before 1816; all freeborn persons who had arrived after 1816 and possessed a passport or an official function as a civil servant; and anyone else who already had citizenship rights in any other Dutch colony. Those freedmen who were liberated before 1831 and lived in Surinam, as well as their children, would obtain citizenship rights 'insofar as they do not belong to the caste of slaves [*Slavenstand*]'. Regarding the enslaved who were to be freed, the period of one year and one day waiting time was extended:

> Persons who will receive Letters of Manumission . . . will only be able to fully enjoy the right of Citizenship two years after the Letters of Freedom will have been given them, provided they can also show a certificate of good behaviour: they will thus obtain the status of 'Residents of the Colony' [*Ingezetenen der Kolonie*].[66]

Manumission, vagrancy and patronage

In 1843, a new tax was announced for slave owners who liberated their slaves. Moreover, the waiting period for freedmen to obtain citizenship rights and the requirement of extra paperwork was further extended in October 1844. Then a new law against vagrancy was announced, with the explanation that this phenomenon had recently increased. From now on, slaves could no longer just be liberated, but were bound to declare a profession and to work at it immediately after their liberation or face charges of vagrancy. Slaves thus freed were held to a 10-year period of ambiguous status, similar to the British apprenticeship. Every 'liberated' slave was assigned a *patron* ('guardian'). In the case that the *patron* died or left the colony, the 'authority over the manumitted person' would be given to the Commissioner over the Domestic

Population (Commissaris over de Inlandsche Bevolking). No freed person could leave the colony on his or her own; only in very special cases would permission to leave the colony be granted by the governor general.[67]

This reconstruction of legal history explains why the abolition of slavery did not lead to any significant increase of colonial migration to the Netherlands during the nineteenth century. Migration was actively obstructed and thus travelling away from the colonies remained as exceptional as it had been during the centuries of enslavement. The high cost of manumission also limited the frequency of blacks travelling to the Netherlands until 1848, when the so-called 'Recognition taxes' were abolished, and 1850, when the manumission fees were significantly reduced. While this could have resulted in increased migration to the Netherlands, the government simultaneously issued new regulations on travel permits, prohibiting former slaves from leaving the colony without written permission from the governor and compensation paid to the *patron*. Many additional restrictions limited and controlled the lives of newly manumitted slaves, who risked re-enslavement if they violated the law's provisions.[68]

Abolition and the end of the patronage system

This system of guardianship or patronage remained intact for several decades. In the Netherlands, patronage was introduced while slavery was still intact, and carried on from the former personal relationship between owner and slave to the relationship between a former owner and former slave, until the year 1863 brought about the legal abolition of slavery. Manumission implied an extensive registration of enslaved men, women and children across Suriname. When their application was submitted and accorded, the slave owners received financial compensation for all the enslaved they had been able to register. In sharp contrast, the enslaved were not compensated in any way, but instead forced into a new status, between enslavement and freedom. Patronage was transformed into what was called *Staatstoezigt* – a form of state guardianship over the freedmen and women. It was a form of state supervision that would last for another 10 years until 1873. During this period, the freedmen and women between 15 and 60 years old were obliged to make a labour contract, in practice often with their former owner. Shortly before 1 July 1873, the day when state supervision would end, the governor of Suriname Van Idsinga issued a proclamation to the former enslaved – a large majority of the country – on 14 June 1873. The tone of this proclamation was characteristic in its paternalism, reminding the audience to show 'orderly behaviour, obedience to the Law' and their 'attachment to the King and to the Netherlands, that you are grateful for the rights granted to you'.[69]

Entering the Netherlands: a history of exceptions

The legal history of race and the history of the few black people travelling to Europe are strongly asymmetrical. While white Europeans began to travel, trade and explore far beyond the borders of their continent, and other Europeans wrote, painted, drew and sketched these other worlds on the basis of oral reports and stories, few African, Asian or American men, women and children were able to come to Europe, and most of the very few who were able to come stayed only temporarily. Throughout four centuries, the lack of free access to Europe was a constant factor in its history, produced by numerous decisions, rules, laws and regulations that had the effect of keeping out the 'rest of the world'. In retrospect, only the post-colonial migration of the twentieth century, following the independence of the former colonies in the wake of World War II and the Shoah, was a short period when access to Europe was easier for entire families and multiple generations from overseas countries in the Caribbean, Asia and Africa, because these countries had until recently been part of the European nation and their inhabitants had equal citizenship rights. These last 50 years have changed the face of Europe, but it is equally clear that post-colonial migration was restricted again soon after independence occurred. While the unification of Europe after 1989 extended membership to the former East European countries, further amalgamation with nations to the south and south-east has not materialised and remains controversial. In the two decades after 1989, a 'Fortress Europe' emerged with daily news of asylum-seekers and international migrants seeking access, often at the risk of their own lives, attempting to cross borders in the back of a truck, in small boats or by walking through mountainous areas looking for a loophole in the law and an opportunity to slip through the net that still attempts to keep Europe closed.

Notes

[1] W.P.C. Knuttel, ed., "t Sij bij wege van verdrach, ofte andersints bij wege van gewelt bevordert worde ende uytgewrocht de relaxatie van de voorsz. gevangen Christenen, suchtende onder 't jock der Turcken ende jammerlicken slavernie." *Acta der Particuliere Synoden van Zuid-Holland, 1621–1700*, vol. 4, *1657–1672* (The Hague: Nijhoff, 1912). Rijks Geschiedkundige Publicatiën, Kleine Serie, deel 11. *Acta Synodi*, 1660, article 41, Rotterdam, 5–22 July 1660. See also Bartolomé Benassar and Lucile Benassar, *Les Chrétiens d'Allah: l'histoire extraordinaire des renégats* (Paris: Perrin, 1989). Chapter 3 contains many examples of enslaved European children.

[2] Linda M. Heywood and John K. Thornton, *Central Africans, Atlantic Creoles, and the Foundation of the Americas, 1585–1660* (Cambridge: Cambridge University Press, 2007), 299.

[3] For their comments on earlier versions of this text, I thank the editors and Allison Blakely, Thomas Spijkerboer, Margaret Hunt, Gert Oostindie, Sue Peabody, Susan Amussen, Alyson Poska, Susan Legêne, Kwame Nimako, Siep Stuurman, Andrea Mosterman, John Thornton and Linda Heywood.[0] A more elaborate discussion of the developments described in this article is included in my manuscript '"Race" in European History'.

[4] 'Freedom was socially constructed – not discovered, for it was an invented value . . . in a specific pair of struggles generated by slavery. One of these inhered in the master–slave relationship itself; the other arose from the confrontation between slaveholders and slaves, on the one hand, and slaveholders and other free persons, on the other.' Orlando Patterson, *Freedom in the Making of Western Culture* (London: Basic Books, 1991), 3.

[5] I thank Siep Stuurman for this (email to author, 16 January 2009). The history of the terminology of slavery merits further research.

[6] Heywood and Thornton, *Central Africans*, 312.

[7] Amsterdam City Archives, Archieven Notariaat, Archive no. 5075, Inventaris no. 941, notaris Daniel Bredan, Minuutacten 1632. Additional information was found in Archive no. 5372,

Amsterdamse Notarissen 16e–18e eeuw, ongeinventariseerde archieven. For their help with this research I am indebted to Lydia Hagoort and Eric Schmitz of the Amsterdam City Archives.

[8] Kathleen Chater, 'Job Mobility amongst Black People in England and Wales during the Long Eighteenth Century', *Immigrants and Minorities* 28, nos. 2–3 (2010): 113–130. See also Kathleen Chater, *Untold Histories: Black People in England and Wales during the period of the British Slave Trade, 1660–1807* (Manchester: Manchester University Press, 2009).

[9] A first outline of this article was presented as 'The "Dark Dimension" of Dutch History: Recent Developments in the Historiography of Black Africans in Early Modern Europe' at a roundtable discussion on 'Nation, Race, and Gender: Colonial Challenges to Early Modern Historiography' during the American Historical Association conference, New York, 4 January 2009.

[10] Steven A. Epstein, *Speaking of Slavery: Color, Ethnicity and Human Bondage in Italy* (Ithaca, NY: Cornell University Press, 2001), 191.

[11] Nell Irvin Painter, *The History of White People* (New York: Norton, 2010).

[12] Seymour Drescher, 'The Long Goodbye: Dutch Capitalism and Antislavery in Comparative Perspective', *American Historical Review* 99, no. 1 (1994): 44–69 (49).

[13] Seymour Drescher, *The Mighty Experiment: Free Labor versus Slavery in British Emancipation* (Oxford: Oxford University Press, 2004), 12–13.

[14] Amsterdam City Archives, Archive no. 5075, Inventaris no. 2271, ff. 764v, 766, 1 November 1656, notaris Adriaen Lock.

[15] Arend H. Huussen, Jr., 'The Dutch Constitution of 1798 and the Problem of Slavery', *Legal History Review* 67, nos. 1–2 (1999): 99–114 (113).

[16] For more details on this history, see Dienke Hondius, 'Black Africans in Seventeenth-Century Amsterdam', *Renaissance and Reformation/Renaissance et Réforme* 31, no. 2 (2008): 89–108; Dienke Hondius, 'Blacks in Early Modern Europe: New Research from the Netherlands', in *Black Europe and the African Diaspora*, ed. Darlene Clark Hine, Trica Danielle Keaton and Stephen Small (Urbana: University of Illinois Press, 2009), 29–47.

[17] Amsterdam City Archives, Archieven Notariaat, Archive no. 5075, Inventaris no. 941, notaris Daniel Bredan, Minuutacten 1632. Additional information was found in Archive no. 5372, Amsterdamse Notarissen 16e–18e eeuw, ongeinventariseerde archieven.

[18] Lydia Hagoort, *Het Beth Haim in Ouderkerk aan de Amstel: De Begraafplaats van de Portugese Joden in Amsterdam, 1614–1945* (Hilversum: Verloren, 2005), 39.

[19] Amsterdam City Archives, Archieven Notariaat, Archive no. 5075, Inventaris no. 3403, 19 February 1626.

[20] The main Dutch Jewish studies journal, *Studia Rosenthaliana*, published English translations of the Amsterdam Portuguese Jewish community records for several years in its volumes from 1967–2002, covering a selection of the original Portuguese records from 1610–1627. The English translations are by E.M. Koen, W. Hamelink-Verweel, S. Hart and W.C. Pieterse. *Studia Rosenthaliana* 32–33 (1998–1999), Amsterdam City Archives, Archieven Notariaat, Archive no. 5075, Inventaris no. 3403, 19 February 1626. See also E.M. Koen, '*The Portuguese Jews in the Municipal Archives of Amsterdam up to 1620*, Brochure, no. Br Ros 309–315', *Studia Rosenthaliana* [1, no. 1 (1967): 111ff.], University Library of Amsterdam.

[21] *Studia Rosenthaliana* 32–33 (1998–1999), Amsterdam City Archives, Archieven Notariaat, Archive no. 392A, ff. 84–84v, notarissen Jacob and Nicolaes Jacobs.

[22] Amsterdam City Archives, Archive no. 5075, Inventaris no. 2271/764, f. 764, 1 November 1656, notaris Adriaen Lock. I thank Boston University PhD candidate Andrea Mosterman very much for her help in the transcription of this document.

[23] Ibid. ff. 764v, 766.

[24] Jonathan Schorsch, *Jews and Blacks in the Early Modern World* (Cambridge: Cambridge University Press, 2004), 57. Schorsch shows that there was rivalry between the Reformed Church ministers and aldermen and the Portuguese Jewish community about whether or not Christians

could or should work as domestic servants in Jewish homes. More fascinating ambiguities in the interactions between Blacks, Jews and Christians in Europe in Jonathan Schorsch, *Swimming the Christian Atlantic: Judeoconversos, Afroiberians and Amerindians in the 17th century* (Leiden: Brill, 2009), 434, 496. Amsterdam City Archives, Archive no. 5075, Inventaris no. 2271/764–766, 1 November 1656, notaris Adriaen Lock.

[25] Amsterdam City Archives, Archieven Notariaat, Archive no. 5075, Inventaris no. 941, notaris Daniel Bredan, Minuutacten 1632.

[26] Hagoort, *Beth Haim*, 39.

[27] See Hondius, 'Black Africans'.

[28] Schorsch, 95.

[29] Sue Peabody, *'There Are No Slaves in France': The Political Culture of Race and Slavery in the Ancien Régime* (New York: Oxford University Press, 1996), 114–115; Dwain Pruitt, '"The Opposition of the Law to the Law": Race, Slavery, and the Law in Nantes, 1715–1778', *French Historical Studies* 30, no. 2 (2007): 149–152.

[30] Daniel J. Hulsebosch, 'Nothing but Liberty: "Somerset's Case" and the British Empire', *Law and History Review* 24, no. 3 (2006): 647–657. Hulsebosch concludes that Somerset's lawyers' primary goal was 'to keep slavery an ocean away': 'The empire's legal pluralism allowed Mansfield to rationalise the brutality of slavery while locating it offshore, thus facilitating the coexistence of slavery and freedom'. See also Daniel J. Hulsebosch, *Constituting Empire: New York and the Transformation of Constitutionalism in the Atlantic World, 1664–1830* (Chapel Hill: University of North Carolina Press, 2005). For more similar and other cases in the British Atlantic world, see Eliga H. Gould, 'Zones of Law, Zones of Violence: The Legal Geography of the British Atlantic, circa 1772', *William and Mary Quarterly* 3rd ser. 60, no. 3 (2003): 471–510. Mansfield sought to 'insulate' England from colonial 'contagion'.

[31] Peabody, *'There Are No Slaves'*; Pierre Boulle, *Race et esclavage dans la France de l'Ancien Régime* (Paris: Perrin, 2007); Pruitt, '"Opposition of the Law"', 147–174. According to Peabody, baptism was separated from the free soil notion in France by the early eighteenth century. She also indicates that 'in 1736 the States General overruled the Court of Amsterdam on the basis of Roman law: That may have effectively ended the validity of the Free soil principle for the remainder of the eighteenth century' (email to author, 2008). I thank Sue Peabody and John Cairns for their stimulating and concrete suggestions for research in Dutch sources.

[32] John Cairns, private communication. Among the Dutch jurists who have mentioned cases that emerged following the 1776 statute establishing free soil in the Netherlands, are Arnoldus Vinnius, J.G.Heineccius, Simon van Leeuwen, as well as Christin, Grotius, and Zyp. I thank John Cairns for these indications. See also Sue Peabody, 'Slavery, Freedom, Statehood and the Law' (paper presented at Maastricht Centre for Transatlantic Studies third interdisciplinary conference on Democracy and Culture in the Transatlantic World, Maastricht, 27–30 October 2004).

[33] Bankton, Andrew MacDowall, Lord, An institute of the laws of Scotland in civil rights: with observations upon the agreement or diversity between them and the laws of England. In four books. Edinburgh, 1751–56, p. 9–11. Slavery is 'so local to the states abovementioned, that so soon as a slave makes his escape, and sets foot in any other nation, they can not only not be vindicated by their former masters, but ipso facto become free, that is, as free as the native born subjects of that state. That it is so in France, is asserted by Vin.lib.I tit.3. instit. Par. 3. In Gallia servi, licet peregrinorum, ut primum regni fines penetraverint, eodem momento liberos fieri, exempla rerum judicatorum ostendunt'. For the Dutch decision to liberate 'Spanish slaves', the reference is 'Groenwegn. De. Leg. Abrog'. For Germany, he refers to 'Heinc'. This case is also discussed in Peabody, *'There Are No Slaves'*, 23–40.

[34] Deuteronomy 23:15–16.

[35] Hulsebosch, 'Nothing but Liberty', 15–16. Whether this policy was also tried and confirmed in cases in other parts of the Netherlands is the subject of further research.

[36] 'The *Akte van Verlatinge*, the 1581 Dutch declaration of independence from Spain, which may have been a model for the American Declaration of Independence, justifies the revolt against the King of Spain by arguing that "God did not create the People Slaves to their Prince". Like the Americans, the Dutch conceived of the foundation of their nation as a rejection of slavery. The right of revolution was further justified thus: "[when the Prince, i.e. the King of Spain] oppresses [the People], ... exacting from them slavish Compliance, then he is no longer a Prince but a Tyrant"'. See also Johanna C. Kardux, Monuments of the Black Atlantic. Slavery Memorials in the United States and the Netherlands. in Heike Raphael-Hernandez (ed.), *Blackening Europe: The African American Presence* (London: Routledge, 2004), 87–105. Johanna Kardux, quoting Stephen E. Lucas, 'The *Plakkaat van Verlatinge*: A Neglected Model for the American Declaration of Independence', in *Connecting Cultures: The Netherlands in Five Centuries of Transatlantic Exchange*, ed. Rosemarijn Hoefte and Johanna C. Kardux (Amsterdam: VU University Press, 1992), 192.

[37] Many Dutch reprints of texts by Bartolomé de las Casas celebrated this image of the Dutch as a nation in pursuit of freedom from their Spanish oppressors, and self-identifying as victims of history. Benjamin Schmidt, *Innocence Abroad: The Dutch Imagination and the New World, 1570–1670* (Cambridge: Cambridge University Press, 2001).

[38] David Eltis and Martin Halpert, Voyages: The Transatlantic Slave Trade Database, Introductory essays: http://www.slavevoyages.org/tast/assessment/essays-intro-01.faces. See also: Henk den Heijer, De geschiedenis van de WIC, Waanders, Zutphen 2002. The provincial Zeeuws Archief in Middelburg and National Archives, The Hague are major archives for further research: www.zeeuwsarchief.nl and www.nationaalarchief.nl

[39] See 'Déclaration pour la police des noirs, 9 August 1777', in Pruitt, '"Opposition of the Law"'. See also Peabody, *'There Are No Slaves'*, 106–120; Cristina Nogueira da Silva and Keila Grinberg, this issue.

[40] J.A. Schiltkamp and J.T. de Smidt, eds., *West-Indische Plakkaatboeken*, vol. 1A and 1B, Suriname I and II; vol. 2A and 2B, Curaçao, Aruba and Bonaire; vol. 3 St. Maarten and St. Eustatius and Saba (The Hague: Nijhoff, 1973–1979).

[41] Ibid., vol. 2A, Curaçao, 6, Article 1: 'De direkteur zal het niet toelaten dat eenige van onse christenen met wilde vrouwen ofte zwartinnen souden trouwen voor ende aleer deselve naer voorgaende genoechsame onderwijsinge gedoopt ende de gemeente Christi ingelijft zijn'. "The director will not allow that any of our Christians would be able to marry 'wild women' (Native American women) or 'swartinnen' (black women) before they would have been properly baptised, educated, and had been incorporated in the community of Christ." The unchanged 1739 rule is no. 139 (38).

[42] Ibid., vol. 1A, Suriname I, 277; no. 240, 28 January 1711.

[43] In the colonies, the Roman law had been accepted in the *Orde van Regeringe*, and this included the law *de fugitivis servis* ('on escaped slaves'): they should always be returned to their owner. Emy Maduro, 'Nos a bai Ulanda: Antillianen in Nederland 1634–1954', in *In het land van de overheerser II: Antillianen en Surinamers in Nederland, 1634/1667 – 1954*, by Gert Oostindie and Emy Maduro (Dordrecht: Foris, 1986), 155 ref.; Cornelis van Bijnkershoek, *Observationes Tumultuariae*, (A.M. Meijers, H.F.W.D. Fischer, and M.S. van Oosten (eds.), Cornelli van Bijnkershoek, Observationes Tumultuariae. Tomus Quartus, Harlemi, Tjeenk Willink 1962, 4; M.S. van Oosten, ed., *Systematisch compendium der observationes tumultuariae van Cornelis van Bijnkershoek* (Haarlem: Tjeenk Willink, 1962), 1.

[44] Peabody, *'There Are No Slaves'*, 39–41.

[45] Maduro, 'Nos a bai Ulanda', 146 ref. ARA, WIC, 421/122–123.

[46] Schiltkamp and de Smidt, *West-Indische Plakkaatboeken*, vol. 1A, Suriname I, 295; no. 245, 1755.

[47] Maduro, 'Nos a bai Ulanda', 155 ref.; R. Buve, 'Surinaamse slaven en vrije negers in Amsterdam gedurende de achttiende eeuw', *Bijdragen tot de Taal-, Land- en Volkenkunde* 119, no. 1 (1963): 8–17 (15–16).

[48] Gert Oostindie, 'Kondreman in Bakrakondre: Surinamers in Nederland 1667–1954', in Oostindie and Maduro, *In het land*, 14.

[49] Schiltkamp and de Smidt, *West-Indische Plakkaatboeken*, vol. IB, Suriname II, 864; no. 739, 17 December 1773. See also National Archive, The Hague, Archief Raden van Politie, Suriname, 219, no. 906; Archief Societeyt van Suriname, SAS 403, vol. 6.

[50] Oostindie, 'Kondreman in Bakrakondre', 15–16; Maduro, 'Nos a bai Ulanda', 155–157. They refer to National Archive, The Hague, Archief Societeyt van Suriname, SAS 406, no. 31; 403, vol. 6, 111; Archief Raden van Politie, Suriname, 220, no. 965; 224, no. 279.

[51] Maduro, 'Nos a bai Ulanda', 158–159. Maduro presents the case of a Curaçao slave owner who as late as 1852 tried very persistently to keep his enslaved Virginie and her daughters as his possessions, which was ultimately turned down by the Minister of Colonies (162).

[52] George M. Fredrickson, 'Race, Ethnicity, and National Identity in France and the United States: A Comparative Historical Overview' (paper presented at fifth annual Gilder Lehrman Center international conference on Collective Degradation: Slavery and the Construction of Race, Yale University, 7–8 November 2003), http://www.yale.edu/glc/events/race/Fredrickson.pdf. See also Peabody, *'There Are No Slaves'*, 128–131.

[53] Jennifer Heuer, 'The One-Drop Rule in Reverse? Interracial Marriages in Napoleonic and Restoration France', *Law and History Review* 27, no. 3 (2009): 515–548; Jaap Toes, 'Een zwarte bruidegom en een blanke bruid', *Pro Memorie* 3, no. 2 (2001): 313–315. Exceptions did occur: in Amsterdam on 5 February 1815, the 53-year-old musician Jan Andries Machielse, who was born in Curaçao, married Gerardina Hellendoorn, who was born in Emmen.

[54] Carl Haarnack and Dienke Hondius, '"Swart" (Black) in the Netherlands: Africans and Creoles in the Northern Netherlands from the Middle Ages to the Twentieth Century', in *Black Is Beautiful: Rubens to Dumas*, ed. Esther Schreuder and Elmer Kolfin (Zwolle: Waanders, 2008), 94; Dirk Tang, Passagiersoverzicht Sociëteit van Suriname, tussen Suriname en Nederland, 1729–1775. Source: Society of Surinam Archive, National Archives, The Hague. Gouvernementsjournaelen 1682–1795, archive entrance nr. 1.05.03, inv.nos. 171–347. I am grateful to Dirk Tang for making available this data from his research. Of a total of 456 black people known to date, 47 per cent (216) were men, 35 per cent (161) were women, 15 per cent (65) were boys, 2 per cent (9) were 'mulatto girls' and 1 per cent (5) was small children (calculated from Tang's data). The estimates of Gert Oostindie are slightly higher, with a total of 101 persons travelling from Suriname to the Netherlands between 1729 and 1749, and 648 between 1749 and 1781. Oostindie, 'Kondreman in Bakrakondre', 7 (Table 1).

[55] A.M. de Rouville, *Is Nederland verplicht om bij de emancipatie der slaven in West-Indië de eigenaren der slaven schadevergoeding te betalen?* (Themis, 1860), 55, 187–242, quoted in Jaap Toes, 'Wanklanken rond een wingewest: in de nadagen van de Surinaamse slavernij' (PhD diss., VU University, 1992), (Hoorn: Drukkerij Noordholland, 1992), 18.

[56] See Glenn Willemsen, *Dagen van gejuich en gejubel: viering en herdenking van de afschaffing van de slavernij in Nederland, Suriname en de Nederlandse Antillen* (The Hague: Amrit, 2006); Cynthia MacLeod, *Slavernij en de Memorie* (Alkmaar: Conserve, 2002).

[57] *Gouvernementsblad Suriname*, 1813–1828, 2 delen, University Library, University of Amsterdam, Bijzondere collecties, TS 5557, Register, vol. 1: 'Hoofdgeld op de slaven, behoorende tot de houtgronden en Plantaadjen 6% op de uit te voerene produkten, ten aanzien van vaartuigen', 4, 2–4–6 March 1816.

[58] Gouvernementsblad Suriname, 1825. See also Publicatieblad, 1 January 1831, and Emy Maduro, 'Nos a bai Ulanda', p. 158.

[59] *Reglement op het beleid der regering van de Nederlandsche West-Indische bezittingen*, 21 July 1828, Suriname, Engelbracht 1828, Articles 116 and 117, 47 (copy at KIT Library, Amsterdam). I thank Susan Legéne for her reference to a rare copy of the original text of the 1828 *Reglement* at the KIT Library, Amsterdam. See also Jaap Toes, 'Wanklanken rond een wingewest: in de nadagen van de Surinaamse slavernij' (PhD diss., VU University, 1992), (Hoorn: Drukkerij

Noordholland, 1992), 37, who refers to a letter of Raad-fiscaal aan Gouverneur in the Manuscript of Mr A.T. Lammens, member and later president of the Court, Surinaams Museum IX, afd. Aanmerkingen, no. 9. See also M.L. Wijnholt, *Strafrecht in Suriname* (Deventer: Kluwer, 1965), 31.

[60] Susan Legêne, 'De bagage van Blomhoff en Van Breugel: Japan, Java, Tripoli en Suriname in de negentiende-eeuwse Nederlandse cultuur van het imperialisme' (KIT, Amsterdam 1998: Dissertation Erasmus University Rotterdam, 1998), 154–155.

[61] In 1832, the new rules were 'simplified' and published in a new Royal Decree (*Koninklijk Besluit*). The separation of powers (*trias politica*) from 1828 was revoked. In the colonies, 'the separated powers of legislative, legal and executive powers, were merged and reunited again': see J. Wolbers in *Geschiedenis van Suriname* (1861; Amsterdam: H. de Hoogh, 1970), 672–676, 813–814.

[62] *Slavenreglement*, Article 3, regarding food for slaves in 1851 and 1856. See Wolbers, *Geschiedenis van Suriname*, 276.

[63] *Gouvernementsblad Suriname*, no. 11, 1816: Notificatie 16 December 1816, of a Resolutie, taken by the Hof van Policie. Paramaribo, 16 Dec. 1816, Ter Ordonnantie van den Hove, P.J. Changuion, secretaris.

[64] Herman Daniël Benjamins and Joh. F. Snelleman, eds., *Encyclopedie van Nederlandsch West-Indië* (Leiden, 1914–1917). *The Encyclopedia of the Netherlands West Indies (1914–1917)* contains paragraphs on the subjects 'Slavery', 'Leave of Absence', payment during leaves of absence. Leiden: Brill. Herman Daniël Benjamins en Joh. F. Snelleman (eds.). There were changes in these rules in 1887 and 1908–1910.

[65] *Gouvernementsblad Suriname*, no. 13, 25 July 1831: *Reglement op het Burgerregt in de Nederlandsche West-Indische Koloniën.*

[66] Ibid., 156, Articles 6–20: Paramaribo, De Algemeene Secretaris, G.A. van der Mee, en Cantz'laar, Ter Ordonnantie van Zijne Excellentie.

[67] Nadere voorziening omtrent het manumitteren van Slaven in de Nederlandsche West-Indische Bezittingen. (Specifications regarding manumission of Slaves in the Netherlands West Indian possessions.) De Gouverneur-Generaal, 22 augustus 1843; artikel 1- 12. 3 oktober 1844, B.J. Elias, ter ordonnantie van den Gouverneur Generaal, de Gouvernements-Secretaris, G.S. de Veer. (p. 260–261).

[68] *Gouvernementsblad Suriname*, no. 2, 24 January 1850, Article 11: bepalingen, door aankomende en vertrekkende Personen, in de Kolonie Suriname in acht te nemen. (Article 11: rules to be taken into consideration by persons arriving into and leaving from the Colony Suriname.)

[69] Ibid., no. 19, 14 June 1873: Paramaribo, Proclamatie. Gouverneur Van Idsinga. 'Proclamatie. De Gouverneur aan de onder Staatstoezigt geplaatste bevolking in de kolonie Suriname'. (Proclamation: from the Governor to the Population placed under State Supervision in the colony Suriname.)

Infidels at the Oar: A Mediterranean Exception to France's Free Soil Principle

Gillian Weiss

Ottomans and Moroccans on France's galleys from the sixteenth to the eighteenth century violated the kingdom's 'free soil' principle. Evaluating naval, spatial, strategic, theological and juridical explanations, this article argues that employing Muslim rowers served pragmatic and symbolic ends, while provoking relatively little consternation among French leaders. Only after colonial slaves began claiming liberty in the metropole did questions about the lawfulness of keeping esclaves turcs *arise. The rationales proposed suggest that a categorical shift in French understandings of servitude accompanied more limited access to freedom as the Atlantic slave trade eclipsed the Mediterranean one.*

'There are no slaves in France'. So went the adage that any serf, bondservant, captive or chattel entering French territory be immediately freed. On these grounds, as Sue Peabody has shown for the eighteenth century, hundreds of colonial slaves won manumission in the metropole.[1] When French kings, nobles and jurists in the sixteenth century began applying municipal customs of 'free soil' to the entire kingdom, however, their benchmark was generally not sub-Saharan pagans but Ottoman and Moroccan 'infidels'. Second-hand reports have the Duke de Guise refusing to turn over the 'Moorish or Turkish slave' of a Spanish general during the 1552 siege of Metz, according to 'the privilege of France from time immemorial . . . that the least barbarian or foreigner, having put only his foot on French soil is immediately free and removed from all slavery and captivity'. They show King Henry III liberating 'Turks, Moors and Barbarians' from a Spanish galley that wrecked on a sandbar near Calais.[2] Most famously, they cite a 1571 judgment from the Parlement of Bordeaux, barring the sale of several 'Moors' acquired by a Norman trader on the Barbary Coast, as contemporaries called North Africa.[3]

Muslims unbound thus became central to conceptions of French liberty. But this did not prevent natives of the Levant and the Maghreb, southern or eastern Europe from becoming slaves in France. Traces remain of domestic slaves with such origins in sixteenth-century Marseille.[4] By 1544, once demand for manpower outstripped supplies of voluntary oarsmen, an inventory listed 210 'Turks' and 79 'Moors', representing more than a third of the slaves and convicts on galleys stationed in the city.[5] Early commercial concessions from the Ottoman sultan[6] and the pashas, *deys* and *beys* who governed the regencies of Algiers, Tunis and Tripoli all mentioned the return of enslaved rowers. Charles IX, for example, promised to pay compensation to local captains after repatriating 60 Algerians in 1562.[7] In an ode likely composed during the 1590s, poet François de Malherbe celebrated France's 'warships brave' that unloaded 'Moorish slaves'.[8]

The first Franco-Tunisian treaty of 1604 guaranteed the exchange of any French slaves in Tunis for all the 'Turks and Muslims detained in Provence'.[9] Three years later, Henry IV ordered Marseille's leadership to turn over the men, but he quickly restricted emancipation to 'only the least useful ... and least able to support work'.[10] During the decades that followed, the perceived worth of Muslims as rowers would repeatedly trump both diplomatic arrangements and ideals about France's 'free soil'.

Port-city slavery

Subjugated Muslims in the port cities of Marseille, Toulon and Dunkirk, briefly Bordeaux, and afterwards Brest and Rochefort, spent spring and summer at sea. Chained to benches below deck for months at a stretch, whipped as they rowed and fed mostly hard tack, bean soup and water, they were left to sleep, 'eat and shit altogether' where they sat.[11] During fall and winter ashore, they endured nights on docked galleys beneath two-ply woollen tents or, by the turn of the eighteenth century, inside barracks known as *bagnes*. On payment of a daily surety, they toiled in naval arsenals and shipbuilding yards, and eventually in proto-factories at the wharves. Some peddled clothes and coffee, or pulled teeth in small stalls along the quay.[12] Whether allowed to roam unrestrained or paired with convicts known as *forçats* and accompanied by guards[13], others were hired out to local businesses and households – as valets and longshoremen, water haulers and construction workers, minions in the production of soap and every sort of manufactured good. In theory, if not always in practice, these valuable slaves were steered away from dangerous employment; significantly, most seem to have been spared the job of burying corpses during the 1720 plague. With accrued earnings, slaves bought extra food, frequented taverns and even hired prostitutes. With varying degrees of censorship and confiscation, they posted and received letters.[14] Though naval ministers did their best to prevent this, slaves met with dignitaries from their home countries.[15] They buried their own dead and, in later periods, prayed under some covering at a designated cemetery.[16]

Relative freedom of movement, contact and worship, however, could not allay the misery of French thralldom, from which only the luckiest or high-born Ottomans and Moroccans ever escaped. 'A Turk on the galleys is a slave in perpetuity', asserted a former chaplain in 1708, 'unless when he is old, he finds patrons to secure his liberty for the price of money'.[17] In fact, the Crown – with resistance from galley officers – sometimes accepted payments[18] or made gifts of young, fit rowers with good connections. But old age, infirmity and money did not guarantee emancipation: in some periods, only replacements would do. More common than ransom were exchanges for North African-held French slaves, organised by family members and religious orders, or stipulated by peace accords. Flight was another option. Absconding across the Mediterranean in a stolen boat sometimes worked. Distinguishing headgear (a red cap), hairstyle (shaved with a tuft in back), dress (long shirt and short pants), bare feet and chains (see Figure 1), combined with unfamiliar language and terrain, made overland evasion difficult, however, especially once mutilated or branded a runaway.[19] Still, both techniques succeeded often enough to warrant laws for prevention and compensation.[20]

Diverse geographic origins, occasional Jewish or Orthodox allegiances and invariably dependent status were concealed behind just two appellations: 'Turk' and 'Moor'. There is no doubt, however, that in common usage *turc* had become a quasi-synonym for *esclave* by the mid sixteenth century, as would *nègre* more than 100 years later.[21] For until the kingdom became significantly implicated in transporting black chattel across the Atlantic Ocean[22], France's primary reference point for servitude remained the Mediterranean Sea, where Christian and Muslim powers regularly captured and kept each other's subjects for labour and profit.[23] Among French officials and ordinary people, the detention of both Catholic and Protestant compatriots in North Africa stirred anxieties about economic depletion, social instability, physical corruption, political betrayal and religious conversion.[24] Meanwhile, the presence of ostensibly Muslim slaves on French ships and shores challenged traditional commitments to personal freedom, as well as royal bids for confessional uniformity. It often contravened bilateral treaties. Why, then, did Louis XIV more than other kings not only tolerate but also promote the enslavement of Ottomans and Moroccans? Indeed, the era of his personal rule saw a tenfold increase in the size of the galleys' servile labour force, requiring an annual influx of 150–200 slaves, for an estimated total of 10–12,000 slaves, over a period of 50 years.[25]

In seeking an explanation for such growth despite legal, religious and diplomatic impediments, this article will evaluate the significance of five possible factors: naval ambitions in the Mediterranean whose fulfilment seemingly required infidel rowers; spatial judgments about peripheries and centres that made licit otherwise forbidden Christian–Muslim contact; strategic deference to the customs of foreign lands; theological distinctions between believers and non-believers; and juridical suppositions about the right of reprisal.

Naval ambitions

France's galley fleet was an aesthetic marvel. Even before its restoration under the direction of Jean-Baptiste Colbert, seventeenth-century voyagers described ornate carvings, gilded bows, multicoloured flags and the rhythmic sweep of oars. Some also dwelled on the stench and misery within. Flemish nobleman Emanuel d'Aranda, who owed his release from Algerian servitude to a privately arranged slave exchange, remarked that the 'hundred Turkish slaves' he saw in Dunkirk, crammed into 'a miserable cave [were] not better treated than the Christians in Barbary'.[26] Writer Madeleine de Scudéry noted from Marseille that the word *esclave*, which appears metaphorically in poems of love and novels, 'here floods the imagination with heavy iron chains, red bonnets, blue shirts, shaved heads, the faces of Turks and other similar things'.[27] Though one essayist insisted that 'France is so in love with liberty that she cannot abide a slave: such that Turks and Moors, let alone Christians can never wear irons'[28], eyewitnesses glimpsed hell in the sight of 'naked men ... enchained'[29] and

> convicts and slaves indifferently mixed and chained to one another, crawling with vermin and scabies, beaten morning and night, having as their only clothing a nasty sort of shorts and wide cassock, no stockings, no shoes, not even a bit of straw to lie down on.[30]

For the Sun King, galleys made effective coastal patrols, helping to assure the safe passage of merchants, while expressing power and majesty. 'Nothing manifests his sovereignty more than these battleships, stern aloft and underfoot three hundred slaves in chains', declared his galley intendant, observing, 'Roman emperors triumphed with less'.[31] In order to obtain these slaves, Louis XIV considered land raids but opted for purchase, spending tens of thousands of *livres* yearly – expenditures that represented more than two per cent of the overall budget for the galleys in the second half of the seventeenth century.[32] (During this period, Ottoman or Moroccan oarsmen cost 300–400 *livres* each plus 30 per cent in taxes and fees, about the same as both French and sub-Saharan African slaves.)[33] Often on the sly[34], royal representatives scoured the Mediterranean, signing contracts with consuls in Muslim trading ports, agents in Livorno and Malta, and merchants in Provence to furnish set numbers. *Forçats* sometimes managed to obtain *turcs* as substitutes.[35] Playing on both sides of the fence, petty traders both ransomed Muslims from other Christian countries and sold them to France.[36] One slaver was a former slave. 'I bought a vessel, half merchant, half-armed for privateering to avenge the cruelties I had suffered during my slavery', recounted Jean Bonnet, who had escaped from Tunis after three years' detention. In 1672, he delivered 20 slaves to Marseille.[37]

The recruitment of 'Turks' as opposed to other ethnic groups brought additional perceived benefits – both practical and symbolic. 'Extremely vigorous, resistant to fatigue and very tall', Muslims were reputed the best rowers, and thus placed in technically demanding positions at the oar. Certainly, in 1662, the head of France's forces in the Mediterranean could imagine 'no better men nor as strong as those who accompany the pirates of Algiers and other parts of Barbary'[38], and had put 2000 French seamen into North African servitude.[39] Failed experiments with Iroquois and sub-Saharan Africans between 1679 and 1681 purportedly upheld this instinct.[40] Why Moroccans, Anatolians, Bosnians or even European converts to Islam fared physically better, despite their varied ethnic background, was unexplained. Why Greeks, Albanians and Russians made viable slaves, despite their Christian faith, is another question. Whatever the initial rationale for enslaving so-called 'Schismatics', Colbert seems to have halted the practice after 1677, telling France's consul in Genoa to buy 'the largest number of Turks possible ... but take care not to purchase any that are Christian, His Majesty not wanting any to serve on his galleys'. Ten years later, the conviction that a galley's power depended on the power of 'Turks' inspired a royal ordinance prescribing that one-quarter of rowers be slaves.[41]

Rightly or wrongly assumed to be Muslims, 'Turks' as slaves also had propaganda value for a monarch posturing as 'the Most Christian King'. No wonder the galley intendant dispatched two to work as models at the École des Beaux Arts or had others pose on pedestals 'with collars of silver and chains on their feet' as *tableaux vivants* to amuse touring princes.[42] Staffing galleys with 'infidels', like bombarding North African cities and freeing Christians from North African bondage, enhanced Louis XIV's crusading credentials.[43] Doing so not only masked conflicts between the Gallican Church and the papacy, but also distracted the attention of a turcophobic public from the king's willingness to sign accords with the Ottoman Empire and its dependencies.[44]

Spatial judgments

Thus, for the sake of brawn and the display of belief, French naval officials wanted slaves whom they could pass off as Muslims, and in the 1660s, 1670s and 1680s seem to have expressed not a single scruple about violating the kingdom's customs to buy them. Muslim 'merchandise' – to use the galley intendant's term – appears on lists of other expenses like provisions and custom duties.[45] Nor did anyone question the legality of capturing Muslims at sea during periods of open warfare with North Africa. What did stir some debate in these decades was whether or not to enslave shipwreck victims and runaways, for France's right of refuge, known to *mudejar* and *morisco* slaves fleeing the Iberian Peninsula in the fifteenth and sixteenth centuries[46], had been enshrined in Franco-North African peace treaties from 1628 onwards – and publicised when fugitives decided to repudiate Islam.[47] Clearly related to the free soil principle, it was claimed as an inheritance from both the Roman Empire and the Christian Church, which granted asylum in holy places.[48]

When two Algerian barks with 114 'Turks' on-board crashed on the Languedoc coast in 1669, therefore, what seemed like a boon for the galleys turned into a lost opportunity. After some dithering, Louis XIV ordered the survivors repatriated. He did the same for some 'Turks and Moors' saved from a sinking ship in 1674, and for the 130-man crew of the *Golden Crescent*, which in 1686 made an emergency landing in Brittany.[49] Also, against the inclinations of galley commanders hungry for labour and ship captains hungry for profit, the king regularly returned to North Africa and the Levant individuals who had escaped from slavery elsewhere in Europe. French failure to send home absconding Muslims risked the lives and livelihoods of Frenchmen in Muslim trading ports, which is why he probably responded quickly to a 1696 petition by four Algerians who, as fugitives from the Portuguese galleys, 'took refuge under the banner of France', only to be sold off in Genoa.[50] In order to keep the peace during the minority of Louis XV, the regent went so far as to pay ransoms for slaves in Sicily captured from a French vessel.[51] In order to enhance the reputation of France overseas, naval ministers in the later eighteenth century often charged Marseille's Chamber of Commerce with the upkeep and transport of former slaves.[52]

While the notion of asylum undermined the detention of 'Turks' who arrived in France by fortune, then, it might well have smoothed acceptance of Muslims brought involuntarily to live among Christians. Independent from France until 1486 and defined by its proximity to the Mediterranean, Marseille had long welcomed goods and people from the Levant and the Maghreb, and long suffered accusations of overfamiliarity with 'infidels'. Municipal leaders in the sixteenth century preferred to present their 'maritime and limitrophe city' as a bulwark against both Protestantism and the literal and figurative contagion purportedly emanating from lands of Islam.[53] In the seventeenth century, after ritually claiming possession over Marseille, Louis XIV made this role official. A royal edict promulgated in March 1669, which affirmed Marseille's status as a free port, naval base and site for quarantine, also envisioned the city as a place of refuge: 'His majesty has wished that this famous town become the common fatherland of all peoples, even more than Rome was in its day. The most barbarous and backward nation will find asylum there with no more foreignness.'[54] For the sake of commerce, Louis XIV was willing to suspend on France's periphery those legal disabilities that came with birth outside his territories and overlook that religious pluralism which he and his predecessors endeavoured to erase at France's centre.

This new regime helped insert Marseille into the global economy[55] and brought even more diversity to the population. Eighteenth-century travellers and painters depicted the city's port as a place of 'perpetual movement', thanks to the constant flow 'of people of every country and condition, men and women, Turks, Greeks, Egyptian and Moors', who wore a blur of national costumes and spoke a babel of tongues.[56] The city's multi-ethnic character did not necessarily translate into harmonious relations among constituent elements. It did, however, make *turcs* – whether free or unfree – less noticeable.

Strategic deference

Ottoman and Moroccan rowers, as well as their relatives and rulers, had long objected to the practice of Muslim servitude in France. They certainly had reason to protest illegal captures and incarcerations, insufficient rations and brutal treatments, oarsmen hidden from North African envoys or denied entrance to burial grounds, and the wilful confusion of political divides, which resulted in, say, Tunisian invalids let go in place of able-bodied Tripolitans. 'We are told after this campaign liberty, and this liberty never comes', wrote *ra'is* Mehmet Soulreys in July 1681, in the name of all the 'slaves of Algiers'. Galley officers 'stroked [the Moroccan ambassador] on one side and stole his shirt on another, for they prevented him from seeing a single one of us', complained Muhammad bin Ha'ider of Salé in an intercepted missive dated May 1682.[57]

Only in the last decade of the seventeenth century, however, did any French leaders question the principle of holding Muslim slaves. These rare administrative and theological musings of the 1690s marked the confluence of three developments. First was the achievement of a 60-per-cent expansion of the royal galley fleet to 40 ships, creating an even higher demand for 'Turks'.[58] Second was a violent push – a series of bombardments – to repatriate all the French slaves in North Africa, resulting in bilateral treaties that obliged the discharge of all North African slaves in France.[59] Third was the steady growth of colonial slavery, creating the first opportunities for blacks to claim liberty in the metropole. With the addition of 1000 Muslims needed to achieve an ideal *esclave* to *forçat* ratio and the outflow of approximately 700 Algerians, Tunisians and Tripolitans under way, the pressure was on – to hold or acquire as many new *turcs* as possible.[60] In this context, the manumission of two sub-Saharan Africans fleeing Caribbean bondage posed a challenge. It pointed up the contradiction of Muslims in chains.

Newly appointed Minister of the Marine Louis Phélypeaux, Comte de Pontchartrain, charged with both naval and colonial affairs, had the job of articulating Louis XIV's inconsistent application of a freedom principle to slaves from the Mediterranean and the Atlantic. In the case of stowaways from Martinique, he reported in October 1691 that the king 'did not judge it apropos to return them to the isles, their liberty being acquired by the laws of the kingdom concerning slaves as soon as they touch the soil'.[61] For the same reason, Pontchartrain rejected a Sr. Marin gift of a *nègre* for his galleys in October 1694. The only people exempt from territorial liberation, he asserted, even as the first dictionary of the *Académie Française* recapitulated its universality[62], were 'Turks and Moors who are sent to Marseille for service on the galleys'. According to the minister, the distinction had nothing to do with religion or race. Rather, he attributed it to respect – for the inviolability of alien customs and the sanctity of contracts. Muslim slaves, the minister emphasised, 'before arriving [in a French port] are *purchased* in foreign countries where this kind of commerce is established'.[63] Perhaps Pontchartrain was genuinely seeking a competing principle for allowing slaves in France; more likely he was just practising sophistry for the sake of his sovereign.

Theological distinctions

Four years later, the Sorbonne's 'Court of Conscience' put a religious spin on the matter, asking why '[o]ur Most Christian King has no qualms about buying Turkish slaves, even though very few embrace Christianity'. Implicit in this 1698 formulation were the beliefs that a previous monarch had authorised enslavement as an effective means of evangelising to pagans; and that the current one employed the galleys as an effective means of evangelising to heretics.[64] Implicit in the presiding judge's response was the pertinence of a 'just war' doctrine for rationalising the seizure of infidels. While Christians may not capture and keep believers, ruled Germain Fromageau, they have every right 'to deprive [unbelievers] of their liberty and make them slaves'.[65] Following different logic, the theologian agreed with the minister. As long as hostile Christian powers lawfully made Muslims slaves, officially friendly states like France lawfully bought them – or at least tried to do so, with diminishing success in the eighteenth century.

As in the colonies, where the *Code Noir* now regulated the treatment and religious instruction of sub-Saharan Africans, faith had no necessary bearing on freedom. Political theorist Antoine Loisel had insisted 90 years prior that: 'All persons are free in this kingdom, and as soon as a slave has arrived at the borders of this place, being baptised, is freed.'[66] Instead, over the objections of both galley chaplains belonging to the Congrégation de la Mission (Lazarists) founded by Saint Vincent de Paul and of the Inquisitor to the Order of Saint John of Jerusalem (Knights of Malta), most 'Christianised Turks' received only special outfits, a designated chapel, extra rations and symbolic payments.[67] In July 1676, for example, Colbert admonished galley intendant Jean-Baptiste Brodart for allowing newly christened 'Louis Bonneau' to appeal for manumission in Paris. On further investigation, Brodart discovered that the North African had been excused from the oar by working at the Lazarist-run hospital. 'This *turc* is a very bad man, a great sodomist', he informed the minister, who 'only became a Christian to escape ... I beg you not to grant his liberty'.[68]

Just before Protestantism became illegal in France with the 1685 'Revocation of the Edict of Nantes', a royal edict had ordered that 'Mohammedans and idolaters' be catechised in Catholicism rather than the 'false doctrine' of 'the said R.P.R. [*Religion Prétendu Reformée* (so-called reformed religion)]'.[69] Inland, such instructions may have swayed a few potential converts from Islam, but on the galleys, mutual adversity appears to have drawn the two groups together rather than drive them apart. Jean Marteilhe, '*Forçat* for the Faith' between 1700 and 1713, praised the *esclave turc* who smuggled on-board letters and alms for condemned Protestants. On the galleys, 'Turks are only Turks in name and Christians in effect', wrote priest-turned-minister Jean-François Bion. He charged Catholics with 'the barbarity of infidels', claiming that Muslims 'would rather be changed into dogs than embrace such a cruel religion'.[70] Of course, unknown numbers did convert. The last ones, lingering in Toulon in 1776, subsisted on municipal charity.[71]

For a couple of highly placed individuals, then, detention without conversion raised theoretical issues about provenance and procurement. In practice, however, the most important consideration continued to be diplomatic reciprocity – and its effect on the freedom and prosperity of France's trans-Mediterranean communities. How many Muslims could France keep without starting a war? How many French slaves could be sacrificed to prevent the return of prized rowers to their countries of origin? Fear of repercussions during the 1680s resulted in compulsory 'Turk' letter-writing to North African *deys*.[72] Its invocation served as a weapon of the weak for an Algerian galley slave, who threatened the marine minister with a smear campaign should his grievances not be addressed.[73] In 1710, it even lay behind deliberations about enforcing France's free soil principle in the case of an Ottoman merchant in the Provençal town of La Ciotat whose prepubescent black slave became Christian. Explain that 'liberty is acquired by right to every slave who finds himself in the lands of the king's obedience', Louis XIV ordered galley intendant Pierre Arnoul. Then get a testimony signed by three 'Turks' 'to shut the mouths' of any foreign leaders 'who might take up his cause'.[74] Even after plague killed off the great majority of *forçats* and *turcs* and galleys became technologically obsolete, slaves remained a factor in France's overseas standing. Though the fleet's size contracted dramatically in the eighteenth century, Muslims continued to pull a portion of its remaining oars.[75]

What does this evaluation of naval ambitions, spatial judgments, strategic deference and theological distinctions reveal about France's use of Muslim rowers in violation of its free soil principle? Most importantly, for most of the seventeenth century no one noticed any problem. The desire for prestige at home and abroad drove the illegal detention of 'Turks', while the pragmatic exigencies of international relations partially mitigated it. Meanwhile, port-city cosmopolitanism helped obscure the compromises made for commerce. Reservations expressed and rationales ventured for buying slaves in Mediterranean markets only appeared once French colonists began employing large numbers of chattel in the Atlantic.

Juridical suppositions

The last reflections on the juridical status of Muslim oarsmen date to the second half of the eighteenth century. According to a distiller of customary law and a contributor to the *Encyclopédie*, 'Turks' could be slaves in France precisely because they had power, not because they were powerless. When not rowing, Muslims were roving, both texts implied, on heavily armed sailing ships in pursuit of Christians. The entry 'galérien' from 1757 was the more explicit: calling galley slaves 'men taken in war against the infidels', it acknowledged that 'by the right of war, these should only be regarded as prisoners; but we reduce them to a sort of slavery by the right of reprisal'.[76] In fact, by the time these lines appeared, the matter was metaphysical. 'Cannon diplomacy' had made sure North Africa's corsairs no longer threatened French shipping. Furthermore, while two edicts and several court cases were seeking to reconcile black colonial slavery with metropolitan freedom, 11 decommissioned galleys had been transferred from Marseille to Toulon, where a vestigial population of 200 *turcs* was dwindling towards three.[77]

The second edition of jurist François Bourjon's *Le Droit commun de la France* was published posthumously in 1770. It also invoked the 'just right of reprisal' – but without naming names. French common law, based on religion, nature and reason, holds that all men are free, it asserted. Two exceptions confirmed the rule. 'Negroes brought to France by masters who intend to take them back to the other hemisphere remain under the power of their masters', in accordance with legislation from 1738.[78] In addition, the kingdom also tolerates one other type of servitude, 'in order to treat certain nations the way they treat subjects of the king when any of them fall under their power whom they were the first to exploit'.[79] As the author of this article would have it, 'Turks' themselves bore responsibility for the quandary of slavery on free soil because in some mythical past they had made the first move.

Jacques-Henri Bernardin de Saint Pierre did not buy it. Writing in 1784, this noted abolitionist remembered a *turc esclave* he had met in Toulon more than 20 years before – not as an 'enemy combatant' but a 'good Muslim . . . who never did any harm'. The author of novels and plays that decried both Caribbean and North African bondage here mocked the values of kings who sought stature in the subjugation of human beings. 'Given that our kings want to have Turks, like the kings of Asia have elephants', he remarked, 'it strikes me as more befitting their grandeur to put [the slaves] in a good hospice than on a galley'. For Bernardin de Saint Pierre, slavery in France represented not so much an infringement of a legal tradition as an abdication of a universal right.[80]

Categorical shifts

Today, many scholars would not classify *turcs* in France as real slaves. Since they could gain release through ransom, exchange or treaty, since they could correspond with family members and transmit property, and since they could not pass on servile status, Ottoman and Moroccan subjects in French bondage were neither 'natally alienated' nor 'socially dead'.[81] As such, they might seem to qualify better as hostages or prisoners of war. To the political theorists, naval officers, jurists and judges of early modern France, however, Muslim rowers helped define both liberty and slavery. Their emancipation provided the basis of France's freedom myth in the sixteenth century and into the eighteenth century also served as the leading examples of *esclaves*.

That from the 1690s to the 1780s the status of 'Turks' provoked any uncertainty relates to the expansion of French slaveholding rather than the incongruity of the category. In France, before the rise of the Atlantic trade, neither inheritance nor permanence was an essential component of slavery. The kingdom's 'freedom principle' developed in a Mediterranean world where Christians and Muslims, whether captured or purchased, experienced degrees of unfreedom – and liberty could be bought, negotiated, traded or won. Ottoman and Moroccan rowers did not need to invoke sayings about France *franc* (free France). They had other options. By the eighteenth century, however, the vast majority of slaves in colonial and metropolitan France were black. Just as these sub-Saharan Africans reshaped understandings of slavery, so too did they adapt the maxim, 'There are no slaves in France'.

Acknowledgements

A version of this article was presented at the Sixteenth Century Society and Conference annual meeting in Geneva, Switzerland, May 2009. The author wishes to thank her co-panellists Megan Armstrong, Molly Greene and Claire Norton, as well as Marcy Norton, Sue Peabody, Elliot Posner and Nicolas Vatin for their useful comments and suggestions.

Notes

[1] Sue Peabody, *'There Are No Slaves in France': The Political Culture of Race and Slavery in the Ancien Régime* (New York: Oxford University Press, 1996).

[2] Pierre de Bourdeille, *Œuvres complètes de Pierre de Bourdeille, seigneur de Brantôme*, ed. Ludovic Lalanne, 11 vols. (Paris: Veuve J. Renouard, 1864–1882), 4: 193; Pierre de Saint-Romuald, *Annales chronologiques et historiques...* (Paris: Clouzier, 1665), cited in Ernest Nys, *Études de droit international et de droit politique*, 2 vols. (Brussels: Castaigne, 1896–1901), 1:257.

[3] Commonly cited twentieth-century scholars – Charles de la Roncière, *Nègres et négriers* (Paris: Éditions des Portiques, 1933), 15–16; Shelby T. McCloy, *The Negro in France* (Lexington: University Press of Kentucky, 1961), 12 – assume sub-Saharan origins for the slaves based on two versions of the *Chronique bordeloise* by Gabriel de Lurbe (Bordeaux: Simon Millanges, 1594), 47v and (Bordeaux: Simon Boé, 1703), 33, which refer to *nègres et mores*; and by Jean de Gaufreteau, 2 vols. (Bordeaux: Charles Lefébvre, 1877–1878), 1: 158–159, which notes that the inhabitants of Bordeaux called the slaves *mores* because of the black colour of their bodies and faces and white undersides of their hands. The slaves' complexion may well have been dark, but in the sixteenth century the term 'Moor' was commonly understood to mean Muslim.

[4] For examples, see Wolfgang Kaiser, 'Les "Hommes de credit" dans l'échange et le rachat des prisonniers en Méditerranée', in *Le Commerce des captifs: les intermédiaires dans l'échange et le Rachat des prisonniers en Méditerranée, XVe–XVIIIe siècle* (Rome: École Française de Rome, 2008), 291n2; 'Les Paradoxes d'une ville frontière: conflits et compromis à Marseille au XVIe siècle', in *La Ville à la Renaissance: espaces, représentations, pouvoirs*, ed. Gérald Chaix, Marie-Luce Demonet and Robert Sauzet (Paris: H. Champion, 2008), 293–294.

[5] Jean Bérenger, 'La Politique française en Méditerranée au XVIe siècle et l'alliance ottomane', in *La Guerre de course en Méditerranée (1515–1830)*, ed. Michel Vergé-Franceschi and Antoine-Marie Graziani (Paris: Presses de l'Université Paris-Sorbonne, 2000), 2004; Gabriel Audisio, 'Galériens dans le port de Marseille au XVIe siècle', in *Marseille, face au(x) pouvoir(s): [Texte imprimé]: actes du colloque, Marseille, 4 et 5 février 2000* [organisé par le Counseil géneral des Bouches-du-Rhône] (Marseille: Archives Départementales des Bouches-du-Rhône, 2002), 48–49.

[6] On the Ottoman 'capitulations' (*ahdname*), see Gilles Veinstein, 'Les Capitulations franco-ottomanes de 1536: sont-elles encore controversable?', in *Living in the Ottoman Ecumenical Community: Essays in Honour of Suraiya Faroqhi*, ed. Suraiya Faroqhi and Halil Inalcik (Leiden: Brill, 2008), 71–88.

[7] King Charles IX to naval commissaries for the Levant, Roville, 7 October 1562, Bibliothèque Nationale, Paris, Nouvelles acquisitions latines, 1324, ff. 397–398, reprinted in Paul Deslandres, *L'Ordre des Trinitaires pour le rachat des captifs*, 2 vols. (Toulouse: Privat, 1903), 2: 198–200.

[8] François de Malherbe, *Poésies complètes de Malherbe*, ed. Pierre Jannet (Paris: E. Picard, 1867), 198.

[9] For the text, see Edgard Rouard de Card, *Traités de la France avec les pays de l'Afrique du Nord: Algérie, Tunisie, Tripolitaine, Maroc* (Paris: A. Pédone, 1906), 113–115.

[10] King Henry IV to Marseille's consuls, 28 September 1607, Archives Municipales de Marseille, BB59, f. 15v; Jean Pignon-Reix, 'Un document inédit sur les relations franco-tunisiennes au début du XVIIe siècle', *Revue de l'Occident Musulman et de la Méditerranée* 20 (1975): 107–108, 120–121n29.

[11] Provençal poem *c.*1666, quoted in René Burlet, André Zysberg and Jean Carrière, 'Mais comment pouvait-on ramer sur les galères du Roi-Soleil?', *Histoire et Mesure* 1, nos. 3–4 (1986): 151. On living conditions at sea more generally, see Zysberg, *Marseille au temps du Roi-Soleil: la ville, les galères, l'arsenal* (Marseille: Jeanne Lafitte, 2007), 122–124; Paul Bamford, *Fighting Ships and Prisons: The Mediterranean Galleys of France in the Age of Louis XIV* (Minneapolis: University of Minnesota Press, 1973), chap. 9, who notes that slaves may have received slightly larger rations than convicts (203). A census from 1664 suggests a slightly lower sick rate, argues Ernest Dottain in 'Un chapitre de l'histoire de la marine sous Louis XIV: la justice et les galères', *Revue Contemporaine* 29 (1862): 491.

[12] The sale of coffee by *turcs* – confirmed by Jean de La Roque, *Voyage de l'arabie heureuse*...(Amsterdam: Steenhouwer and Uyterf, 1716), 365; Jean Marteilhe, *Mémoires d'un protestant condamné aux galères de France pour cause de religion* (1757; Paris: Michel Lévy Frères, 1865), 489 – also strayed from the port towards the centre of Marseille (Zysberg, *Marseille*, 133). The city's (and the kingdom's) first café opened in 1671 before coffee was outlawed eight years later. Ina Baghdiantz McCabe, *Orientalism in Early Modern France: Eurasian Trade, Exoticism, and the Ancien Régime* (Oxford: Berg, 2008), chaps. 6, 7. Descriptions of stalls maintained by galley slaves appear as late as 23 December 1765. James Boswell, *Boswell on the Grand Tour: Italy, Corsica, and France, 1765–1766* (New York: McGraw-Hill, 1955), 243.

[13] For descriptions, see Jean-Jacques Bouchard, *Les Confessions de Jean-Jacques Bouchard, parisien* (Paris: Isidore Liseux, 1881), 174; John Evelyn, *Diary and Correspondence of John Evelyn, F.R.S.*, ed. William Bray, 4 vols. (London: George Bell, 1889), 1: 85. Paul Masson, *Les Galères de France, 1481–1781: Marseille, port de guerre* (Paris: Hachette, 1938), 303, dates the coupling of *turcs* and *forçats* to a 29 November 1675 ordinance. Archives Nationales (hereafter AN), Paris, $A^3$13, 81. References to this practice can be found in AN, Marine D^5 and elsewhere.

[14] On off-season living conditions for slaves in Marseille, see Zysberg, *Marseille*, 124–137; Bamford, *Fighting Ships*, chap. 10; Masson, *Les Galères de France*, 292–306.

[15] On meetings with envoys allowed and averted, see, for example, AN, Marine $B^2$5, f. 209, cited in Eugène Plantet, ed., *Correspondance des beys de Tunis et des consuls de France avec la cour, 1577–1830*, 3 vols. (Paris: Félix Alcan, 1893–1899), 1: 202.

[16] On Muslim cemeteries, see Régis Bertrand, 'Les Cimetières des "esclaves turcs" des arsenaux de Marseille et Toulon au XVIIIe siècle', *Revue des Mondes Musulmans et de la Méditerranée* 99–100 (2002): 205–217.

[17] Jean François Bion, *Relation des tourments qu'on fait souffrir aux Protestants qui sont sur les galères de France* (Paris: Grassart, 1881), 31.

[18] On modes of manumission, see Bamford, *Fighting Ships*, 260–267. See also the contract between Assan Cavalhier of Tunis and Mahamet of Tunis registered in Marseille (notaire Aymay Champorcin), 20 June 1578, ADBR, 357 E 72, ff. 1717r–1718r, excerpted in Kaiser, '"Hommes de credit"', 300.

[19] On 'Turks' as substitutes, see Auguste Laforet, *Étude sur la marine des galères* (Paris: A. Aubry, 1861), 84–88. For examples of exchanges, see AN, Marine $B^6$26, ff. 447–448. For examples of slaves released from Marseille by the king's favour and occasional escapes, see Archives de la Chambre de Commerce de Marseille (hereafter ACCM), G51; AN, Marine B^6 and B^7. France's treaties with Algiers, Tunis, Tripoli and Morocco resulted in hundreds of slaves freed (and hundreds more illegally detained). Despite the expense, until the early eighteenth century Louis XIV preferred to warehouse invalids in France or sell them in Livorno rather than sending them home or to the Caribbean. Masson, *Les Galères de France*, 309–310.

[20] For example, a 1695 law requiring employers to pay 1000 *livres* in compensation per fugitive. AN, Marine $A^3$12, 247, cited in Bamford, *Fighting Ships*, 230. An agreement from 1725 had guards and 'Turks' contribute to a pool for remunerating the king for escapes and fines levied on locals who aided fugitives. AN, Marine $B^6$116, f. 32, A^3XIII, cited in Masson, *Les Galères de France*, 406.

[21] Lucette Valensi and Simone Delesalle, 'Le Mot "nègre" dans les dictionnaires français d'Ancien régime; histoire et lexicographie', *Langue Française, 'Langage et Histoire'* 15 (1972): 79–104.

[22] For the latest estimates of the scale before 1715, see James Pritchard, David Eltis and David Richardson, 'The Significance of the French Slave Trade to the Evolution of the French Atlantic World before 1716', in *Extending the Frontiers: Essays on the New Transatlantic Slave Trade Database*, ed. David Eltis and David Richardson (New Haven, CT: Yale University Press, 2008), 205–227.

[23] On Ottoman and Moroccan galley slaves in Malta, see Godfrey Wettinger, *Slavery in the Islands of Malta and Gozo ca. 1000–1812* (San Gwann, Malta: Publishers Enterprises Group, 2002); in Italian seaports and papal lands, see Salvatore Bono, *Schiavi musulmani nell'Italia moderna:*

galeotti, un' cumprà, domestici (Naples: Edizioni Scientifiche Italienne, 1999); in the Iberian Peninsula, see Ruth Pike, *Penal Servitude in Early Modern Spain* (Madison: University of Wisconsin Press, 1983); in the Balkans and Central Europe, see Géza Dávid and Pál Fodor, eds., *Ransom Slavery along the Ottoman Borders: Early Fifteenth–Early Eighteenth Centuries* (Leiden: Brill, 2007); in Europe generally, see Nabil I. Matar, *Europe through Arab Eyes, 1578–1727* (New York: Columbia University Press, 2009), pt. 1, chap. 1; Mohamed Moudine, 'Le Rachat des esclaves musulmans en Europe méridionale du XIIIe siècle à la fin du XVIIIe siècle: le cas du Maroc' (PhD diss., Université d'Aix-Marseille I, 1996); P.S. Van Koningsveld, 'Muslim Slaves and Captives in Western Europe during the Late Middle Ages', *Islam and Christian–Muslim Relations* 6, no. 1 (1995): 5–23.

[24] On French slaves in North Africa, see Gillian Weiss, *Captives and Corsairs: France and Slavery in the Early Modern Mediterranean* (Stanford, CA: Stanford University Press, 2011).

[25] Michel Fontenay, 'L'Esclave galérien dans la Méditerranée des temps modernes', in *Figures de l'esclave au Moyen Age et dans le monde moderne*, ed. Henri Bresc (Paris: L'Harmattan, 1996), 120–121. From 300 *turcs* (out of 2507 rowers) in 1664, their number rose to 2000 in 1670 and 1673, reaching 2040 (out of 7970) in 1685–1687. By the first decade of the eighteenth century, the number in both groups had begun to decline: from 1663 *turcs* (out of 9496 rowers) in 1709, down to 1002 (out of 5600) in 1712. Knight of Malta de Gout, cited in Dottain, 'Un chapitre', 491; Nointel to minister, 19 August 1670 and 'Etat de la chiourme des galères du roy', 1673, AN, AE B^{I}373 and AN, Marine B^{6}105, f. 358, cited in Bamford, *Fighting Ships*, 138, 280; Pierre Boyer, 'La Chiourme turque des galères de France de 1685 à 1687', *Revue de l'Occident Musulman et de la Méditerranée* 6 (1969): 56; Bibliothèque Nationale, Paris, Nouvelles acquisitions latines, 21348, f. 115, cited in Marteilhe, *Mémoires d'un protestant*, 344n61.

[26] Emanuel d'Aranda, *Les Captifs d'Alger*, ed. Latifa Z'Rari (Paris: Jean-Paul Rocher, 1997), 173.

[27] Madeleine de Scudéry to Mlle. Paulet, Marseille, 27 December 1644, in Edmé-Jacques-Benoît Rathéry and Boutron, eds., *Mademoiselle de Scudéry, sa vie et sa correspondance, avec un choix de ses poésies* (Paris: Léon Techener, 1873), 173.

[28] François Savinien d'Alquié, *Les Délices de la France, ou il est traité de l'estat present de ce royaume, de son gouvernement, de ses officiers et de sa politique* (Paris: J. Cottin, 1670), 246.

[29] Anne-Louise d'Orléans, duchesse de Montpensier, *Mémoires de Mlle de Montpensier, petite-fille de Henri IV*, ed. A. Chéruel, 4 vols., 2nd ed. (Paris: Charpentier, 1858), 3: 434.

[30] Letter *c.*1690, in Jean Dumont, *Voyages de Mr. Du Mont en France, en Italie...*, 4 vols. (The Hague: Etienne Foulque and François l'Honoré, 1699), cited in Zysberg, *Marseille*, 29.

[31] Galley intendant Nicolas Arnoul to marine minister Jean-Baptiste Colbert, 11 May 1669, AN, Marine B^{6}78, f. 186, cited in Zysberg, 'Galères et galériens du royaume de France', in *Le Genti del mare mediterraneo*, ed. Rosalba Ragosta, 2 vols. (Naples: Lucio Pironti, 1981), 2: 790.

[32] Louis XIV to François de Vendôme, Duc de Beaufort, 19 May 1662, and Colbert to navy intendant, Louis Testard de la Guette, 8 December 1662. AN, Marine, Recueil des diverses lettres, ff. 1, 184, reprinted in Pierre Clément, ed., *Lettres, instructions et mémoires de Colbert*, 8 vols. (Paris: Imprimerie Impériale, 1861–1873), 3: 3, 27–28; Zysberg, 'Un audit rétrospectif: analyse du budget des galères de France entre 1669 et 1716', in *Histoire des familles, de la démographie et des comportements*, ed. Jean-Pierre Poussou and Isabelle Robin-Romero (Paris: Presses de l'Université de Paris-Sorbonne, 2007), 1068.

[33] Dottain, 'Un chapitre', 493; Peabody, '*There Are No Slaves*', 13.

[34] Jean-Baptiste Colbert, Marquis de Seignelay told the Marseille Chamber of Commerce to instruct a French captain to use a foreign ship – one from Livorno, for instance – when purchasing Turkish slaves, to avoid Ottoman complaints about violating the Capitulations. Versailles, 30 November 1680, ACCM, G50.

[35] On modes of procurement, see Laforet, *Étude sur la marine*, chap. 7; Zysberg, *Les Galériens: vies et destins de 60,000 forçats sur les galères de France, 1680–1748* (Paris: Edition du Seuill, 1987). 130; Bamford, *Fighting Ships*, chap. 7 (esp. 253).

[36] On 17 March 1684, for example, the French merchant community of Candia attested that one of their number had successfully completed a mission to ransom 13 *esclaves turqs*. One of the witnesses was a trader with a contract to supply 'Turks' to the royal galleys. ACCM, G51.

[37] Antoine Galland, *Histoire de l'esclavage d'un marchand de la ville de Cassis, à Tunis*, ed. Catherine Guénot and Nadia Vasquez (Paris: Éditions de la Bibliothèque, 1992), 134–135. See also 5–12.

[38] Beaufort to French consul in Majorca, 25 April 1662, reprinted in Georg Bernhard Depping, ed., *Correspondance administrative sous le règne de Louis XIV*, 4 vols. (Paris: Imprimerie Nationale, 1850), 2: 884n1.

[39] On the number of French slaves in North Africa during the 1660s, see Weiss, *Captives and Corsaires*, chap. 3, app. 1.

[40] Bamford, *Fighting Ships*, 154–160.

[41] The marginalia reads: 'We made less of this distinction at an earlier time and it was even believed that we should prefer Christians. We worked as hard as we could, though capriciously, to make Turks enter the Christian religion and gave a *sol* per day to those Turks who converted'. ACCM, Fonds Arnoul 28 (destroyed in 1944), cited in Masson, *Les Galères de France*, 28; 11 February 1687, cited in Boyer, 'La Chiourme turque', 55–56.

[42] Paul Bonnefon, 'Charles Perrault commis de Colbert l'administration des arts sous Louis XIV d'après des documents inédits', *Gazette de Beaux Arts* (1908): 430; Joseph François Duché de Vancy, *Lettres inédites de Duché de Vanci . . .*, ed. Colin and Reynaud (Paris: Lacroix, 1830), 266.

[43] Weiss, *Captives and Corsaires*, chaps. 3, 4.

[44] Bamford, *Fighting Ships*, 151.

[45] Laforet, *Étude sur la marine*, 102.

[46] Debra Blumenthal, *Enemies and Familiars: Slavery and Mastery in Fifteenth-Century Valencia* (Ithaca, NY: Cornell University Press, 2009), 235–236; Mary Elizabeth Perry, *The Handless Maiden: Moriscos and the Politics of Religion in Early Modern Spain* (Princeton: Princeton University Press, 2005), 169.

[47] See the first Article of the peace treaty signed in Algiers on 19 September 1628, cited in Pierre Dan, *Histoire de Barbarie et de ses corsaires...* (Paris: Pierre Rocolet, 1637), 134–135. Léonce Coutoure, 'Baptême d'un turc à Orthez', *Revue de Gascogne* 21 (1880): 90, excerpts the original 1644 publication, announcing the conversion of two fugitives from the Spanish galleys.

[48] On the right of refuge in the early modern and modern periods, see Jean-François Dubost, 'Refuge religieux et politique en France', in *Dictionnaire de l'Ancien Régime*, ed. Lucien Bély (Paris: Presses Universitaires de France, 1996), 1061–1063; Greg Burgess, *Refuge in the Land of Liberty: France and Its Refugees, from the Revolution to the End of Asylum, 1787–1939* (New York: Palgrave Macmillan, 2008).

[49] AN, Marine B^{6}78, ff. 172–178, cited in Marc Vigié, *Les Galériens du Roi, 1661–1715* (Paris: Fayard, 1985), 70 and Bamford, *Fighting Ships*, 144; marine minister Seignelay to galley intendant Nicolas Arnoul, Versailles, 9 April 1674, AN, Ordres du roi concernant les galères, 1674, f. 114, reprinted in Clément, *Lettres*, 3: 519n1; Louis XIV to Jean Rouillé de Meslay, intendant of Provence, Besançon, 23 May 1674, Archives Municipales de Marseilles (hereafter AMM), GL154; Seignelay to naval intendant Desclouzeau in Brest, 15 June 1686, cited in Dottain, 'Un chapitre', 487; Seignelay to Morant, AN, Marine B^{7}59, f. 89v.

[50] Ibrahim Berkilim, Moustafa, Omer and Ali to the *dey* of Algiers (copy), Genoa, June 1686, ACCM, G51. See also extract from the registers of the ACCM, Marseille, 14 March 1737 and other examples at ACCM, G51.

[51] On this episode from 1716–1718, see galley intendant Arnoul to Conseil de la Marine (copy), Paris, 25 July 1718, ACCM, G51; M. Le Roy, *Etat général et particulier du royaume et de la ville d'Alger, de son gouvernement, de ses forces de terre et de mer* (The Hague: Antoine Van Dole, 1750), 203–204, which reproduces a plea from the slaves.

[52] See multiple late eighteenth-century examples at ACCM, G50.

[53] On this self-depiction, see Kaiser, 'Les Paradoxes', 286–287.

[54] Charles Carrière, *Négociants marseillais au XVIIIe siècle: contribution à l'étude des économies maritimes* (Marseille: Institut Historique de Provence, 1973), 7–8, translated in Peter Sahlins, *Unnaturally French: Foreign Citizens in the Old Regime and After* (Ithaca, NY: Cornell University Press, 2004), 358n118.

[55] On the transformation of Marseille from 'Mediterranean emporium to international port', with increasing numbers of foreigners, see Zysberg, *Marseille*, chap. 6; Junko Thérèse Takeda, 'French Absolutism, Marseillais Civic Humanism and the Languages of the Public Good', *Historical Journal* 49, no. 3 (2006): 707–734, and 'Levantines and Marseille: The Politics of Naturalization and Neutralization in Early Modern France, 1660–1720', *Seventeenth-Century French Studies* 30 (2008): 170–181.

[56] See similar descriptions from 1739 and 1774 in Charles de Brosses, *Le Président de Brosses en Italie...*, 2nd ed., 2 vols. (Paris: Didier, 1858), 35; Philippe Vandebrande, *Voyage de Languedoc, Provence et Comtat d'Avignon* (Paris: 1774), cited in Carrière, *Négociants marseillais*, 178; as well as the well-known *c.*1750 painting by Joseph Vernet, *Vue du port de Marseille.*

[57] Captain Mehmet Soulreys (*ra'is*?) to galley intendant Jean-Louis Girardin de Vauvré, 'A Marseille sur la galère', 4 July 1681, AN, Marine $B^3$37, f. 113; Muhammad bin Ha'ider to Ali 'Mercher', Marseille, 9 May 1682, reprinted in Henry de Castries, Pierre de Cenival and Philippe de Cossé Brissac, eds., *Les Sources inédites de l'histoire du Maroc de 1530 à 1845*, 30 vols. (Paris: Ernest Leroux, 1905–1960), 2nd ser. 1: 691–693.

[58] Zysberg, *Les Galériens*, annex 2.

[59] Weiss, *Captives and Corsaires*, chap. 4.

[60] AN, Marine, Dépôt des cartes et plans 49 (272), pièce 14, 'Mémoire sur l'état des chiourmes', *c.*1690, cited in Bamford, *Fighting Ships*, 161.

[61] Pontchartrain to governor of Martinique d'Esragny, 4 October 1691, AN, Colonies B 14, f. 312, cited in Peabody, *'There Are No Slaves'*, 12.

[62] The *Dictionnaire de l'Académie française* defines *esclave* as one 'who is in servitude and at the entire disposition of a master', as in *esclave More, esclave Turc, esclave Chrestien*, noting that 'as soon as a slave touches the soil of France, he is free'. This wording remains consistent in the first (1694), fourth (1762) and fifth (1798) editions (see The Project for American and French Research on the Treasury of the French Language (ARTFL)). Antoine Furetière, *Le Dictionnaire universel*, 3 vols. (The Hague and Rotterdam: Arnout and Reiner Leers, 1690) and the second edition of 1691 also insist that 'as soon as a slave reaches France, he is free'.

[63] Pontchartrain to Sr. Marin, 20 October 1694, AN, Marine $B^6$26, f. 431 (my emphasis).

[64] On Louis XIII's reticence to allow black slavery in France's Caribbean colonies and supposed acceptance for the sake of conversion, various authors cite Jean-Baptiste Labat, *Nouveau voyage aux isles de l'Amérique*, 6 vols. (Paris, 1722), 4: 114. On Louis XIV's condemnation of approximately 3000 recalcitrant Protestants to the galleys after the 1685 revocation of the Edict of Nantes, see Gaston Tournier, *Les Galères de France et les galériens protestants des XVIIe et XVIIIe siècles*, 2 vols. (Montpellier: Les Presses de Languedoc, 1984); Zysberg, *Les Galériens*, chap. 6.

[65] Simon Michel Treuvé, ed., *Le Dictionnaire des cas de conscience*, 2 vols. (Paris: J.B. Cignard and H.L. Guérin, 1733), cited in Russell Parsons Jameson, *Montesquieu et l'esclavage: étude sur les origines de l'opinion antiesclavagiste en France au XVIIIe siècle* (New York: B. Franklin, 1971), 130–132.

[66] Antoine Loisel, *Institutes coutumières* (Paris: Abel l'Angelier, 1608), 1.

[67] Reports of *turc* baptisms (from 1623, 1632, 1673 and 1669) include: Louis Abelly, *Vie de S. Vincent de Paul, instituteur et premier supérieur général de a Congrégation de la Mission*, 2 vols. (1668; Paris: Poussielgue-Rusand, 1854), 1: 66, 277–278; Jean Louis Guey, *Mémoires ou livre de raison d'un bourgeois de Marseille, 1674–1726*, ed. J.-F. Thénard (Paris: Maisonneuve, 1881), 22; *Mercure Galant*, May 1699, 61, cited in Guy Turbet-Delof, *La Presse périodique française et l'Afrique barbaresque au XVIIe siècle (1611–1715)* (Geneva: Droz, 1973), 162.

On freedoms but not freedom for converted rowers, see AN, Marine, Dépêches sur les galères, 1676, f. 123, reprinted in Clément, *Lettres*, 3: 32; Bamford, *Fighting Ships*, 154; Laforet, *Étude sur la marine*, 99–100.

[68] Colbert to Brodart, Versailles, 26 July 1676, AN, Marine, Ordres du roi pour les galères, 1676, f. 90, cited in Clément, *Lettres*, 3: 28; AN, Marine B^{6}82, ff. 32–34, cited in Bamford, *Fighting Ships*, 217.

[69] 'Déclaration portant que les Mahométans et idolâtres qui voudront se convertir ne pourront être instruits que dans la religion catholique', Versailles, 25 January 1683 (registered at the Parlement of Paris on 13 February 1683), reproduced in François André Isambert, *Recueil général des anciennes lois françaises depuis l'an 420 jusqu'à la révolution de 1789*, 28 vols. (Paris: Verdière, 1829), 19: 414r–415r.

[70] Marteilhe, *Mémoires d'un protestant*, 260–262, 267; Bion, *Relation des tourments*, 28.

[71] Vincent Félix Brun, *Guerres maritimes de la France: port de Toulon, ses armements, son administration, depuis son origine jusqu'à nos jours* (Paris: H. Plon, 1861), 546–547.

[72] 'Mistreat them for that purpose if you must, but his Majesty thinks the threat alone will suffice', the marine minister instructed Brodart. AN, Marine B^{6}14, ff. 91–92, cited in Bamford, *Fighting Ships*, 161. Agy Abdalla, a slave on the *Patronne*, to the *dey* of Tunis, Marseille, February 1685, ACCM, G50.

[73] Caseu l'Algérien, a slave on the *Patronne*, to Louis XIV [1707], AN, Colonies F^{2A}1, ff. 200–203.

[74] Louis XIV to Pierre Arnoul, Marly and Versailles, May–June 1710, AN, Marine B^{7}85, ff. 97–99, 147v–152r, 152–153v.

[75] On mortality rates from 1720–1721, see Bamford, *Fighting Ships*, 246. On the acquisition of 'Turks' in the years afterwards, see Masson, *Les Galères de France*, 401, 451.

[76] 'Galérien' [by M. Durival le jeune], in *Encyclopédie, ou dictionnaire raisonné des sciences, des arts et de métiers par une société de gens des lettres*, http://diderot.alembert.free.fr/F.html.

[77] AN, Marine B^{6}123, f. 168, cited in Bamford, *Fighting Ships*, 172; Laforet, *Étude sur la marine*, 168; Brun, *Guerres maritimes*, 461, 546–547.

[78] Peabody, *'There Are No Slaves'*, 37–39.

[79] François Bourjon, *Le Droit commun de la France et la coutume de Paris réduits en principes*, 2nd ed., 2 vols. (Paris: Grangé and Cellot, 1770), 1: 2. The relevant passage does not appear in the first edition of 1747.

[80] Jacques-Henri Bernardin de Saint-Pierre, *Études de la Nature*, 2nd ed. (Basel: Tourneizen, 1797), 183–185.

[81] Orlando Patterson, *Slavery and Social Death: A Comparative Study* (Cambridge, MA: Harvard University Press, 1982).

'Lucky to be born in Pennsylvania': Free Soil, Fugitive Slaves and the Making of Pennsylvania's Anti-Slavery Borderland

Richard S. Newman

This essay examines the creation and meaning of the Pennsylvania anti-slavery borderland that developed in the United States during the late eighteenth and early nineteenth centuries. Drawing on the voluminous legal files of the Pennsylvania Abolition Society (the world's oldest anti-slavery organisation), as well as recent insights by scholars working on both emancipation and borderlands history in the Atlantic world, I argue that enslaved people and their allies defined Pennsylvania's territorial boundaries in ways that abetted black freedom claims. Indeed, though a seemingly small outpost of Atlantic slave culture, the Pennsylvania borderland became a crossroads of freedom for generations of enslaved people and kidnapped free blacks in the United States.

In the fall of 1814, an enslaved woman named Charity Castle had an unfortunate accident. Shortly before leaving Philadelphia for Maryland with her mistress, she fell 'violently' while getting some firewood. According to a local physician, Charity's broken leg prevented her from travelling below the Mason–Dixon Line. She would have to remain in Philadelphia indefinitely. From that moment onward, Charity's convalescence created a political stir. Because the injury occurred suspiciously on the eve of an important date – the end of a grace period which allowed Charity's family to stay in the Quaker state without emancipating her – abolitionists, lawyers and politicians entered the fray, debating whether or not the hobbled bondwoman would eventually be returned to Maryland. According to abolitionists, section 10 of Pennsylvania's 1780 Abolition Act provided immediate freedom for Charity on technical grounds: she had remained in the state beyond the six-month window for visiting slaveholders and was therefore entitled to the fullest protection of the law. Charity's owners argued that their intent to return her to Maryland before the accident trumped the dictates of the

Abolition Act. With the two sides vehemently disagreeing, Charity's freedom claim remained undecided for months. Then, on Christmas Eve, one abolitionist lawyer dashed off a cool missive informing Charity's Maryland masters that he had 'advised the Husband of Charity' – evidently a free black man in Philadelphia – 'to take her to himself'. If they wanted her back, Charity's owners would have to come to Philadelphia themselves and pursue more vigorous legal means.[1]

Tantalising evidence notwithstanding, Charity's ultimate fate remains unknown. No freedom certificate exists and scholars cannot verify whether or not she ever gained freedom. Like so many enslaved people, Charity disappears into the historical record. Nevertheless, Charity's case illuminates a key development in early national Pennsylvania: the advent of an anti-slavery borderland that separated free territory (and the supposedly free political culture it represented) from slave territory (with its supposedly circumscribed social and political landscape). Indeed, as both Charity's abolitionist lawyer and her Maryland master quickly recognised, Pennsylvania soil could make a key difference in an enslaved person's freedom claim. More importantly, perhaps, Charity's 'violent' accident itself may be interpreted as a conscious recognition of what some scholars are now referring to as the 'geopolitics of freedom'.[2] Serving as an unfree labourer in an emancipating state may have convinced Charity that, as Rebecca Scott has observed in another context, she could claim certain 'public rights', including her own freedom via Pennsylvania's Abolition Act.[3] Like an impressive number of enslaved people before and after her, Charity knew that geography could alter her destiny.

This essay examines the creation and wider meaning of the Pennsylvania anti-slavery borderland Charity came to inhabit by the early nineteenth century. Drawing on the voluminous legal files of the Pennsylvania Abolition Society (or PAS, the world's oldest anti-slavery organisation), as well as recent insights by scholars working on both emancipation and borderlands history in the Atlantic world, I argue that Pennsylvania became one of the first battlegrounds of what Sue Peabody has termed the 'free soil principle': the belief among enslaved people and their allies that certain geographies and territorial domains abetted black freedom claims.[4] Free soil principles impacted a wide terrain, from North Atlantic metropolitan centres (Britain and France) to revolutionising Caribbean locales. Though a seemingly small outpost of Atlantic slave culture – 'a society with slaves', in Ira Berlin's iconic phrasing – Pennsylvania became a crossroads of freedom for generations of enslaved people and kidnapped free blacks in the United States.[5] The state's Emancipation Act of 1 March 1780, the first post-nati abolition law in the western hemisphere, was a key step in this direction. By liberating the children of Quaker state slaves born after 1780 (roughly 7000 people), white Pennsylvanians vowed to rid themselves of bondage far in the future.[6]

But the decision of Pennsylvania lawmakers to institute abolitionist policy was only part of the state's emerging free soil identity. Indeed, the wilful actions of people of colour throughout the mid-Atlantic region reconfigured the meaning of Pennsylvania's Abolition Act and, with it, the free soil dimensions of the state's very borders. Within a decade of its passage in 1780, in fact, both enslaved people and free blacks alike began envisioning Pennsylvania as a haven from slaveholders' national power – a place where their broader freedom claims might be heard and even legitimised. Worrying little about the technical nature of the Abolition Act (which, for instance, did not offer liberty to fugitive slaves), African Americans instead came to view Pennsylvania's geography in moral terms. For many black freedom-seekers, Pennsylvania was, in the words of black activist James Forten, who wrote around the same time that Charity Castle had her unfortunate accident in Philadelphia, 'almost the only state in the Union wherein the African [has] boasted of rational liberty and the protection of laws'.[7]

Re-examining early national Pennsylvania's development as a free soil borderland is important for several reasons. First, it illuminates the way in which people of African descent altered the map of slavery and freedom in the early United States. By registering consistent awareness of abolitionist laws, bondage's borders and the potentially helpful role of abolitionists in non-slaveholding locales, African Americans discovered free spaces – soft spots, as it were – that undermined the national operation of slavery. Though the political impact of runaway slaves and kidnapped free blacks is well known for the antebellum United States, it remains an understudied phenomenon in the late eighteenth and early nineteenth centuries. Yet, as their experiences along the Pennsylvania borderland indicate, African Americans began searching for ways to challenge slavery as soon as the United States secured a new Constitution in the 1780s and attempted to codify bondage as a national institution. According to David Waldstreicher, 11 of the Constitution's 86 clauses dealt with slavery, either directly or indirectly. 'In growing their government', he concludes, the founders 'created fundamental laws that sustained bondage'.[8] By viewing Pennsylvania as a potential zone of freedom, African Americans and their allies hoped to undercut this notion and make slavery a regional institution at best.[9]

Second, the advent of Pennsylvania's free soil landscape set crucial precedents for subsequent slave liberation in the United States. Although scholars of gradual emancipation recognise its many failings, they also understand that northern gradualism was not an isolated part of a national abolition process. As Steven Hahn has recently argued, the United States may have witnessed the longest-running debate over emancipation in the Atlantic world – from the 1770s through to the 1860s.[10] An early lesson of this debate was that manifestations of the state, broadly conceived, could and, under the right circumstances, would be manipulated for black liberation. During the Civil War, Union blue came to symbolise the emancipatory power of the nation. Similarly, in early national Pennsylvania, people of colour came to see justices of the peace, courts and abolitionist lawyers as extensions of the state's free borders – emancipation personified. By reaching Pennsylvania, African Americans believed that they had at least a chance of achieving freedom. Put another way, Pennsylvania's anti-slavery borderland offered an early version of the Civil War emancipation borderland. In both cases, alliances between white officials and black activists cleaved slavery by creating a haven for people of colour.

Needless to say, black freedom claims in early national Pennsylvania (as during the Civil War) did not go unchallenged by slaveholders and their allies, north or south.

The result, I contend, was a borderland: a contested space, where competing notions of ideology, legal culture and territorial use battled one another.[11] Borderlands history recognises competing perspectives as a formative part of regional and national identity. On Pennsylvania's contested soil, there were many slave rescues, but many more slave renditions and kidnappings. Nonetheless, looking at this space as a borderland of competing perspectives allows scholars to bring enslaved people and their allies into the very heart of national (and international) consideration of bondage. Blacks' attempt to map their ideological understanding of freedom onto a geographical border engendered debate over slavery's and slaveholders' power. Was it limitless? For many white as well as black Pennsylvanians, the answer by the early 1800s was clearly 'no'. Looking at Pennsylvania as a borderland, then, offers a key starting point and place from which to follow the evolution of free soil principles in the United States.

Defining a borderland in black and white

Looking north as a young man, Maryland slave William Parker dreamed of freedom. When he told childhood friends about his visions, some laughed and wondered if he was serious about running away. How could a slave escape? After watching the domestic slave trade claim friends and loved ones, Parker fled towards Pennsylvania. Heading out of Baltimore, he and a friend went first to York and then Lancaster. Parker eventually settled in Christiana, 12 miles from the Maryland line, where he aided other fugitives and defended his home against the incursions of slave trackers. In September 1851, Parker heard a disturbing story about slave hunters in the area. Never one to wait, he confronted a posse of white men at his front gate. The meeting turned violent when one white man tried to force his way into Parker's home. Parker and his defenders retaliated, leaving a white Maryland master dead. A bounty on his head, Parker knew again what to do: escape to another border, this time Canada.[12]

Years after he left the United States, Parker issued a blistering critique of white Americans north and south – an entire nation, in his eyes, of racist thinkers. Yet Parker also underscored the saliency of Pennsylvania's borders in his struggles against bondage. While British Canada offered the fullest expression of North American free soil principles (Parliament's Abolition Act banned bondage throughout the British Empire, beginning in 1834), Parker viewed Pennsylvania as a contested northern borderland of slavery, an often violent place where black conceptions of liberty vied against masters' property rights. An unsuspecting white man riding the rails with an escaping Parker near Rochester, New York, testified to this notion when he commented that the Christiana rebels (like Parker) would not, and should not, be executed for battling masters. 'I do not know', he said,

> but the laws of Pennsylvania would not hang him – they might imprison him. But it would be different, very different, should they get him into Maryland. The people in all the Slave States are so prejudiced against colored people, that they never give them justice. But I don't believe they will get Parker. I think he is in Canada by

> this time; at least, I hope so – for I believe he did right, and, had I been in his place, I would have done as he did.

The conversation brought a smile to Parker's face. It told him that slaveholders' power might not cross some borders.[13]

If most blacks did not – could not – leave the type of testimony that Parker did about their rough-and-tumble experiences along Pennsylvania's anti-slavery borderland, their stories did register in other ways. Going back to the early national period and the advent of abolitionist legislation in Pennsylvania, it is clear that both enslaved people and free blacks sought to use the Quaker state as the new American nation's first dividing line between slavery and freedom. How do we know? Between the 1770s and 1830s, African Americans found themselves enmeshed in several hundred freedom suits in and around Pennsylvania. Why? For many people of colour, Pennsylvania's Abolition Act made the Quaker state an American Eden: a seemingly mythic place where black equality might reign. The reality was much different, as fugitive slaves and transplanted free blacks would learn again and again. But because the Abolition Act had been passed amidst the turmoil of the American Revolution, when African Americans began moving in large numbers to borders which conferred freedom, blacks may have wilfully misinterpreted it as yet another freedom Act. Lord Dunmore's Proclamation of 1775 and the Phillipsburg Proclamation of 1779 offered freedom to escaped slaves reaching British lines in Virginia and New York, respectively. In the late 1770s, British forces occupied Philadelphia, leading to an increase in fugitive slaves to south-eastern Pennsylvania. By the early 1780s, many blacks may not have worried about the details of Quaker state emancipation law. They interpreted Pennsylvania's borders as a free soil haven.[14]

The result was a large caseload of black freedom-seekers. The PAS, which had originally formed to protect, and perhaps expand, the state's abolition law, found itself inundated with black appeals for legal help during the late eighteenth and early nineteenth centuries. Already by the late 1780s, the group had to deploy more lawyers and legal aids to keep pace with black freedom suits. Three types of case confronted Pennsylvania abolitionists. Unlawfully detained people of colour seeking freedom, usually from within the Quaker state, constituted the first grouping; kidnapped free blacks hoping for restitution of their free status, either from Pennsylvania or surrounding states, formed the second; and fugitive slaves from beyond Pennsylvania hoping to find freedom within the Quaker state formed the third. Key differences marked each caseload. A fugitive slave seeking refuge within the Quaker state was not accorded the same theoretical legal protections as a kidnapped free Pennsylvanian. The former involved national principles of comity, while the latter revolved around the application of state laws.

While white reformers' aid was an essential part of defining Pennsylvania as a free soil borderland, African Americans themselves often initiated the process. In fact, obvious differences aside, these three types of case offer strong evidence that African Americans were at the forefront of a movement to envision Pennsylvania as a refuge from slaveholders' power nationally. Although it is impossible to gauge the overall number of unlawfully detained people of colour, runaway slaves and kidnapped free blacks along the Pennsylvania borderland, evidence indicates that it was rather sizable over an extended period of time. When local and state abolition societies began holding national meetings in the 1790s, with groups from New York to Virginia attending, Pennsylvania reformers usually reported the largest docket of kidnapping cases – dozens or more every quarterly session, hundreds over the space of just a few years and even more still over the course of a decade.[15] All the same, Pennsylvania abolitionists estimated that for every case that came to their attention, several more never did. By the time famed Underground Railroad operative William Still began secretly keeping notes on fugitive slave escapes in the Philadelphia area during the 1850s, the number had hardly changed, with dozens of people seeking aid in any given month and several hundred adding up over the space of just a few years. Though the majority of Still's roughly 900 escapees resolved to go to Canada, many recognised Pennsylvania's borders as a crucial step towards freedom. 'What are your impressions from what little you have seen of freedom?', Still asked a Virginia escapee named George who ventured to Philadelphia in 1857. 'I think it is intended for all men', he replied, 'and all men ought to have it'. George felt secure in making that declaration, Still noted, only on Pennsylvania soil.[16]

In the years before 1850, endangered free people of colour were among the first to interpret Pennsylvania's borders as a dividing line between slavery and freedom. By reading the Emancipation Act of 1780 in the broadest possible terms as a document that protected their personal liberty and independence, many free people of colour came to see Pennsylvania itself as a freedom zone. In 1804, a free black woman being carried through Tennessee as a slave convinced a local sheriff to check her freedom claim in the Quaker state. A similar case occurred around the same time in the Mississippi Territory. In both instances, the very word 'Pennsylvania' set off alarm bells for local constables, who contacted Pennsylvania abolitionists. The group verified black claimants' stories (by checking their bulging stack of manumission files), restoring them to freedom. The PAS's legal files include many similar cases of kidnapped free blacks desperately claiming Pennsylvania residency.[17] In 1819, famed anti-slavery reformer Isaac Hopper served a writ to a Maryland man who 'unlawfully detained' a black woman on his plantation. Approached by the woman's free husband in Philadelphia, who claimed that she had been liberated and had lived in Pennsylvania, Hopper went directly to a Philadelphia magistrate for a writ of 'habeas corpus ... to the said [slaveholder] commanding him to bring the body of said [woman] before you in order that right may be done in the premises'. The woman was returned to Philadelphia when Pennsylvania jurists declared her 'forever' free.[18]

How did free black kidnapping victims get help in Pennsylvania in the first place? Utilising diverse communication networks both within and beyond the black community, they often secured abolitionist aid through a series of mediators or go-betweens. Many people of colour passed information along via word of mouth, eventually prevailing upon white authorities to intervene legally. Others issued their own written appeals or notes. Still others used black leaders in various communities to secure aid from Pennsylvania abolitionists. Richard Allen, the founder of the African Methodist Episcopal Church and himself a former slave who had once been grabbed as a suspected fugitive, served as a go-between for Pennsylvania abolitionist lawyers, forwarding information from kidnapped blacks and their families to white lawyers on a case-by-case basis. For this reason, Allen's church and homes became well-known safe havens among mid-Atlantic African Americans. James Forten, Absalom Jones, Robert Purvis and a range of other black leaders in Pennsylvania served similar 'go-between' roles.[19]

By the turn of the century, these communication networks between black freedom-seekers and black leaders, and black leaders and white abolitionists, were securely in place. That the networks usually came back to Pennsylvania illustrated the state's standing among endangered people of colour. A moving example emanated from beyond Pennsylvania's borders. In the early 1800s, a New Jersey family asked Pennsylvania abolitionists to track down the whereabouts of a man named Bill Coachman after he disappeared under a cloud of suspicion. Through artful negotiation with his New Jersey master, Coachman had reduced bondage for life to a seven-year labour agreement. Before the deal matured, however, Coachman's family claimed that his master sold the soon-to-be-free man into Maryland slavery. In a sworn deposition, Coachman's first master even claimed that the enslaved man knew 'to the day' when his freedom agreement matured. Despite this and other compelling evidence, Coachman was never located by Pennsylvania abolitionists.[20]

Still, Coachman's case illuminates two important components of a free soil consciousness developing among people of colour in early national society. First, it shows that African Americans believed they were entitled to broader legal protections when within the vicinity of emancipating locales like Pennsylvania. Whether or not one chooses to call this a vernacular sense of the law, in Rebecca Scott's phrasing (a right to claim 'public rights'), or Elsa Barkley Brown's notion of 'pivoting the centre' (meaning that we redefine where the push for freedom begins), the point remains that both Coachman and his family understood the sanctity of their freedom contract and therefore their rights as would-be freemen, particularly (though not exclusively) in northern locales.[21] With Pennsylvania close by, blacks believed, slaveholders did not have national authority to dispose of property when and how they desired. Indeed, Coachman's proud recollection of his freedom date prefigures Charity Castle's intricate knowledge of her master's expiring grace period in Pennsylvania just a few years later. In these and other cases, people of colour in a variety of situations attempted to convert their basic understanding of freedom law into tactical ammunition against bondage.

The second point revolves around the connections people of colour drew between geography and freedom, for Bill Coachman's friends and family knew precisely what they were doing when they approached Pennsylvania abolitionists for legal aid. Located near Pennsylvania's anti-slavery borderland, Coachman's family heard tales of black aid networks in Philadelphia, the PAS's legal and political lobbying for black freedom, and Pennsylvania sheriffs' and jurists' sympathies to some black liberty claims. The very words 'Pennsylvania' and 'Pennsylvania Abolition Society' came to signify more than a state boundary line or an organisation in the next state. For people of colour throughout the mid-Atlantic region, Pennsylvania represented a place where courts, politics and people could be mobilised on behalf of black freedom. Even when northern freedom turned sour, many black activists attempted to rally around a symbolic version of a free soil Pennsylvania: a place within American culture that had once sanctified black liberty. After being disfranchised by a new Constitution in 1838, one group of Afro-Pennsylvania reformers appealed to Pennsylvania's long-standing tradition of interracial egalitarianism. 'We are PENNSYLVANIANS', the group declared, referring to the state's 1790 Constitution that refused (against some white politicians' objections) to separate blacks' from whites' rights. Black and white citizens were equal in 1790, the group maintained, and that heritage must be maintained in the antebellum era.[22]

If not as numerous, fugitive slave cases impacted the definition of 'free' Pennsylvania as well. As word spread about black and white aid networks in Pennsylvania, enslaved people made the Quaker state a freedom destination. Although the Pennsylvania Abolition Act provided masters with clear legal recourse against runaway slaves, fugitives eagerly sought out the state's borders. A runaway slave advertisement published in Philadelphia in 1802 indicates just how concerned southern masters were about the possibility of enslaved people reaching the Quaker state. 'Ran away from the subscriber near ... Jefferson County, Virginia sometime in December 1799', a slaveholder named Levi Martin wrote. After giving a detailed physical description of a man calling himself 'Jerry Arthur', Martin suggested that the escaped man might very well seek refuge in a major Pennsylvania city, perhaps Philadelphia or Harrisburg. He then set up an elaborate pay scale based on geography to reward Jerry Arthur's prospective captors. 'If he is taken within 10 miles of home', Martin promised to give a $10 reward; 'if 20 miles, $15, if 40 miles $20'. Martin eventually ended his rising reward rate at '150 miles and beyond', in which case he would pay the incredible sum of 'one hundred dollars' to a person who recovered the absconded slave. That sum amounted to nearly a quarter of an average labourer's annual salary in early national Philadelphia! But Martin was convinced that he needed to offer that princely sum, for he believed that Pennsylvania was not so far away in the minds of men like Jerry Arthur.[23]

Like other Chesapeake masters, Martin knew that state and federal courts were supposed to provide him with the fullest protection of the law when attempting to recover fugitive slaves. In practice, however, he probably would have agreed with a rising number of Chesapeake slaveholders who believed that a solid contingent of Pennsylvanians sought to undermine fugitive slave recoveries whenever and however they could. Martin testified to this belief with money. Other masters did so via literary appeals. In the space of two years at the dawn of the nineteenth century, five separate Maryland masters contacted the chief justice of the Pennsylvania Supreme Court to complain about the state's status as a free soil sanctuary. One master referred to the 'rash of runaways' to Pennsylvania and the impact their absence had on plantation discipline below the Mason–Dixon Line.[24] Would blacks' flight to Pennsylvania ever stop, he wondered? More broadly, in a catalogue of fugitive slave cases considered by the PAS between 1780 and the 1820s, Virginia and Maryland alone accounted for nearly half of the overall number.[25] By the 1820s, the Maryland legislature increased its pressure on Pennsylvania to curtail abolitionist aid to fugitive slaves. But such overtures usually failed.

Even the most powerful of southern masters had difficulty navigating Pennsylvania's anti-slavery borderland. Before the national government moved to Washington, DC, in 1800, several southern congressmen lost slaves while attending their federal duties in Pennsylvania. Two of President George Washington's nine slaves fled in the mid 1790s, neither of whom was ever returned. Though upset, Washington could hardly have been surprised. Even before the departures of seamstress Oney Judge and chef Hercules, the steely Washington had instructed his long-time aid Tobias Lear to make sure that his presidential slaves were shuttled in and out of Pennsylvania at appropriate times to comply with the Abolition Act's grace period of six months. Tacit recognition of slaves' geopolitical consciousness was only part of Washington's concern. He also had to contend with a vibrant free black community in Philadelphia, who might mix with his own slaves on market days and tell tales of how to escape slavery's grasp.[26]

Northern masters also found themselves dealing with Pennsylvania's seemingly free borders. As the first emancipating state, Pennsylvania became a key destination for northern fugitive slaves and other endangered blacks. Nearby New Jersey (which did not pass its own gradual Abolition Act until 1804) became an eastern borderland of slavery. In 1790, the PAS used a writ to secure the release of 'Negro Silas', a former enslaved man from New Jersey who had been sold south in violation of an indenture agreement with his master. After interviewing black as well as white witnesses, the PAS restored Silas to his liberty. Other examples abounded, but the point remains the same: by the early 1800s, nineteenth-century African Americans saw Pennsylvania as a free soil boundary line.[27]

Abolitionist mediators on the Pennsylvania borderland

Although early abolitionists remained dedicated to gradualist principles, they also served a key function in defining the Pennsylvania borderland as a potential freedom zone. Unlike second-wave abolitionists, who often extrapolated big anti-slavery lessons from the smallest of legal cases, PAS lawyers did not usually make grand demands for universal human freedom. They focused more on the facts of individual black freedom claims, particularly the way technicalities and loopholes might enable African American liberty. Thus, as one Pennsylvania reformer would note in 1822, PAS activists would always be torn between the heart and head. 'If it were in my power', this PAS member wrote,

> I would declare without hesitation that every fugitive slave setting foot on the soil of Pennsylvania should be free and emancipated at once. Born and educated in Pennsylvania, the sentiments are so deeply rooted in my heart that they can never be . . . shaken.

But, he went on, the American constitutional order protected southern slaveholders' property rights. No Pennsylvania abolitionist could therefore seek to liberate fugitives and runaways in an unquestioned manner.[28]

Nevertheless, by creating a legal aid system that helped blacks from around the nation (not just Pennsylvania), the PAS hoped to accumulate enough victories in court that slavery would either lose its judicial sanction in key locales or become an inefficient and legally troublesome institution for masters to maintain. When white settlers from the Chesapeake came to the Quaker state with little intention of submitting to abolitionist laws (which allowed visitors no more than six months' grace before registering slaves), they often found abolitionist lawyers ready to represent black claimants in Pennsylvania courts. In the words of Richard Allen and Absalom Jones, Pennsylvania abolitionists were 'the Friends of him who hath no helper': legal experts who translated black conceptions of freedom into technically ramifying arguments.[29]

In this sense, early white abolitionists remain undervalued partners in the development of Pennsylvania's version of the free soil principle. Indeed, while scholars have been rather harsh on early white abolitionists' gradualism, they often miss the way PAS legal manoeuvring enhanced black protest along the Pennsylvania borderline. Through a broad array of legal work, white abolitionists helped ground the black freedom struggle in specific legal precepts – like the use of writs of habeas corpus to engender formal legal inquiries into masters' rendition of fugitive slaves in Pennsylvania – thereby infusing Quaker state jurisprudence with a self-conscious sense of anti-slavery exceptionalism. The son of slain Maryland master Edward Gorsuch discovered this in 1851, when he demanded that black defenders – whom he called 'rebels, confederates and treasonous' figures – be summarily rounded up and convicted. Pennsylvania Governor William Johnston, an anti-slavery Democrat who moved to Whig circles, rebuffed Gorsuch by delaying warrants for Parker's arrest. While some fugitive slaves were returned to Pennsylvania in the wake of the incident, Christiana stood as a stark reminder that slaveholders' interests were less than secure above the Mason–Dixon Line. Indeed, many of the defendants were acquitted over the most serious charge – treason.[30]

Early abolitionist lawyers abetted such notions by ingeniously foiling masters' power. For instance, they consistently deployed writs of habeas corpus to initiate examinations of a black person's claim to freedom, often using this bureaucratic manoeuvre to win African American liberty. By calling literally for the body of a detained person to be delivered up, writs compelled southern masters to comply with a different brand of jurisprudence. Here, a conception of 'localised law', in Laura Edwards' phrasing, prevailed, with even anti-abolition judges respecting abolitionists' rights to investigate certain cases.[31] In some instances, merely the request to deliver the body alerted slaveholders and their allies that they were on different terrain – a legal geography not automatically favourable to property rights in human beings. In 1805, Pennsylvania reformers served a writ to a Philadelphia woman accused of slave trading. She fled before the case could be adjudicated. But like other cases, it put slave traders, slave catchers and masters on notice. Abolitionists would police the wharves and streets, jails and almshouses in search of black claimants. Between 1796 and 1798, Pennsylvania abolitionists used writs to secure the release of five free black men detained illegally. In 1800, Pennsylvania abolitionists helped liberate a free black man in Winchester, Virginia. He, too, had been illegally detained, this time by a mistress who claimed that she could dispose of her property in any manner she saw fit, former agreements be damned. Working again with family and local reformers, the PAS discovered that an indenture agreement had been brokered and that the woman had no claim on the man's liberty. He, too, was soon freed.[32]

Southern masters saw the impact that meddling abolitionists could have on Pennsylvania's free borders as early as 1782. Just two years after the passage of Pennsylvania's gradual Abolition Act, a Virginia master named Samuel Blackmore moved to Pennsylvania with his two female slaves. He did not register them, thereby failing to comply with the state's new anti-slavery law. Blackmore wrongly believed that he still lived in the Old Dominion (a boundary dispute had, in fact, occurred over the south-western counties in which Blackmore lived, though it was settled in Pennsylvania's favour by the time he moved to the Quaker state). Learning of their master's error, and perhaps buoyed by their newfound status as inhabitants of emancipating Pennsylvania, Blackmore's slaves eventually claimed their freedom by getting word to the PAS. Though the case came to trial much later (1797) in a federal district court, it illustrated that, in Pennsylvania at least, slavery was not conceived of as a national institution.[33]

Indeed, when Blackmore's legal counsel claimed that his client had belatedly attempted to comply with Pennsylvania's abolition law after he discovered his geographical error, the PAS scoffed, using the technicality to argue broadly for the enslaved women's freedom. As soon as Blackmore made his mistake (and failed to register his slaves), the PAS lectured the court, the women were forever free as inhabitants of Pennsylvania. The court could not, in effect, re-enslave them now. 'Can the legislature by a law, declare a free person to be a slave when the [state] constitution declares all men [or in this case, women] free?', the PAS counsel wondered. 'No', he told the court. The federal judges agreed and the two women gained their freedom. Blackmore's lawyers complained that the case boded ill for southern slaveholders.[34]

As the Blackmore case showed, the PAS used black action on the ground to alter the very meaning of the state's gradual Emancipation Act, a piece of parchment paper that, like all legal documents, awaited interpretation and use to come alive. In this case, as in others, abolitionist lawyers moved well beyond the specific intent of the abolition law – delayed freedom for Pennsylvania slaves – in order to argue for immediate freedom for their clients. Though decided on a technicality, abolitionist lawyers hoped that the case would send a stern message to American masters: know your geography.

Even masters who did not enter Pennsylvania with their slaves had to be cognisant of the state's borderland status. In 1825, a federal court considered the case of a Maryland master who unwittingly provided the legal grounds for his slave's liberation in Pennsylvania. The case revolved around the ingenious ploy of an enslaved man named Marshall Green, who asked permission from his master to enter Pennsylvania temporarily. Why? Green said that he wanted to visit family and that he would return expeditiously. When that did not happen, his Maryland master sued. Pennsylvania abolitionists easily found a technicality that conferred freedom on Green. Arguing that he did not plan to flee, they claimed that Green could not be labelled a fugitive slave. He had his master's permission to visit a known free state! The judge bought this argument, finding that Green had not engaged in 'presumptive flight'. It was as if the master himself had walked across the Mason–Dixon Line with Green, thereby opening the door to his freedom. While latter-day readers might marvel at the judge's decision in this case, Maryland masters fumed at PAS meddlers, going so far as to petition against abolitionist legal exertions.[35]

If these legal and political tactics are a guide, the PAS and African American reformers forged a complex relationship – or, as one might more properly refer to it, an interrelationship. That blacks themselves were a key part of remaking Pennsylvania's image into that of a free state was not lost on white abolitionists. By the early nineteenth century, many members of the PAS agreed with black litigants that Pennsylvania functioned as the United States' inaugural free soil territory – an emancipating polity still surrounded by slaveholding states hostile to the broader cause of black freedom. But the partnership between black litigants and white abolitionists was in no way equal, and resulted in disappointment for many people of colour. Fugitive slaves without technicalities or compelling facts on their side were told frankly by PAS legal counsellors that they would not be freed (though perhaps, abolitionists might assert, enslaved people could use white reformers' aid to bargain slavery down to an indenture contract). Moreover, as even accomplished black leaders like Richard Allen would discover, white abolitionists could hide behind legalisms and remain diffident about full social and political equality for people of colour. Neither Allen nor any other early national African American figure was ever allowed to join the segregated PAS.

Still, to ignore the many ways in which black and white activists did work together to create a free soil borderland in Pennsylvania misses something crucial. For both black litigants and white reformers hoped to show that American slavery's borders were not national; they were, in fact, sectional and, in some key cases, even contingent. Slaveholders had power, to be sure, but the slaveholding republic was anything but secure geographically, legally or culturally. One of the most intriguing freedom cases in this regard occurred in 1815 when a self-emancipated woman living in the Quaker state was claimed by a Virginia family. The case came to the attention of the PAS when the woman's free husband asked the group for legal aid – not only for his wife but his children, who were born in Pennsylvania but now being claimed as slave property in the Old Dominion. *Kitty* v. *Chittier* was the resulting federal court case and it became one of the first to determine the status of children of fugitive parents.[36]

Indeed, though worried about her own liberty, the enslaved woman Kitty registered even more concern for her children's free future, fighting back against her mistress's attempts to claim the children as well. With the help of several high-profile members of the PAS, including a one-time United States senator from Pennsylvania, Kitty's children remained free citizens of Pennsylvania. In a series of written opinions to prepare for the case, abolitionist lawyers generally agreed that Pennsylvania had a diverging conception of black freedom from that of Virginia. While the latter rejected the very idea of black equality before state law, the former, as Peter Du Ponceau observed, guaranteed freedom to all its native inhabitants, black or white. Though nothing in the original Abolition Act guided the abolitionist lawyers, they argued that Pennsylvania had, over time, become a 'free' state. And as long as blacks were born within its geographical boundaries, they could claim forever freedom. 'It was the good fortune of these children to have been born here', Deponceau summarised in rather blunt non-legalese. DePonceau was right: the case in the federal court resulted in the children's freedom.[37]

Such legal victories advertised Pennsylvania's 'free' borders internationally. As early as 1795, for instance, British Quaker David Barclay approached Pennsylvania abolitionists and African American reformers about the prospect of emancipating a group of nearly 30 Jamaican slaves he had inherited as part of a debt obligation.[38] Barclay's choice of Pennsylvania is, indeed, interesting, for he was a businessman and sometime reformer with transatlantic connections. Though the British mainland had been cleared of slaves, and the French Empire had declared bondage incompatible with the Declaration of the Rights of Man and of the Citizen, Barclay believed that Pennsylvania represented these former bondmen's best hope. Slavery had been non-violently cut down, free black communities and institutions ascended, and the state's legal and political culture respected black liberties to a rather extraordinary degree.

For some, the very word 'Pennsylvania' belonged in the same category as revolutionary Saint-Domingue. Both signified freedom in the Atlantic world. Julien Raimond, the mixed-race planter and political activist who pushed for slavery's end in what would become Haiti, became a corresponding member of the PAS in the 1790s precisely because he felt a kinship to those fighting for racial justice thousands of miles away.[39]

Creating free cultural spaces

Like borderlands elsewhere in the Atlantic world, Pennsylvania's anti-slavery boundaries acquired a variety of meanings through time. For communities of colour, abolition laws and legal decisions were only part of evolving notions of the free soil principle. Already by the close of the eighteenth century, for instance, black reformers viewed access to an abolitionist press as an important analogue of Pennsylvania's Abolition Act of 1780. Indeed, for black activists, occupying the cultural space of print was nearly as valuable as crossing a physical border to attain liberty. Both acts asserted one's free status and underlined black civil rights.

While literary emancipation of black voices was constricted below the Mason–Dixon Line – only a few pamphlets and printed works authored by people of colour saw the light of day during the early national period – it thrived in Pennsylvania. Not only did the PAS have a public directory listing, but African Americans became an active presence in the public sphere, printing protest documents, petitions, church constitutions, records of various benevolent societies and spiritual narratives. Richard Allen alone published three important abolitionist pamphlets during the 1790s, while Philadelphia's black community initiated three major petition drives to the federal congress before the close of the nineteenth century. Throughout, Afro-Pennsylvanians pictured themselves as equal citizens. Whether or not white Pennsylvanians agreed, they believed that Pennsylvania's abolitionist heritage conferred upon blacks the basic right to express themselves.

By the 1810s, African Americans exploited the concept of cultural freedom to hold public rallies celebrating the end of the overseas slave trade. These 'January 1st' festivities looked forward as well as backward by challenging white citizens to end domestic slavery. Many of these commemorative celebrations were codified in pamphlets and distributed to white, as well as black, reformers. By the 1820s and 1830s, as new generations of black activists emerged, January 1st days morphed into regional and national conventions aimed at achieving racial justice throughout American culture. It is no coincidence that every major black convention in antebellum culture took place on northern soil.

Interestingly, when waves of white rioters sought to disrupt African American meetings and rallies, black activists referred to their birth on, or cultivation of what became, free soil to claim their equality. As Richard Allen observed in 1827: 'America is now our Mother Country . . . We have watered it with our tears and blood'.[40] Drawing on black anti-colonisationist writings from a decade earlier, Allen argued that African Americans' long residency (and toil) on American lands must be viewed as a legitimate claim to equal citizenship. Allen's line of thinking would echo in essays by other black activists, from Maria Stewart to Frederick Douglass.[41] By referring specifically to the soil as an ally in their freedom struggle (the literal foundation of black freedom claims), Allen and other black reformers paid homage to a generation of freedom-seekers who had creatively used geographic borders in the struggle for justice. It was, indeed, significant that Allen publicly proclaimed these words on what he believed was the free soil territory of Pennsylvania.

Neither Allen nor his successors were naive about northern freedom, however. Recognising that Pennsylvania's free borders required constant protection, African Americans redoubled their efforts to aid fugitive slaves and kidnapped free blacks during the antebellum era. In the 1830s, for instance, informal networks of black activists created the Vigilant Association. One of several black-led resistance groups in the northern states, the association was formed in 1837 to protect free people of colour and fugitive slaves from more brazen attempts by southern masters to (re)claim slave property in the Quaker state. Robert Purvis, a wealthy man of colour with South Carolina roots, helped organise the group after a Pennsylvania magistrate liberated an enslaved Maryland family who had crossed into free territory hotly pursued by slave catchers. Convinced that this was a harbinger of things to come, Purvis joined with a dedicated group of black activists to form an aid network that would, among other things, provide money, safe houses and public support to runaway slaves.[42]

The Vigilant Association picked up where the PAS left off, particularly as old abolitionists died or tempered their activism. Purvis's group confronted slave catchers in

Philadelphia and secured writs to investigate fugitive slave cases in and around Pennsylvania. By the late 1830s, it was just one of several vigilance groups attempting to spread free soil principles throughout the north. David Ruggles, who formed the New York Vigilance Committee in 1835, sought to make 'immediate emancipation' a fact of life 'in every individual case that may come within the sphere of our influence'. And that sphere of influence began at New York's borders – its wharves, bridges and streets. 'Let [enslaved men and women] come within the reach of our hand', Ruggles continued, 'and [they] shall rise to liberty and peace, and the light of truth, and the blessings of social life'.[43] In Philadelphia, Purvis likewise hoped to patrol and protect Pennsylvania's free borders.[44]

Although an advocate of Garrisonian non-resistance for much of his life, Purvis increasingly embraced blacks' right to physical self-defence, particularly after the passage of the Fugitive Slave Law of 1850.[45] When the Vigilant Association folded in 1852, Purvis helped create the General Vigilance Committee. Though secret – Purvis burned his notes – the new (and interracial) group offered to help any fugitive coming through Philadelphia. With as many as 100 requests for aid per year from fugitive slaves, Purvis and his fellow activists remained constantly busy.

One case above all others signifies how far the free soil principle had come by then. In the summer of 1855, members of the group learned that an enslaved woman from North Carolina was staying in a Philadelphia hotel with her master, who was en route to Nicaragua for a ministerial post in the Pierce administration. A black hotel worker informed William Still, a leading operative in the Philadelphia anti-slavery community, that the woman, Jane Johnson, desired her freedom now that she and her children were in 'free' Pennsylvania. Once again, nothing in Pennsylvania statutory law supported her claim. Johnson's master had a clear right to bring her into northern territory. But, by then, black and white reformers had imbued Pennsylvania's very name and borders with free soil principles, convincing many jurists and citizens that slavery could not be tolerated within the Quaker state. Still and his white associate Passmore Williamson (who would spend several months in prison for his actions) interdicted the master's passage by telling the woman that she had, indeed, crossed into a geographical terrain that would honour her freedom claim. A tussle ensued, but when the North Carolina master, named John Wheeler, attempted to prevent Johnson's escape, five black waterfront workers intervened. She and her two children escaped with Still into a carriage and liberty (Wheeler had left one of Johnson's children behind in North Carolina as a potential deterrent; she did not gain freedom).[46] The entire episode took less than an hour but was, in no small way, decades in the making.

Pennsylvania's borderland extended

In the spring of 1862, African American Civil War correspondent George Stephens reported an important development from the Maryland battlefront. Every day, he wrote in the New York *Anglo-African*, dozens of fugitive slaves streamed into Union lines. Although the Civil War was less than a year old, Stephens predicted that self-emancipated slaves would destroy the Confederacy. They are, he declared, 'a power that cannot be ignored'. A free black man whose parents had left Virginia after Nat Turner's rebellion to settle in Philadelphia, Stephens knew that people on the ground could reshape the meaning of borders and legal codes every bit as much as presidents, generals and congressmen. For Stephens, the boundary between slavery and freedom was no longer the Pennsylvania landscape; rather, enslaved people had made any Union-occupied territory a free soil destination. The anti-slavery borderland of Stephens' youth had become mobile, penetrating the heart of the slavocracy. So obvious was this fact that Stephens hailed Abraham Lincoln's Emancipation Proclamation not for its originality, but for solidifying a freedom movement already taking shape on the front lines.[47]

This emerging Civil War borderland flowed from decades of both black and white abolitionist attempts to charge specific landscapes with anti-slavery meaning. Pennsylvania's anti-slavery borderland was the first major dividing line between slavery and freedom – a proving ground of an emerging free soil principle that used local readings of the law to counteract slaveholders' national power. At its heart, Pennsylvania's anti-slavery borderland was not a geographical terrain so much as a moral one. For, in the minds of escaped slaves and kidnapped free blacks, Pennsylvania was re-imagined and remapped as a 'free space'. The implications of that effort to overlay a moral vision on geographical space would resonate in the creation of future anti-slavery borderlands where African Americans and their allies extended the boundaries of freedom.

In fact, African Americans' attempt to redefine Pennsylvania as a free soil state was part of a transatlantic process already occurring at the close of the eighteenth century. As Douglas Egerton has recently shown, Lord Mansfield's famous 1772 decision that Britain would not tolerate slavery prompted black restiveness from Massachusetts to South Carolina.[48] In revolutionary Saint-Domingue, Toussaint L'Ouverture's famous volte-face – shifting his support from the Spanish to the French government in the early 1790s – symbolised the aspirations of tens of thousands of Caribbean enslaved people who would trade bondage in one locale for freedom in another. As these examples illustrate, blacks throughout Atlantic society had more than a vague understanding of geopolitics – which laws, borders and allies might confer freedom upon them. While African Americans might not have had the power to destroy racial injustice in the Quaker state, their struggle to imbue Pennsylvania's borderland with free soil principles undermined slaveholders' national power and allowed people of colour to imagine a day when freedom would be firmly inscribed not only in the land, but the law.

Notes

[1] Phillip R. Seitz, 'Tales from the Chew Family Papers: The Charity Castle Story', *Pennsylvania Magazine of History and Biography* 132, no. 1 (2008): 65–86.

[2] See, for example, Edlie L. Wong, *Neither Fugitive nor Free: Atlantic Slavery, Freedom Suits, and the Legal Culture of Travel* (New York: New York University Press, 2009); Phillip Troutman,

'Grapevine in the Slave Market: African-American Geopolitical Literacy and the 1841 Creel Revolt', in *The Chattel Principle: Internal Slave Trades in the Americas*, ed. Walter Johnson (New Haven, CT: Yale University Press, 2004), 206–207.

[3] This theme is treated most fully in Rebecca Scott, *Degrees of Freedom: Louisiana and Cuba after Slavery* (New York: Cambridge University Press, 2005). See also Rebecca Scott, 'Public Rights, Social Equality, and the Conceptual Roots of the Plessy Challenge', *Michigan Law Review* 106, no. 5 (2008): 777–804.

[4] See, for example, Sue Peabody, *'There Are No Slaves in France': The Political Culture of Race and Slavery in the Ancien Régime* (New York: Oxford University Press, 1996).

[5] Ira Berlin, *Generations of Captivity* (Cambridge, MA: Belknap Press, 2003), 87.

[6] 'Pennsylvania – An Act for the Gradual Abolition of Slavery, 1780', passed on 1 March 1780 and posted at the Yale Law School's online Avalon Project, http://avalon.law.yale.edu/18th_century/pennst01.asp. See also Gary B. Nash and Jean Soderlund, *Freedom by Degrees: Emancipation and Its Aftermath* (New York: Oxford University Press, 1991).

[7] James Forten, '"Series of Letters by a Man of Colour" (1813)', in *Pamphlets of Protest: An Anthology of Early African American Protest Writing, 1790–1860*, ed. Richard S. Newman, Patrick Rael and Phillip Lapsansky (New York: Routledge, 2001), 67.

[8] David Waldstreicher, *Slavery's Constitution: From Revolution to Ratification* (New York: Hill and Wang, 2009), 3.

[9] On black uses of the law in the antebellum United States, see, for example, Martha Jones, 'Leave of Court: African-American Legal Claims Making in the Era of *Dred Scott* v. *Sandford*', in *Contested Democracy: Politics, Ideology and Race in American History*, ed. Manisha Sinha and Penny Von Eschen (New York: Columbia University Press, 2007), Wong, *Neither Fugitive nor Free*.

[10] Steven Hahn, *The Political Worlds of Slavery and Freedom* (Cambridge, MA: Harvard University Press, 2009).

[11] On borderlands perspectives, see generally Karl Jacoby, *Shadows at Dawn: A Borderlands Massacre and the Violence of History* (New York: Penguin, 2008); Daniel K. Richter, *Facing East from Indian Country* (Cambridge, MA: Harvard University Press, 2003). On Pennsylvania, see especially Patrick Spero's fine literature review, 'Matters of Perspective: Interpreting the Revolutionary Frontier', *Pennsylvania Magazine of History and Biography* 132, no. 3 (2008): 261–270.

[12] For a slightly different reading of Parker's escape, see Hahn, *Political Worlds.*

[13] William Parker, 'The Freedman's Story: In Two Parts', *Atlantic Monthly* 17 (February 1866): 152–166; 17 (March 1866): 276–295 (290), http://docsouth.unc.edu/neh/parker1/menu.html.

[14] See Gary B. Nash, *The Forgotten Fifth* (Cambridge, MA: Harvard University Press, 2004); Douglas Egerton, *Death or Liberty* (New York: Oxford University Press, 2008).

[15] Carol Wilson, *Freedom at Risk: The Kidnapping of Free Blacks in American Society, 1780–1865* (Lexington: University Press of Kentucky, 1994).

[16] William Still, *The Underground Railroad* (Philadelphia: Porter and Coates, 1872), 149.

[17] Alexander McLean to William Silas Densmore, June 1804, in 'Cases in Which Slaves Were Awarded Freedom in Court, 1773–1833', *PAS Papers*, microfilm ed., Reel 24.

[18] 'Writ of Habeas Corpus' sworn out by Isaac Hopper, in 'Cases in Which Slaves'.

[19] On Allen's role as a mediator, see Newman, *Freedom's Prophet: Bishop Richard, the AME Church, and the Black Founding Fathers* (New York: NYU Press, 2008), chap. 5.

[20] See the case of *William Coachman* v. *George Hand*, Cape May, NJ, 1802–1804, in 'Cases in Which Slaves'.

[21] See Elsa Barkley Brown, 'African-American Women's Quilting: A Framework for Conceptualizing and Teaching African-American Women's History', *Signs* 14, no. 4 (1989): 921–929. See also, Scott, *Degrees of Freedom.*

[22] Robert Purvis, '"Appeal of Forty Thousand Citizens, Threatened with Disenfranchisement, to the People of Pennsylvania" (1837)', in Newman, Rael and Lapsansky, *Pamphlets of Protest*, 135.
[23] 'One Hundred Dollars Reward', *Philadelphia Gazette*, 27 October 1802, runaway slave advertisement posted on the Historical Society of Pennsylvania's 'Fugitive Slaves and the Underground Railroad Exhibit', http://www.hsp.org/files/1802ad2.pdf.
[24] See Newman, *Transformation of American Abolitionism: Fighting Slavery in the Early Republic* (University of North Carolina Press: Chapel Hill, NC, 2002), app. 1, 185.
[25] Ibid., 68.
[26] For more on Washington and the president's house in Philadelphia, see Newman, *Freedom's Prophet*, chap. 5.
[27] See 'In res: Negro Silas', in 'Cases in Which Slaves'.
[28] Quoted in Newman, *Transformation of American Abolitionism*, 85.
[29] See Absalom Jones and Richard Allen, '"A Narrative of the Proceedings of the Black People during the Late Awful Calamity in Philadelphia" (1794)', in Newman, Rael and Lapsansky, *Pamphlets of Protest*, 33–42.
[30] See G.S. Gorsuch to Governor William H. Johnston, 18 September 1851, in *A Full and Correct Report of the Christiana Tragedy* (Lancaster, PA, 1851).
[31] Laura F. Edwards, *The People and Their Peace: Legal Culture and the Transformation of Inequality in the Post-Revolutionary South* (Chapel Hill: University of North Carolina Press, 2009), 3–4.
[32] For information on the many PAS cases from the 1790s, see 'Cases in Which Slaves'.
[33] See *Respublica* v. *Aberilla Blackmore*, 2 Yeates 234 (1797). See also Newman, *Transformation of American Abolitionism*, 60–85.
[34] The case was decided in 1797. See Newman, *Transformation of American Abolitionism*, 76–78.
[35] *Green* v. *Brickell* (1825). See Newman, *Transformation of American Abolitionism*, 79.
[36] The case *Respublica* v. *Chittier* (1815) went unreported. See 'Cases in Which Slaves'.
[37] See Newman, *Transformation of American Abolitionsim*, 76–78.
[38] See David Barclay, *An Account of the Emancipation of the Slaves of Unity Valley Pen, in Jamaica* (London, 1801).
[39] See *Centennial Anniversary of the Pennsylvania Society, for Promoting the Abolition of Slavery, the Relief of Free Negroes, Unlawfully held in Bondage: and for Improving the Condition of the African Race* (Philadelphia: Grant, Faires and Rodgers, 1875), 59–60, http://www.archive.org/stream/centennialannive00penn/centennialannive00penn_djvu.txt
[40] *Freedom's Journal*, 2 November 1827.
[41] On black freedom claims and the notion of being born on free soil within the United States, see Richard S. Newman and Roy Finkenbine, eds., 'Black Founders in the New Republic: Introduction', *William and Mary Quarterly* 61, no. 1 (2007): 83–94 (esp. n13).
[42] See Margaret Hope Bacon, *But One Race: The Life of Robert Purvis* (Albany: State University of New York Press, 2007), 78–79.
[43] David Ruggles, '"New York Committee of Vigilance for the Year 1837, together with Important Facts Relative to Their Proceedings" (1837)', in Newman, Rael and Lapsansky, *Pamphlets of Protest*, 149.
[44] Bacon, *But One Race*, 78–79.
[45] Ibid., 77, 120.
[46] Nat Brandt and Yanna Koyt Brandt, *In the Shadow of Civil War: Passmore Williamson and the Rescue of Jane Johnson* (Columbia: University of South Carolina Press, 2007).
[47] Stephens to the *Anglo-African*, 5 April 1862, in *A Voice of Thunder: The Civil War Letters of George Stephens*, ed. Donald Yacovone (Champaign: University of Illinois Press, 1997), 203–204.
[48] See Egerton, *Death or Liberty*, 275, 293.

Soil Free from Slaves: Slave Law in Late Eighteenth- and Early Nineteenth-Century Portugal

Cristina Nogueira Da Silva and Keila Grinberg

In 1761, when the kingdom of Portugal was home to a large slave population, particularly in the south, a decree was published prohibiting the transportation of slaves to the kingdom and declaring all those that arrived after that date to be free.[1] At the same time, in France and England, people were discussing the 'free' nature of the respective metropolitan territories an argument that some attorneys in these countries used successfully in freedom lawsuits involving slaves who were or had been in France and England. A special debate on this matter would soon take place during the case of the slave Somerset, culminating in the 1772 decision which was understood to establish that all slaves who landed in England were free.[2]

It is possible that some of these cases were known in Portugal. Sebastião de Carvalho e Mello, later known as the Marquis of Pombal (1699–1782), the minister of King D. José I who helped to define the terms of the king's 1761 decree, was certainly aware of them, especially in light of his diplomatic career in several European courts.[3] Even so, would the kingdom of Portugal at the end of the eighteenth century become free soil for those slaves who travelled through the capital city of the Portuguese Empire? In this article, we intend to discuss the different meanings of the decree of 1761: Pombal's intentions in publishing it, the way the decree was used by slaves in the Portuguese and Brazilian courts from the end of the eighteenth to the middle of the nineteenth century, and, finally, its importance in legal doctrine and in the construction of the myth that slavery had been abolished in Portugal during the Pombal period.

In the second half of the eighteenth century, the Portuguese Empire underwent a crisis, caused by the low price of sugar from the north-east of Brazil and by the drop in gold production in Minas Gerais. It was in this context that the future Marquis of Pombal was appointed by King D. José I as the Secretary of War and Foreign Business of Portugal. With this appointment, the Portuguese Crown sought, among other objectives, to increase the income derived from its American territory, which was experiencing an increase in slavery and agricultural slave labour production.[4] Recent estimates show that the Portuguese controlled some 38 per cent of the transatlantic slave trade at the end of the eighteenth century.[5] Between 1751 and 1775, 476,596 slaves landed in Brazil under the Portuguese flag.[6] A similar increase in the number of slaves also occurred in the kingdom of Portugal. A recent study shows that almost 50 per cent of the inhabitants of the Capitania of Rio de Janeiro in 1789 were enslaved and, in Salvador, 41.7 per cent of the population in 1775 were enslaved; meanwhile, between 1771 and 1775, some 3000 Africans were transported to the kingdom of Portugal, most to the south of the country.[7] The presence of slaves in the city of Lisbon was widely noted by travellers at the time, such as Richard Twiss and the Duke of Châtelet, who was reported to have said in 1777 that some 15,000 blacks and mulattoes 'infested' the city, 'becoming a source of disorder, bastardisation and lessening of the Portuguese race'.[8]

It was precisely within this context that the decree of 1761 was promulgated. The decree manifested more a desire to 'free' the kingdom of slaves than to put into effect a doctrine of 'free soil' in the terms in which it was then being debated in French courts. As we will show, the intention of this decree was not to grant freedom to all the slaves who 'stepped on' the kingdom's soil, although this could be a consequence of its use. It was, instead, to guarantee that the soil of the kingdom was not 'stepped on' by them. Or, to put it another way, it was not a matter of advocating the freedom of the slaves who landed in the kingdom, much less of the slaves who already lived there. What was intended was to threaten the owners and traffickers of slaves, dissuading them from unloading new slaves in the kingdom, whether for their own use or to sell them. If they did so, those slaves would be free.

For this reason, the king's decree explicitly stated that it did not alter the legal condition of the slaves already residing there and would not serve as a pretext for other slaves to come and seek freedom in the kingdom:

> However, it is not my intention, neither with respect to the black men and women who are already present in these Kingdoms as well as to those who come here within the aforementioned terms, to change anything through this law; nor for slaves to leave my overseas domains under the pretext of this law. Much to the contrary, I order that all free black men and women who come to these Kingdoms to live, trade or serve, using their full freedom to which they are entitled, necessarily bring the papers from the respective Chambers from which they left showing their sex, age and figure, so that their identity is given and that state whether they are black, freed and free. And that if any come without these papers as stated, they will be arrested and fed and sent back to the places from whence they came, at the expense of the people in whose company or the ships came or are.[9]

If the objective of the decree was not to change the status of slaves who then lived in the kingdom of Portugal, nor to free those who landed there, it is of the utmost importance to understand the reasons behind its publication.

The decree of 1761 and the defence of metropolitan public order

The text of the decree of 1761 clearly states that its origin is the 'noticeable need' for slaves in the plantations and mines of Brazil. Clearly, one of its goals was to divert the traffic of slaves from the kingdom to 'overseas domains'. But another reason, perhaps stronger and more directly related to the territory of the kingdom, was the establishment and defence of public order. The presence of slaves left the *moços de servir* ('service boys' or servants) unoccupied. According to the decree, they were affected by competition from slave labour and became idle, and, therefore, socially dangerous.[10]

Such concerns were not new. Since the sixteenth century, public order was often used as an argument in petitions sent to the Cortes, whose authors denounced the excessive number of slaves and the harm that followed from it. In addition to consuming food reserves, it was stated that slaves indulged in idleness and vagrancy, theft and prostitution. Some legal scholars and bishops of the sixteenth and seventeenth centuries had similar opinions about the presence of slaves.[11] And there are signs that this perception was generalised and shared by the government, which reflected it in the laws that were published.[12]

Alongside public order, and strongly related to it, was the idea that a space free of slaves was a more 'civilised' space. The decree of 1761 stated that the transportation of 'black slaves' to the kingdom went against the 'laws and customs of other polished Courts'. This reference to the 'laws and customs of other polished Courts' reminds us of those laws from the *Nações Cristãs, iluminadas e polidas* that would come to be converted into sources of the Portuguese by the Law of 'Good Reason' by 18 August 1769, a law in which the same concern with the 'civility' of the kingdom would be noted.[13] The size of the slave population in the kingdom, which foreign travellers never failed to mention, harmed this image of civility.[14] The presence of slaves contributed nothing to dignifying places, even less so the urban space of Lisbon. For the minister, it was important to free the soil of the kingdom of slaves so that it could become part of the modern, civilised world, the world which already, at least according to some well-known authors, was (or should be) a world without slaves. With regard to the 'overseas domains', these were other worlds, where people lived in a different stage of civilisation. Montesquieu, an author always quoted in Portuguese political and legal literature of the end of the eighteenth century and first half of the nineteenth century, had already explained this in his famous work, *De l'esprit des lois* (1748).[15]

The decree of 1761 may have also been the result of racial prejudice because of the presence of both blacks and mulattoes in the kingdom, which was similar to the prejudice evinced by French officials of that time.[16] The treatment of non-whites as a single, undifferentiated class can be seen in a subsequent declaration of 1767 which, contrary to the prevailing understanding of the Customs Service of the city of Lisbon, ruled that the 1761 legislation applied not just to blacks, but also to mulatto slaves, who would also be free upon landing in the kingdom of Portugal. The king declared:

> I order you to hand down the necessary orders so that in the Casa da India the same treatment be given to the mulattoes who from now on arrive from the aforementioned ports of America, Africa and Asia, as is given to blacks who arrive from those same ports.[17]

It was also within this context, and with the same intention of freeing the soil of the kingdom of slaves, that in 1773 (following the English 1772 Somerset decision) another important law was published. This law determined that all slaves whose condition went back to their great-grandmothers (but not those for whom it only went back to their mothers or grandmothers), as well as all those who were born after the publication of the law, were free. This 'free birth law' put an immediate end to captivity of fourth-generation slaves born in the metropole and prepared for gradual abolition in the kingdom.[18] Of course, an important part – perhaps the majority – of the slave population would remain slaves, since only those fourth-generation slaves who were most integrated into Portuguese culture would be freed.[19] In any case, the law had important economic and social consequences, above all in the south of Portugal, where farmers relied upon slave labour.[20]

The 1773 decree refers to major losses that would result for the state from the legal status of slaves, which made them incapable of participating in economic activities such as agriculture and commerce, which suggests an economic motive for the law. Pombal's policy of economic 'modernisation' pursued after the earthquake of 1755 had created new needs for free labour in the kingdom, especially for the factories that Pombal wanted to develop.[21] There was also a relation between the 1761 decree and this one. The new decree was designed, in part, to overcome an unforeseen effect of the decree of 1761: the intensification by slave owners of reproductive strategies for slaves who already lived in the metropole.[22]

To this objective was added the desire to prepare for the gradual abolition of slavery. Abolition would only apply to the soil of the metropole, a place where, despite everything, a relatively small number of slaves lived. There was no anti-slavery intent in this decree and slavery itself was not condemned either in this decree or in the *lex naturalis* doctrines that D. José included in the syllabus of the Law School.[23] While the 'free soil' of Portugal was established in 1761, and a gradual emancipation policy implemented in 1773, neither resulted from a popular anti-slavery philosophy or movement. Nevertheless, slaves themselves saw these developments in a very different light. What it is important to clarify is not so much the intention of those who framed the law, but rather the other interpretations that came to be made of this legislation, whether in terms of jurisprudence or in legal thought, in the subsequent decades in Brazil and in Portugal.

The decree of 1761 and the actions of the slaves

The decree of 1761 ended up serving as the basis by which enslaved people, for varying reasons and under different circumstances, claimed their freedom, often with help from the Lisbon confraternities, especially Nossa Senhora do Rosário dos Pretos de Lisboa.[24] They gave the decree its own meaning and often achieved manumission, either at customs, upon entry into the kingdom, or in the courts, when they asked for the right to change their legal status. Although it is not known how many of the Africans and Brazilians who arrived as slaves were aware of the existence of the decree, the fact is that, for many of them, the soil of Portugal ended up meaning the land of freedom.[25]

This was the case with 'two blacks who came to the port of this Court [Lisbon] with the crew of a French ship' in 1791. It was to this effect that the intendant, Pina Manique, wrote to the Minister of the Overseas Area, Martinho de Mello e Castro, saying that the two had been abducted while drunk and put on a ship to be sold as slaves in Pará. Upon learning of the situation, the intendant asked the minister to send orders to the governor to send the two blacks back to Lisbon, as well as to arrest the person responsible for their enslavement. He also said that he had no 'intention of releasing them, unless the same slaves reach Lisbon, to give a good example this way'.[26] The minister sent a letter to the governor of Pará on 2 March 1791, ordering that the requested measures be taken. In another instance, Marçal José de Araújo, a resident of the Capitania of Minas Gerais, requested a license in 1795 to 'travel to this Court [Lisbon], or the city of Porto, with his wife, two daughters and two black servants'. He received as a reply that the 'black servants', as a result of the Order of 1761, would be free as soon as they arrived in Portugal.[27]

Such instances demonstrate the means by which many blacks arrived in the metropole: as sailors or colonial servants. The flow of slaves to Portugal, especially sailors, was significant, as has been demonstrated by the ample historiography on this matter.[28] Moreover, such cases demonstrate that many slaves were, in fact, aware of the legislation and used it consciously, even if it took a long time to realise their freedom. For example, Francisco de Paula, a black sailor for more than 27 years and supposedly a slave of the Brazilian Colonel Anselmo da Fonseca Coutinho, sent a letter to the king of Portugal requesting manumission for having travelled from Rio de Janeiro to the port of Lisbon. Francisco de Paula mentions by name the Orders of 19 September 1761 and 16 January 1773 to beg the king to 'declare [him] Free and Exempt from Slavery'.[29]

The metropolitan authorities were apparently surprised at the volume of manumission requests that were filed and granted, especially by sailors, since they put into effect a series of rules (*Notices*) seeking to limit the effects of the decree, excluding its application to slaves who were registered on ship lists.[30] A Notice of 22 February 1776 allowed the temporary entry into Portugal of black slaves who were part of the crew of ships coming from overseas, provided that they were registered on the crew lists and on condition that they returned to the territories from which they came.[31]

Even so, the movement of slaves in the ports and their entry into Portugal seems to have continued, as demonstrated by another decree of 7 January 1788, prompted by a request from four 'blacks who were detained as slaves' on-board a ship. The four argued that they were entitled to freedom, pursuant to the terms of the Order of 1761. The response was surprising: 'the exception of the notice of February 22, 1776, covers only professional sailor slaves and not called so, of the inhabitants of Brazil and other Portuguese colonies'. Since these four were not part of the ship's crew, they could not be kept in slavery, like the other individuals who were in a similar situation. The decree thus seemed to attempt to avoid 'harmful frauds', such as the illegal enslavement by any ship owners who wanted to 'retain the blacks who seemed to be under strict slavery, sell them and transport them to wherever had been agreed upon, under the pretext of belonging to the crew of their ship, as has happened in this Kingdom'.[32]

Thus, the text of the decree seems to confirm both the desire to maintain the soil of the kingdom of Portugal free of slaves and the privileged status of white sailors in the metropolitan ports, while preserving the slave status of black sailors from Brazil, where there were no others who could work in this capacity. After all,

> due to a lack of free white sailors, the crews are composed of slave sailors, it would be a blow to navigation in these ports of Brazil or the other colonies if the slaves who make up the crews of these ships became free as soon as they arrived in the port of this capital or to any other port in this Kingdom.[33]

Two additional orders, with a similar content, were published in 1800 and 1802. The latter emphasised that because of the 'difficulties, which since the publication of the Order of September 19, 1761, have been placed upon the ports of My Overseas Domains against slaves coming to these Kingdoms, in the exercise of sailors', and by the fact that 'of the aforementioned slaves, able sailors, and experts can be found, with which to facilitate navigation, and promote commerce', those who were registered on the crew lists should not be freed, but should return as soon as possible to their ports of origin, without becoming established in the kingdom of Portugal or remaining there 'in a state of slavery'.[34]

From these notices, decrees and orders, we can see that, if the movement of slave sailors to the port of Lisbon was significant, no less important was the desire by the metropolitan authorities to control the entry of individuals onto Portuguese soil without harming the business conducted on both sides of the Atlantic, for which the enslaved sailors seemed to be essential. At the same time, it seems clear that there was a social use of the legislation by the enslaved individuals, who turned to the authorities to demand that their rights be respected. Thus, although the slaves themselves were probably intended to benefit from the 'free soil' decree of 1761 – which was imagined as a penalty against slave masters who would bring them to the metropole – the slaves' actions ended up expanding the effects of the text. On the one hand, they forced the authorities to constantly correct the original text. On the other hand, they favoured the use of the law in other contexts, as we can see in the following examples of freedom suits brought immediately after the independence of Brazil, many of which were through an initiative of the Brotherhood of São Benedito.

In the aftermath of Brazilian independence, the status of slaves migrating from the former colony to the kingdom took on a new political urgency. In one case from 1822, Mariana and her minor children Henriqueta and Carlota argued that, having arrived in Lisbon from Rio de Janeiro as the slaves of Jacinto de Araújo, she and her children should be free by force of the Order of 19 September 1761. Represented by the Brotherhood of São Benedito, the three confirmed their emancipation in 1825 after the judge received orders from the king himself to maintain them in freedom.[35] That same year, Joaquim José da Costa Portugal fought in the courts of Lisbon for the right to keep Luciano, who was born in the Congo, and Carolina, a Creole, as slaves. They had arrived from Maranhão with him and were considered to have been freed and manumitted by the General Administrator of the Alfandega Grande do Açúcar, who granted them liberty on the basis of the Order of 19 September

1761. In spite of the owner's request to keep his slaves until he could return to Brazil, whence he had fled following the proclamation of independence of that country in 1822, the two were freed.[36]

This latter case is exemplary of a very common situation after the independence of Brazil: many allies of the Portuguese cause emigrated to Lisbon during the 1820s with their slaves, whom they had to bring on the trip while they waited for the conflict to be resolved before returning to Brazil. In every case, the argument was the same: since they were only in Lisbon temporarily, their slaves could not be definitively freed.[37] However, the response of the judges was also unwavering: pursuant to the terms of the Order of 1761, the slaves should be freed. It is not known whether it was because of mistrust over whether these owners would ever return to Brazil or due to a belief in the law, but the fact is that the judges in these cases confirmed the maxim that was already established in the eighteenth century: no more slaves would be allowed to enter onto Portuguese soil, and those who did land would be freed.

The decree of 1761 and eighteenth-century Portuguese doctrine

Legislation from the Pombal period constituted a source to which jurisprudence turned to serve as a basis for decisions freeing slaves who landed in the kingdom. It is important to analyse how this legislation was read by nineteenth-century legal scholars seeking to establish the new liberal national doctrine. As we will see, these theorists attributed to that legislation a different meaning than that which the Pombalian legislators intended. These scholars read the Pombalian laws as evidence of an old 'abolitionist tendency' of Portuguese legislation on slavery. This tendency, supposedly maintained and reinforced by the Pombalian laws, was, in turn, read as a sign that the definitive abolition of slavery was at hand throughout Portuguese territory, including the overseas possessions, in the second half of the nineteenth century. All these readings finally constituted yet another piece in the creation of the myth according to which slavery was abolished in Portugal by the Pombal decrees.

If, as we have seen, in 1773 a 'free birth law' created the conditions for slavery to disappear little by little from the European part of Portuguese territory, it would be necessary to wait many years for this to occur in the overseas part of this territory.[38] This happened when, within the context of a long process of the abolition of slavery in the Portuguese overseas provinces, a law was published on 24 July 1856, which declared free the children of slave mothers, with these children obliged to serve their mother's master without wages until they reached the age of 20. Then, on 29 April 1858, a new decree declared that all slavery would be abolished throughout the Portuguese territories, including its overseas territories, within 20 years. This deadline was later advanced by another decree which, on 25 February 1869, abolished slavery throughout that territory, freeing all remaining slaves, who nevertheless became freedmen. These freedmen, known as *libertos*, had a minor civil and political status that involved the obligation to work for their previous masters until 1878. In 1875, another decree declared the abolition of the status of *liberto*, allowing freedom to work throughout Portuguese continental and overseas territories.[39]

However, and in spite of this continuation of slavery throughout the nineteenth century, developing Portuguese legal doctrine produced over the course of three centuries increasingly considered slavery to be an illegitimate institution, without any ethical or legal foundation. Among the legal scholars who developed this interpretation was Vicente Ferrer Neto Paiva (1798–1896), an influential professor of *lex naturalis* at the University of Coimbra:

> If all rational beings exist for themselves and for their own purpose, and under no circumstances should serve as a means to achieve the arbitrary will of another ... it is evident that slavery is unfair. In fact, neither *contract* nor *birth* nor *force* can serve as a pretext for slavery. *If a man sells himself* into slavery, all his possessions become the property of the owner. Therefore, the owner would give nothing, and the slave would receive nothing, and freedom would not be paid for. No less absurd would be the free renunciation of freedom, as this goes against good sense and nature; because it is from freedom that rights and obligations arise ... as does all morality ... *Birth* can also not be invoked; because if a man cannot sell his freedom, much less can he sell that of his child, who has not been heard. Finally, force does not create a right.[40]

For the civil law scholar Manuel Maria da Silva Bruschy (1813–1873), slaves also represented 'a crime and a sin committed, or consented to, by the government' because it was 'unjustifiable to deprive a man of his freedom so that another man could avoid work'.[41] António Ribeiro de Liz Teixeira (1790?–1847), another civil law scholar, considered that 'laws which create slavery were mere facts, or actual crimes by the lawmakers and slave owners'.[42] But these two legal scholars, unlike Vicente Ferrer Neto Paiva, were analysing the law that was in effect, and not just the philosophy of law. For this reason, they could not ignore the fact that there was operative Portuguese legislation that regulated slavery in Portuguese colonies, notably the rules in the *Ordenações do Reino*, one of the most important sources of Portuguese law until the publication of the Civil Code in 1867.[43] When they referred to these rules, Portuguese legal scholars at no time moved away from the idea of the illegitimacy of the institution, in contrast to some Brazilian legal scholars at that time who argued in favour of the relationship between the legality of slavery and its legitimacy.[44] Instead, they opted to describe the condition of the slave on Portuguese territory as a condition that was *only tolerated* and *only in the African possessions*. This was a situation of fact, not of law. It was also a temporary situation: 'black slaves residing in the African colonies, kept in slavery, and in the Cape Verde Islands, and others adjacent to Africa are *temporarily* kept in slavery, because *that is how it is observed*'.[45]

The idea that there were no slaves in the kingdom, but only in the overseas territories, was already present in Portuguese legal thought at the end of the eighteenth century. Despite the clear presence of slaves in the metropole, as well as in Portugal's overseas colonies, in 1789, 16 years after the publication of the 'free birth law' by D. José in 1773, Pascoal José de Mello e Freire guaranteed that 'currently there are no slaves among us'. He admitted that black slaves were tolerated in Brazil. But he insisted, basing himself on the authority of Montesquieu, Adam Smith and Raynal, that there was no legitimate foundation for this. The situation should, for this reason, be rapidly resolved: 'In Brazil and in the other Domains of Discovered

Lands, black slavery was tolerated, but I confess that I know absolutely nothing of the right to hold them'.[46] Later, referring to the rules in the *Ordenações* that still regulated slavery on Portuguese territory, he claimed that 'these *Ordenações*, based on Roman laws, in the provisions in the same law extensively deal with free men and freed slaves, have almost no use currently'. Later, this idea was systematically reviewed by nineteenth-century legal scholars. All these scholars recognised that, according to 'modern principles', all human beings were legal entities, 'a being considered to be capable of rights ... to have rights and to owe other people rights'.[47] The law could not, under any circumstances, convert men into things.[48] If slaves were men, then they had to be, from birth, legal entities, 'true people'.[49] According to them, the Roman law that inspired the *Ordenações* had converted men into things, as Borges Carneiro affirmed: 'Slaves, according to Roman Law, are not people, but things and are reputed to be dead'.[50]

In order to reinforce the legal illegitimacy of slavery in Portuguese law, it was therefore necessary to devalue the importance that the principles of Roman law occupied in Portuguese law. This was what another well-known law professor of that time, Manuel António Coelho da Rocha (1793–1850), did. In order to get around the problem of the Roman origin of Portuguese law, which still regulated slavery on Portuguese territory, Coelho da Rocha, basing himself again on Pombalian legislation, remembered that Portuguese soil was free and, for this reason, the principles of Roman law already had little importance: 'In Roman Law, slaves were not people, because they could not have rights. This principle has little use in Portuguese law; because among us, everyone is free, and black slaves are only tolerated in our African possessions'.[51]

Based on this set of ideas, it was then necessary to explain several things. In the first place, why was slavery 'tolerated', and even more so in a context in which it was in effect throughout all Portuguese territory, including overseas territories, with written constitutions in which freedom and equality had been declared fundamental rights?[52] The few legal scholars who tried to give an explanation for this invoked the 'interests of society' or 'economic obstacles'.[53] But it was also necessary to demonstrate two other statements: that there already were no slaves in the 'civilised space' of the kingdom and that the preservation of slavery in the colonies really was 'temporary'.

In order to demonstrate this latter statement, Portuguese legal scholars sought to reinterpret the Pombalian laws of 19 September 1761 and of 1773. In the narrative that resulted from this interpretation, Portuguese soil had been, since 1761, 'free soil'. For them, the decrees of 1761 and 1773 had not only put an end to the existence of slaves in the kingdom, but were also part of a set of older and broader legislation whose emancipating tendency would eventually extend to the overseas territories. In relation to those first decrees, legal scholars emphasised that they had declared to be free the slaves who stepped on Portuguese soil. Based on this affirmation, most of them celebrated the 'liberating force' of Portuguese soil, as can be seen in the following passage:

> because by the Orders of 19 September 1761 and 10 March 1810, throughout the continent of the Kingdom and adjacent islands, such is the liberating force of the

> soil, or so linked in it are the principles of our Christian origin, that those who step on it are free.[54]

Even so, they recognised, often in footnotes, that 'Portuguese soil' had a restricted geographical meaning, covering only the kingdom and the islands of Madeira and the Azores, and some remembered that the Order of March 1810 had reduced these effects. Nevertheless, the supposedly universal liberating aspect of the law of 1761 created strong roots in Portuguese legal doctrine. It is sufficient to cite the affirmation of Pascoal de Mello e Freire when he stated, in 1789, that 'in Brazil, black slaves are tolerated, and when these go to Portugal, they receive native freedom'.[55]

Read together, the two decrees of D. José were then interpreted as a sign of an abolitionist dynamic in Portuguese legislation. In order to reinforce this idea, the same orders were written by these legal scholars into a larger set of rules, constituted either by articles from the *Ordenações do Reino* or by separate legislative documents. With these references, legal scholars sought to demonstrate an older will of Portuguese legislators to grant rights to slaves, in softening their condition and in treating them like 'people' and not like 'things'.[56] The Roman perception that slaves were things had not 'sullied our legislation', in which slaves were recognised to have rights.[57] Other legal scholars granted even more emphasis to Portuguese law, which they designated as 'favourable to freedom'. Among these scholars, the documents most often mentioned were the laws that favoured the freedom of Indians, of which one in particular stood out: the decree of 1 April 1680 which affirmed, according to one observer, 'that freedom comes from *lex naturalis* and there are stronger reasons in favour of it than there are in favour of slavery'.[58] In the opinion of Liz Teixeira, this decree prepared not only the 'laws in favour of the freedom of Brazilian Indians, and a few years later others in the same sense regarding the Indians of Maranhão … [but also] the great work of the extinction of slavery in Portugal'.[59]

The interpretation that was given to this set of rules – from other contexts and times, but whose meaning was unified under the umbrella of a single emancipating intention of the Portuguese monarchs – was clearly expressed in the words of publicist João de Sande Magalhães Salema in 1841:

> In Portugal the King D. José by the civilising hand of the Marquis of Pombal was the first, who knew slavery well, the object of so many titles in Roman law, supported by so many Lawmakers of the Ancient World, which is nonetheless opposed to the dignity of human nature and induces in the State indecency, confusion and hatred among the Citizens, and renders useless that unfortunate condition for public jobs, and to render other services to the State [Order of 16 January 1773]. Previously, some of his Kingly Predecessors had recognised that the reasons in favour of freedom are stronger than those in favour of slavery [Order of 1 April 1680]; however, its laws were partial, *and will only serve to prepare the great work of extinction of slavery in Portugal.* It was certainly D. José to whom is owed the great restoration, generally on the continent of the *lex naturalis*, with regard to the first human quality.[60]

When referring to the Pombalian orders as legislative measures that sought freedom for all slaves who touched Portuguese 'free soil' and that prepared for emancipation throughout Portuguese territory, including the colonies, these legal scholars attributed an abolitionist sense that they did not have, contributing to the construction of a myth that would last far beyond the nineteenth century.

More than just giving 'liberating force' to Portuguese soil, the Order of 1761 sought, above all, the prohibition of the landing of slaves in the kingdom. The order also threatened slave owners with punishment if they transported slaves to the kingdom. This is precisely what the text of the Pombalian orders shows: that it was not imagined that the process of the extinction of slavery in the kingdom would later extend overseas, as the legal scholars of the nineteenth century suggested. The transportation of slaves to the kingdom should end not only because it was against the 'laws and customs of other polished Courts', but also because the 'black slaves' were much needed in the 'overseas domains'. That it was also not the freedom of the slaves that it had in mind is also proven by the wording of the decree itself, in which it is clearly emphasised that the decree should not serve as a pretext for blacks to come and seek their freedom – although many achieved manumission using the decree – but rather as an instrument to prohibit them from being brought to the kingdom. Curiously, the legal scholars never referred to the jurisprudence previously analysed. The lawsuits that had resulted in the freeing of slaves since the 1790s until at least the 1820s could have served to support their interpretation. But either the legal scholars did not know them or did not consider jurisprudence to be a source of law with sufficient dignity to serve as a basis for their opinions.

The Order of 16 January 1773, which declared the children born to slave mothers in the kingdom to be free, was even more profoundly mischaracterised by nineteenth-century legal scholars as the decree that put an end to slavery in Portugal: 'among us there are no more slaves since the promulgation of the Law of 16 January 1773, which abolished all future slavery';[61] 'by the decree of 16 January 1773, all slaves who existed in the kingdom were declared free and by the Order of 12 April 1761 also deemed free were all slaves who landed on Portuguese shores'.[62] In fact, the 1773 'free birth law' did *not* establish that the slaves who lived in the kingdom at that time would be free, only the children and grandchildren born after its publication, a condition that the legal scholars ignored when they suggested that there had been no slaves in the kingdom of Portugal since its publication. The truth is that slaves *did* exist, since the law did not immediately abolish the status of slave in the kingdom. Moreover, another condition of the law – that slaves seeking freedom be able to prove their descent through four generations of maternal slavery – meant that many would have a hard time proving the slavery status of their great-grandmother as a basis of claiming their freedom.[63]

Finally, the invocation of the decrees that granted freedom to the Indians as a legal basis for the reception of the principle presuming that all men are born free required a strong decontextualisation. What generally happened in this legislation is that slavery of the Indians was clearly separated from slavery of the Africans and their descendants. The latter was preserved as a way to compensate for the lack of workers caused by granting freedom to the Indians. As has been, and continues to be, affirmed by historiography, this legislation 'in no way affected the blacks and mulattoes of Brazil'.[64]

Thus, in Portugal, as in Brazil, legal scholars invented a legal tradition in favour of freedom, attributing to the legislation meanings that it did not have originally and probably amplifying its effects.[65] In so doing, they contributed to the creation of two important effects, one of which is in Portuguese historical memory and the other in the legal system of the time in which they wrote. With regard to the former, the abolitionist reading that they made of the Pombalian decrees transformed their texts into yet another piece in the creation of the myth of Pombalian abolitionism in the Portuguese historical memory. This is a myth which, until the twentieth century, was the object of historical appropriation. With regard to the legal effect, which is more important in this text, we can affirm that these legal scholars reinforced a reading of the Pombalian decrees that favoured freedom for slaves, and that, by doing so, they presented legal arguments in favour of freedom that could condition this meaning upon the jurisprudential decision. Future development of this investigation will make it easier to see how legal doctrine conditioned Portuguese and Brazilian jurisprudence until the definitive abolition of slavery in Portugal in 1869.

Conclusion

Those who drafted the Pombal decrees of 1761 and 1773 were neither anti-slavery nor abolitionist; their objective was to free the kingdom of Portugal from a presence that harmed it, from a symbolic point of view, and was perceived as negative, from the economic viewpoint of the Portuguese kingdom and Empire. However, the fact is that upon publication, the decrees gained a new life. This life was much more strongly conditioned by the particular contexts in which the decrees were read than by the will of the original legislators. They were read by the slaves as an opportunity to achieve freedom. The success of some of them shows two things: first, it confirms that slaves used the law and the courts to achieve their individual goals; second, it shows how the interpretation of the laws was measured by the legal and political culture in effect both at the time of their production and at the time of their reception. This measurement becomes clear if we think about the effort made by the Portuguese legal scholars of the nineteenth century to transform the Pombalian legislation into legislation that tended towards abolitionism. This was one way to show that in Portuguese law, the modern principle, according to which people cannot be things, was already in effect. This principle was in effect in the metropolis and had also to be extended to the colonies.

Notes

[1] See Didier Lahon, 'O escravo africano na vida económica e social portuguesa do Antigo Regime', *Africana Studia* 7 (2004): 73–100 (76–85), in which he provides statistical data on the slave population of Lisbon. According to Lahon, the number of Africans imported into Portugal between the second half of the sixteenth century and 1761 was about 400,000 (75). He also states that between 1756 and 1763, 998 slaves were shipped in Lisbon Customs (76), and that between the late seventeenth century and 1761 the black population, especially

slaves, may have represented 15 per cent of the population of Lisbon, which means 22,500 for a total population of 150,000 (79).

[2] Sue Peabody, *'There Are No Slaves in France': The Political Culture of Race and Slavery in the Ancient Régime* (Oxford: Oxford University Press, 2002); Keila Grinberg, 'Freedom Suits and Civil Law in Brazil and the United States', *Slavery & Abolition* 22, no. 3 (2001): 66–82; Christopher Brown, *Moral Capital: Foundations of British Abolitionism* (Chapel Hill: University of North Carolina Press, 2006).

[3] Kenneth Maxwell, *Pombal: Paradox of the Enlightenment* (Cambridge: Cambridge University Press, 1995); Nuno Gonçalo Monteiro, *D. José* (Lisbon: Círculo de Leitores, 2006).

[4] Rafael Marquese, *Feitores do corpo, missionários da mente* (São Paulo: Companhia das Letras, 2004), 174ff.

[5] João Pedro Marques, *Os sons do silêncio: o Portugal de oitocentos e a abolição do tráfico de escravos* (Lisbon: Imprensa de Ciencias Sociais, 1999), 55.

[6] This data came from the Trans-Atlantic Slave Trade Database, http://www.slavevoyages.org.

[7] Sílvia Lara, *Fragmentos setecentistas: escravidão, cultura e poder na América portuguesa* (São Paulo: Companhia das Letras, 2007), 127; David Eltis and David Richardson, *Atlas of the Atlantic Slave Trade* (New Haven, CT: Yale University Press, 2010), 29.

[8] Maria do Rosário Pimentel, *Viagem ao fundo das consciências* (Lisbon: Edições Colibri, 1995), 58.

[9] Order with the force of law from 19 September 1761. See Sílvia Lara, 'Legislação sobre escravos africanos na América portuguesa', in *Nuevas aportaciones a la historia hurídica de Iberoamérica*, ed. José Andrés-Gallego (Madrid: Colección Proyectos Históricos Tavera, 2000), 345–346.

[10] Lahon, 'O escravo africano', 93. According to Lahon, who considers them to be determining factors, more than the lack of workers in Brazil, the other reasons cited – especially that of public order, slave traffic to the metropolis and the introduction of slaves owned individually – allowed, until the eighteenth century, access to slave labour at a very advantageous price. This situation meant that, until that time, slaves played an important economic role, so much so that at times it led to resistance by some trade guilds (76–85). Lahon also provides information on the accusation of competition of slave labour and the perception of its presence in the degrading of the ways of life of free workers in the kingdom since the sixteenth century (86–87).

[11] Didier Lahon, 'Esclavage et confréries noires au Portugal durant l'Ancien Régime (1441–1830)' (PhD diss., L'École des Hautes Études en Sciences Sociales, Paris, 2001), 102. Lahon has also identified the opposition of some corporations' craftsmen (for example, Lisbon boatmen and goldsmiths) to the employment of slaves in these trades. See Lahon, 'O escravo africano', 84–85.

[12] For example, the legislation that had governed slaves bearing arms since the sixteenth century. See Didier Lahon, 'Violência do estado, violência privada: o verbo e o gesto no caso português', in *Ensaios sobre a escravidão (I)*, ed. Manolo Fiorentino and Cacilda Machado (Belo Horizonte, Brazil: Editora UFMG, 2003), 96. In addition to the reference to these laws, Didier also describes an *Ordenação Real* from the early eighteenth century where serious problems of public order were denounced, in which the slaves would have taken a very active part. Violence within the slave community was also described in notices published in Lisbon's eighteenth-century weekly newspapers (97).

[13] António Manuel Hespanha, *Cultura jurídica europeia: síntese de um milénio*, 3rd ed. (Lisbon: Publicações Europa América), 239ff.

[14] Didier Lahon identifies these kinds of comments from foreign travellers since the fifteenth century (Gerónimo Munzer, 1494, o Humanista flamengo Clenardo (1538). See Lahon, 'O escravo africano', 81. With regard to the eighteenth century, we can count, among others, the examples of Richard Twiss and the Duke of Châtelet, cited earlier.

[15] Mais, comme tous les hommes naissent égaux, il faut dire que l'esclavage est contre la nature, quoique, dans certains pays, il soit fondé sur une raison naturelle; e il faut bien distinguer ces

pays d'avec ceux où les raisons naturelles mêmes les rejettent, comme les pays d'Europe où il a été heureusement aboli'. Montesquieu, *De l'esprit des lois [Spirit of Laws]* (Paris: Gallimard, 1995), bk. 15, chap. 7,. See also Cristina Nogueira da Silva, 'Escravidão e direitos fundamentais no século XIX', *Africana Studia* 14 (2010): 243ff.; Tâmis Parron, 'A nova e curiosa relação (1764): escravidão e ilustração em Portugal durante as reformas pombalinas', *Almanack Brasiliense* 8 (2008): Luis Geraldo Silva, '"Esperanças de liberdade": interpretações populares da abolição ilustrada', *Revista de História* 144 (2001): 107–149.

[16] Sue Peabody, 'The French Free Soil Principle in the Atlantic World', *Africana Studia* 14 (2010): 9–12.

[17] Notice of 5 June 1767, in Lara, 'Legislação sobre escravos africanos', 351n522.

[18] It is interesting to note that this Portuguese iteration of gradual emancipation by generation, or 'free birth', precedes the Pennsylvania legislative iteration promoted by American Quakers by seven years.

[19] '[C]hildren born before the publication of the law remained slaves if they were not of the fourth generation.' Lahon, 'Esclavage et confréries noires', 109. Lahon found processes in which freedom was denied to third-generation slaves who requested it shortly after the law of 1773, with the argument that these slaves were necessary to work the land in Alentejo. Lahon, 'O escravo africano', 95. Until 1830, there are still reports of the presence of slaves in the kingdom.

[20] Lahon, 'Esclavage et confréries noires', 110; Jorge Fonseca, 'As leis pombalinas sobre a escravidão e as suas repercussões em Portugal', *Africana Studia* 14 no. 1 semestre 2010, 29–36.

[21] Lahon, 'Esclavage et confréries noires', 108.

[22] 'I had certain information that throughout the entire Kingdom of Algarve and in some provinces of Portugal there are still people so lacking in feelings of Humanity and Religion that they keep slaves in their homes, some of whom are whiter than them with the name of Blacks and Negros, and others Mulattoes, and others true blacks, for through the reprehensible propagation thereof, they perpetuate this captivity through an abominable Commerce of sin, and of stealing the freedom of the miserable babies born from those successive and lucrative concubines, under the pretext that the Wombs of Slave Mothers cannot produce free Children under Civil Law.' Lara, 'Legislação sobre escravos africanos', 359–360.

[23] Maria do Rosário Pimentel, 'A escravatura na perspectiva do jusnaturalismo', *História, Cultura e Filosofia* 2 (1983): 329–375; 'Escravo ou livre? A condição de filho de escravos nos discursos jurídico-filosóficos', *História, Cultura e Filosofia* 13 (2000/2001): 37–53. With regard to this topic, see also the classic work by David Brion Davis, *The Problem of Slavery in Western Culture* (Ithaca, NY: Cornell University Press, 1975).

[24] The importance of the brotherhoods in the process of granting and registering the manumissions is clear in the Order of 12 August 1763, which states that the manumissions should be registered in the book of the Brotherhood of Nossa Senhora do Rosário dos Pretos. Fonseca, 'As leis pombalinas', 2ff., 11ff. Daniela Buono Calainho, *Metrópole das Mandingas: religiosidade negra e inquisição portuguesa no Antigo Regime* (Rio de Janeiro: Garamond, 2008); Lucilene Reginaldo, 'África em Portugal: devoções, irmandades e escravidão no Reino de Portugal, século XVIII', *Revista História* 28, no. 1 (2009): 289–319.

[25] The study of these processes is still under way, both in Portugal and Brazil. Future studies may serve to indicate more clearly the reach of the actions of the slaves in this context, as well as the result of its requirements.

[26] This case was discovered and analysed by Fernando Novais and Francisco Falcon, 'A extinção da escravatura africana em Portugal no quadro da politica pombalina', in *Aproximações: estudos de historia e historiografia*, by Fernando Novais (São Paulo: Cosac Naif, 2005), 101–102.

[27] Ibid., 100.

[28] See, for example, Peter Linebaugh and Marcus Rediker, *A hidra de muitas cabeças: marinheiros, escravos, plebeus e a história oculta do Atlântico revolucionário* (São Paulo: Companhia das Letras, 2008); Luiz Geraldo Silva, *A faina, a festa e o rito: uma etnografia histórica sobre as gentes do mar (séculos XVII ao XIX)* (Campinas, São Paulo: Papirus, 2001).

[29] This document, filed in the Manuscript Section of the National Library of Rio de Janeiro, C 420, 49 n. 12, was found by Manolo Florentino and reproduced by him in his book *Tráfico, cativeiro e liberdade: Rio de Janeiro, séculos XVI–XIX* (Rio de Janeiro: Civilização Brasileira, 2005), 358 (attachment 1).

[30] Lahon, 'Esclavage et confréries noires', 102.

[31] Notice of 22 February 1776, in Lara, 'Legislação sobre escravos africanos', 361–362.

[32] Decree of 7 January 1788, in Lara, 'Legislação sobre escravos africanos', 362n528.

[33] Ibid.

[34] Order of 10 March 1802, in Novais and Falcon, 'A extinção da escravatura', 102–103.

[35] Juízo da Índia e da Mina, Feitos Findos, Arquivo Nacional da Torre do Tombo, Lisbon, Proceeding No. 12, Set 12, Box 136.

[36] Ibid., Process No. 1, Set 2, Box 126.

[37] Lahon analyses similar cases in 'Esclavage et confréries noires'.

[38] Here, the 'overseas part of this territory' is understood to be the overseas domains of Portugal, except for Brazil, which became independent in 1822. Throughout the nineteenth century, the overseas Portuguese possessions were understood to be the African and Asian territories belonging to Portugal: Angola, Mozambique, São Tomé and Príncipe, Cape Verde, Goa, Macau and Timor.

[39] On this process, see the works of João Pedro Marques and, for a synthesis, João Pedro Marques, *Sá da Bandeira e o fim da escravidão* (Lisbon: ICS, 2008). See also Cristina Nogueira da Silva, *Constitucionalismo e império: a cidadania no ultramar português* (Coimbra, Portugal: Almedina, 2009), 239ff.

[40] Vicente Ferrer Neto Paiva, *Elementos de direito natural ou de philosophia de direito*, 2nd ed. (Coimbra, Portugal: Imprensa da Universidade,), 70.

[41] Manuel Maria da Silva Bruschy, *Manual de direito civil português*, vol. 1 (Lisbon: Editores Rolland e Semiond, 1868), 30.

[42] António Ribeiro de Liz Teixeira, *Curso de direito civil portuguez para o ano lectivo de 1843–44, ou comentário às instituições do sr. Paschoal José de Mello Freire sobre o mesmo direito* (Coimbra, Portugal: Imprensa da Universidade, 1845), 79.

[43] On legislation in the *Ordenações Filipinas* and other laws regulating slavery during the Old Regime, see Lara, 'Legislação sobre escravos africanos', 24–25.

[44] Joseli Maria Nunes Mendonça, *Entre a mão e os anéis: a lei dos sexagenários e os caminhos da abolição no Brasil* (Campinas, São Paulo: Editora da Unicamp, 1999).

[45] José Homem Corrêa Telles, *Digesto portuguêz ou tratado dos direitos e obrigações civis*, vol. 2 (Coimbra, Portugal: Imprensa da Universidade, 1835), 219. Liz Teixeira also notes that 'the black slaves residing in the African Colonies of Cape Verde, and others adjacent to Africa, are *temporarily conserved* '. See Liz Teixeira, *Curso de direito civil*, 129 (our emphasis).

[46] Pascoal José de Mello e Freire, *Instituições de direito civil português, tanto público como particular* (1789), 18, http://www.fd.unl.pt/Default_1024.asp.

[47] Liz Teixeira, *Curso de direito civil*, 68. See also Manuel António Coelho da Rocha, *Instituições de direito civil portuguez*, 2nd ed., vol. 1 (Coimbra, Portugal: Imprensa da Universidade, 1848), 34–35: 'All men are capable of having rights, and therefore, all men are *person*'.

[48] Liz Teixeira, *Curso de direito civil*, 68.

[49] Manuel Borges Carneiro, *Direito civil de Portugal* (Lisbon: Impressão Régia, 1826), 65: 'The children, families and slaves are real people'.

[50] Ibid., 97. 'To the contrary, according to Roman Law, not every man is a person; this is what is seen in the slave, since he is incapable of having or of owing rights.' See Liz Teixeira, *Curso de direito civil*, 68.

[51] Coelho da Rocha, *Instituições de direito civil*, 35. See Silva Bruschy, *Manual de direito civil*, 30.

[52] On this topic, see Nogueira da Silva, 'Escravidão e direitos fundamentais'.

[53] '[It] is not due to a lack of respect for the principle, but rather to the need to serve the interests created many years ago that it would be inconvenient to promptly make cuts without a state of

transition that reconciled the demands of justice with the interests of society.' See Dias Ferreira, *Codigo civil portuguez annotado*, vol. 1 (Lisbon: Imprensa Nacional, 1870), 7. As an example, see also Liz Teixeira, *Curso de direito civil*, 79.

[54] Silva Bruschy, *Manual de direito civil*, 31.

[55] Mello e Freire, *Instituições de direito civil*, 18.

[56] For example, they mentioned the *Ordenações Filipinas*, Liv. V, Tit. 36, para. 1, affirming that in it is expressed the idea of equality of punishment between slaves and servants, or the decree of 30 September 1693 and the Order of 3 October 1758, ordering that owners keep their slaves in jail if they are there as a punishment, and that they be treated like other prisoners. See Liz Teixeira, *Curso de direito civil*, 78; Corrêa Telles, *Digesto portuguêz*, 220; Coelho da Rocha, *Instituições de direito civil*, 35.

[57] Silva Bruschy, *Manual de direito civil*, 30: 'Considered as work instruments, they are still far from the condition of Roman slaves. They are not things, they are men.'

[58] Liz Teixeira, *Curso de direito civil*, 78; Mello e Freire, *Instituições de direito civil*, 16; and Borges Carneiro, *Direito civil de Portugal*, 100–101, which dedicates a subchapter to them, in which it presents the laws 'in favour of the freedom of Indians in Brazil' as proof of the prevalence of the principles against slavery in Portuguese legislation.

[59] Liz Teixeira, *Curso de direito civil*, 78.

[60] João de Sande Magalhães Salema, *Princípios de direito político applicados à constituição política da monarquia portugueza de 1838 ou a theoria moderada dos governos monarchicos constitucionaes representativos* (Coimbra, Portugal: Imprensa de Trovão, 1841), 464.

[61] Liz Teixeira, *Curso de direito civil*, 88.

[62] Basílio Alberto de Sousa Pinto (1777–1849), *Lições de direito público constitucional* (1840), Lição No. 8, 20, http://www.fd.unl.pt/Default_1024.asp.

[63] Lahon, 'Esclavage et confréries noires', 105–109; Fonseca, 'As leis pombalinas', 8.

[64] Sílvia Lara, 'O espírito das leis: tradições legais sobre a escravidão e a liberdade no Brasil escravista', *Africana Studia* 14 (2010): 73–92, which also analyses how the 'judges and legal scholars involved in the debate on freedom actions in the middle of the nineteenth century were leaning over the Portuguese body of legal studies in search of the legal tradition capable of sustaining legal actions in favour of the ... matter of the extinction of slavery' in Brazil (23).

[65] For Brazil, see Lara, 'Legislação sobre escravos africanos', 42–45.

African Freedom Suits and Portuguese Vassal Status: Legal Mechanisms for Fighting Enslavement in Benguela, Angola, 1800–1830

Mariana P. Candido

This article focuses on the vulnerability of free blacks in Benguela, in West Central Africa, during the first decades of the nineteenth century at the height of slave exports. After the British abolition of the transatlantic slave trade in 1807, slavers moved south of the Equator leading to the pressure for more captives and the expansion of violence around Benguela. Focusing on the case of a free black woman, Dona Leonor de Carvalho Fonseca, this study discusses how she was captured, enslaved, transported to the coast, and sold. However she did not remain in captivity for a long time, since she was able to claim the principle of 'original freedom.' A legal mechanism created by the vassalage treaty, the principal of original freedom differentiated the local population between vassals and non vassal, Christians and non-Christians. The case of Dona Leonor illustrates how a free black could be subject to arbitrary capture, but also could claim original freedom and hence be protected from enslavement. Like her, others were able to bring freedom cases to the attention of Portuguese authorities and dispute their enslavement. These cases allow us to explore how, where, and why people were captured. It also shows the importance of vassalage treaties in defining who could or not be enslaved. By the early nineteenth century, Portuguese legislation regulated legal and illegal enslavement opening the space for captives to challenge their status. The freedom suits stress the vulnerability of the population living around the Portuguese settlements, and show how the pressures of the international slave market spread instability, even among those who were supposed to be protected by colonial law.

In 1811, a free mulatto woman could become merely another victim of the slave trade in West Central Africa. Dona Leonor de Carvalho Fonseca, the widow of an established

Portuguese trader, was on a business trip to the Mbailundu state in the Benguela highlands, accompanied by her two daughters. She carried her husband's letters of credit and may have been attempting to collect money from her husband's debtors. The *soba* ('ruler') of Mbailundu summarily ordered that she and her daughters be enslaved. The three were then sold to *sertanejos*, who transported them to the town of Benguela.[1] Separated from her children there, Dona Leonor boarded the slave vessel *Grão Penedo* to Luanda, the capital of the Portuguese establishment in West Central Africa. Upon arrival, Leonor reached the governor of Angola, José de Oliveira Barbosa, claiming that as a vassal of the Portuguese Crown and a mulatto she could not be enslaved. The governor agreed and overruled the governor of Benguela, Antônio de Carvalho Fonseca Henriques Ferreira. When Dona Leonor arrived in Benguela in a slave coffle, he ruled that Ferreira should have recognised her status as a free person and prevented her from being transported or separated from her daughters. Governor Barbosa ordered her immediate release and that she be reunited with her daughters, who remained under Ferreira's custody, employed as domestic slaves.[2]

Dona Leonor's story demonstrates the vulnerability of free blacks in West Central Africa during the early nineteenth century. The expansion of the transatlantic slave trade provoked violence and threatened individuals who lived in the Portuguese colony of Benguela. In this case, Dona Leonor travelled to Mbailundu, an African state that maintained commercial relationships with coastal traders. Dona Leonor and her husband were some of the Benguela merchants who travelled inland to acquire slaves. The colonial apparatus imposed a new legal code which nominally protected subjects of African rulers who had signed diplomatic treaties with the Portuguese Crown. As a resident of Benguela, Dona Leonor was protected by colonial legislation and she was able to fight her enslavement. For the Portuguese, unlike other European imperialists, freedom was not merely geographic. In contrast to the French and the British, who used the principle of free soil to confer freedom to those crossing boundaries[3], in West Central Africa the Portuguese recognised certain attributes – such as vassalage, baptism, Christian names and lighter skin colour – as characteristics of freedom. Thus, the same legal system that promoted violence against and the enslavement of some Africans offered legal spaces for those seen as insiders – the vassals – to appeal to the Portuguese bureaucracy and regain their freedom.

As a result, West Central Africans recognised by the state as Portuguese vassals could claim protection through the Portuguese legal system. Dona Leonor's journey to Mbailundu demonstrates her confidence in precisely this status as a protected person. When this status was violated, Dona Leonor was able to contact Portuguese authorities and insist that she was not the type of person who was supposed to be enslaved, using the principle of 'original freedom' to challenge her capture and possible shipment to Brazil.[4] The governor of Angola affirmed her rights as a free mulatto woman and a Portuguese vassal, supporting her claim. Like Leonor, many Africans were violently seized in regions not far from Benguela, in an area nominally controlled by the Portuguese or African rulers who had sought the protection of the Portuguese Empire. Few relied on the Portuguese judicial system to challenge their fate, claiming rights that separated them from the rest of the population based on their recognition of Portuguese authority.[5] Dona Leonor's story reveals the conflicts and tensions among Portuguese colonial authorities regarding their participation in the slave trade and enslavement of free Africans. By the late seventeenth century, the Overseas Council had already identified European traders and colonial administrators as responsible for capturing free people, regardless of their free status in their societies.[6]

Focusing on a single freedom suit case, I explore how the knowledge of Portuguese jurisprudence offered Dona Leonor, and others, the ability to dialogue with colonial authority and challenge its power. My aim is to emphasise the agency of individuals who challenged assaults on their free status and, by extension, the action of Portuguese agents in and around Benguela. The judicial sources selectively represent each story and often lack conclusions (for example, was Dona Leonor reunited with her daughters?). Reported cases include only those that Portuguese authorities considered worthy of note. Still, these sources offer interesting insights into the enslavement process and the thin line separating freedom from slavery in West Central Africa. The freedom suits stress the vulnerability of the population living around the Portuguese settlement, and show how the pressures of the international slave market spread instability, even for those who were supposed to be protected by colonial law.

Benguela, the transatlantic slave trade and the law

From the late sixteenth century, the Portuguese engaged in trade in the region around the Baía das Vacas, founding Benguela in 1617. Slaves were among the first exports from the new settlement of Benguela and continued as an important economic product in the region, although their volume was eventually surpassed by Luanda, to the north.[7] The Portuguese Crown recognised the profits this trade generated and suggested that local authorities support its expansion, since 'it could provide revenue to his Majesty'.[8] By the mid eighteenth century, Benguela had become pivotal to the exportation of slaves from the heavily populated highlands located in the hinterland and one of the major ports of the slave trade.[9] From 1699 to 1856, more than 630,000 enslaved Africans were exported from Benguela.[10] Yet, the town's permanent residency remained small, due to its relative isolation, unsanitary conditions and poor reputation, maintaining a population of only 2000–2600 people, including free and slaves, over the first half of the nineteenth century.[11] Portuguese royal officials sought to maintain order, uphold legislation and regulate trade, though their numbers were few. Portuguese agents did not control the hinterland, with insufficient soldiers to patrol the coast, although fortresses were established inland.[12]

Benguela and the population under Portuguese rule followed the same legal code as other Portuguese subjects, the *Ordenações Filipinas*, promulgated in 1603 during the reign of King Philip II. The *Ordenações* allowed anyone who did not agree with an unlawful enslavement to challenge it through legal procedures and, in cases where people were challenging their enslavement, 'arguments in favour of freedom always prevail'.[13] As the case of Dona Leonor shows, high-ranking authorities in Benguela acted in connivance with traders and kidnappers to ignore the fine points of the law. A few months after Ferreira assumed his position as governor of Benguela in January

1811, he was already embroiled in Dona Leonor's scandal. The case reveals his tacit agreement with illegal enslavement, despite the prohibitions on either direct or indirect participation of governors and high-ranking officers in the slave trade. Inevitably, situations like this led to conflicts between governors, local magistrates and, in some cases, traders and African rulers. The so-called cases of *liberdade original*, or 'original freedom', raise questions about the role of Portuguese agents in private trading.

Portuguese vassals and unlawful enslavement

Even as late as the nineteenth century, treaties between local African rulers and Portuguese authorities reproduced medieval European categories of vassalage, including their terminology, with subject chiefs characterised as vassals to the King of Portugal and owing tribute, military service, loyalty and obedience in exchange for protection and investiture.[14] Vassals submitted to the incursion of traders and armies into the territory under their control and provided men as soldiers and porters.[15] For example, in the formulaic language of the treaty signed by the ruler of Kilengue in 1804, he signed

> a treaty of voluntary subjugation, without the use of force or payment. This *soba*, one of the most powerful in the region of Libolo, will offer many slaves to the traders who visit his territory. He [will also] facilitate transportation through his land of those interested in reaching other *sobas* and people.[16]

Under the vassalage treaties, populations living in regions under Portuguese rule became subjects of the Portuguese Crown and Portuguese officials had to protect them. Vassals, including their subjects, could not be enslaved since they were considered to have embraced the Christian faith.[17] Christianity alone, however, did not protect many people in Angola.[18] Since the mid eighteenth century, authorities in Lisbon and Luanda had proposed new regulations to prevent administrators from participating directly in the slave trade in Benguela and its neighbouring territories. The 1765 'Regimento dos capitães-mores' [directions to the captains] for example, stated that captains and other authorities in the hinterland must maintain the peace and protect vassals of the Portuguese Crown in order to facilitate trade.[19] The regulations clearly proclaimed the duty of governors to control the slave trade and ensure that no illegal slave exportation occurred, despite the tempting profits.[20] As a way to overcome the enslavement of vassals and free black people, the Portuguese colonial administration introduced in 1769 the *inquisidor da liberdade* ('interrogator of freedom') to 'examine the slaves coming from the interior to be sold and embarked to Brazil, hoping that no free person is among the slaves'.[21] Manoel Gonçalves, the first priest to occupy the position in Benguela, was in charge of baptisms and of inquiring into the conditions of enslavement of each captive. If no claim of original freedom was found, the priest baptised them and then branded them with the royal mark, confirming their slave status. The creation of this position stresses the fact that the enslavement of freeborn people must have been common in Benguela during the eighteenth century.

By law, the enslavement of Dona Leonor was illegal. The use of the title of *Dona*, associated with nobility and prestige, also indicates her position as an important merchant in town. Clearly a vassal of the Portuguese Crown, she was probably baptised in the church of Nossa Senhora do Pópulo, although I was not able to locate her baptism certificate. For this violation, the governor of Angola reprimanded Ferreira and asserted his authority over the new officer.[22]

Petitions of original freedom reveal the contradictions of the Portuguese activities in West Central Africa, which, rather than protecting subjects, threatened their security. In the last decade, several studies have demonstrated that slaves used the legal system to petition for freedom in other parts of the Portuguese Empire – mainly in Brazil, but also in West Central Africa.[23] The *processos de liberdade* [freedom cases] represented an opportunity for slaves to challenge the power of their slave owners, arguing that abuses had been perpetrated. The claims of original freedom have to be understood as part of the changes taking place throughout the Atlantic world during the late eighteenth and early nineteenth centuries regarding the recognition of individual rights.[24] In areas under Portuguese control, new structures, such as the *juiz da liberdade* ('judge of freedom'), allowed people to appeal to the courts 'without the delay of the ordinary procedures'.[25]

In Angola, the same system was applied with some modifications. In the case of Benguela, the high mortality rate of Portuguese authorities inhibited continuity, leading to inevitable conflicts between the administrative and commercial elites. *Juizes de fora* were professional lawyers who mastered Roman law and were assigned for a three-year term. They presided over the town council, oversaw local authorities and ensured respect for judicial proceedings throughout the province.[26] Among other proceedings, the *juiz de fora* assessed cases of illegal enslavement.[27] Between 1776 and 1825, 11 judges were sent to Benguela, spending an average of 4.45 years in office.[28] These short-term appointments not only prevented the establishment of networks of interest, but also generated instability in the position, undermining respect for the law and strengthening the hand of long-term residents involved in slaving. *Juizes de fora* had to offer public audiences twice a week in towns with more than 60 inhabitants, including Benguela.[29]

As a slave trader who moved imported commodities into the interior and brought slaves to the coast, Dona Leonor had probably heard about such protection. She insisted on using the legal authorities, demonstrating her knowledge of the system and the tensions inherent in it. Her case shows the vulnerability of free black people – particularly women – to enslavement. It is not clear why her case reached the attention of the governor of Angola. Maybe he knew her deceased husband. He probably heard about Dona Leonor through the *inquiridor das liberdades* 'interrogators of freedom'. In Angola, and, by extension, Benguela, priests often acted as interrogators of freedom, interrogating slaves before they were sent off on slave ships.[30] However, many priests were disinclined to take these cases seriously; one claimed: 'no Negro will ever say that he had been legally enslaved ... they will always say that they were stolen and captured illegally, in the hope that they will be given their liberty'.[31] As a resident of Benguela, the widow of a slave trader and a merchant herself, Dona Leonor assumed her identity as an urban trader would mark her, and her daughters, out as people who could not be enslaved.

Multiple systems of law

Negotiating diverse legal systems was not alien to African societies in the hinterland of Benguela. They were accustomed to the existence of multiple legal codes. People who engaged in long-distance trade relied on the existence and enforcement of regulations offering protection to merchants. Thus, for the people living around Benguela and its hinterlands, Portuguese law offered another set of legal requirements limiting actions and protecting its subjects. As in other parts of the world, Africans realised the benefits of litigation in the Portuguese legal system.[32] It is in this context that we can understand the debate among West Central Africans and Portuguese authorities over the legality of particular enslavement.

In Benguela, the Portuguese administration regulated the trade and customs of officers, traders, outlaws, expatriates, slaves and a large local population with some level of adherence to the Portuguese language and Catholicism. People living beyond the very fluid frontier circumscribing Portuguese control were also subject to local customary law. Both systems shared similarities, especially pertaining to slavery and who could be enslaved. African and Portuguese authorities sanctioned enslavement through justified wars. Other means – such as trickery, kidnapping and banditry – were clearly considered illegal.[33] The mechanisms of enslavement for Portuguese and different African rulers protected insiders.[34] Portuguese agents, for example, avoided enslaving mulattoes in West Central Africa, since mulattoes were descendants of whites, who, by definition, were free people.[35] African rulers in the interior of Benguela, the *sobas*, established their own rules to determine sanctions and punishments, and protect insiders. These codes corresponded to local conceptions of morality in many parts of Africa; as elsewhere, they appear to have changed according to the external demand for slaves.[36]

Along the coast, the pressure to supply the transatlantic slave traders generated a series of tensions that required the intervention of the Portuguese administration. The erosion of social and political institutions led to an increase in violence and kidnapping, which was particularly threatening to ordinary free people, who had their mobility hindered by fear and insecurity.[37] The constant demand for people along the African coast is intimately linked to the existence of different enslavement strategies. It was through illegal mechanisms, according to Roquinaldo Ferreira, that most of the male slaves were generated, since most of captives in conflicts were women, children and elderly people.[38] Violent means of capturing people were not uncommon throughout the African continent. The slave trade was based on violence and there were very few effective mechanisms in place to prevent illegal activities.[39] The Portuguese authorities respected customary laws in part because they shared similarities with respect to who could be enslaved.[40] In 1828, in order to protect people illegally enslaved, the governor of Benguela ordered the strict inspection of every ship leaving the coast.[41] It is not clear if the authorities and traders respected this decree, or if people enslaved illegally were rescued from slave ships. Cases stress the local clashes between administrative and commercial elites who had different ideas and interests.[42]

Restoring freedom through legal means

Dona Leonor's experience and the governor's abduction of her two daughters demonstrates that the boundary between slavery and freedom was a thin one. Slaves used the courts and judicial systems to fight for their rights, including the authority of slave masters to apply abusive punishments.[43] Yet, the ability of some Africans to present their cases at the judicial courts reinforced the authority of the Portuguese agents, conferring on them the power to regulate Africans' destinies. Jurisdictional disputes can be seen as challenging the boundaries of the Portuguese Empire, but they inevitably reinforced the power of foreign agents over Africans.[44] Merely issuing regulations as to who could or could not be enslaved was not sufficient to protect Portuguese vassals. Dona Leonor went to the interior to trade and collect debts in the *sobado* [state] of Mbailundu during a time of political instability and reconfiguration in the central highlands. New warrior elites committed to slave trading and allied to Benguela's colony replaced the old ruling groups, which resulted in the spread of violence and raids.[45] Perhaps Dona Leonor was confident that her position as a trader, her skin colour and her social network would protect her, and her daughters, from enslavement. However, the *soba* of Mbailundu, unwilling to pay his debts, ignored all these attributes and enslaved them. As women travelling alone, Dona Leonor and her daughters were perceived as easy targets.

The nineteenth century saw an increase in the number of slaves exported from Benguela, which was probably a result of the Anglo-Luso treaties restricting the slave trade to the south of the equator.[46] Besides, the internal use of slave labour also expanded, exacerbating the cycle of violence. In order to deal with the internal and external demand, slavers kidnapped anyone in a defenceless position. Portuguese agents were aware of the vulnerability of free blacks. In order to restore peace, new authorities arrived in Angola, committed to respect the law. In 1812, João de Alvelos Leiria assumed the position of governor of Benguela. He declared that he would follow the regulations, including ensuring that no free person was enslaved.[47] His mandate was to release illegally enslaved people and, in this, he had the support of the Benguela traders, who feared retaliation from African authorities.[48] Traders travelling alone in the interior, such as Dona Leonor, attracted the attention of greedy people, especially when they carried valuable goods such as textiles, alcohol and weapons. They risked not only their merchandise, but also their own freedom. In 1817, four traders operating in the interior of Benguela were kidnapped while travelling. When facing the priest investigating the case, one of the traders managed to tell their story, but not before another of them had had his body branded with the royal stamp.[49] They explained that they were free black men sent to the interior with orders to buy slaves when they were captured by the *gentio* ('heathen'). They had changed hands three times before arriving in Benguela, where they were about to board a slave ship.[50]

Violence continued in the 1820s, threatening free blacks. While travelling in areas outside the regions under nominal Portuguese control, any black person was vulnerable, even if legally they were protected as vassals of the Portuguese Crown. They could easily be captured by anyone who did not, or chose not to, recognise their protected position. Unless they returned to Benguela and found people willing to support their claim for freedom, they could end up enslaved in the Americas.[51] On 4 October 1826, Captain Manoel Joaquim Pinto de Almeida sent 11 captives to be baptised at the church of Nossa Senhora do Pópulo in Benguela. Among the 11 slaves was a soldier, Vicente de Barros. Barros served in the infantry of Benguela before deserting. During the collective baptism, the priest, João Napumoceno e Souza, was close to branding him with the royal stamp when Barros claimed his original freedom.[52] In 1796, the queen (Maria I) had ordered that if there was any doubt, the priest should not brand people claiming freedom. They had to be kept in prison until a further investigation was concluded.[53] Following the rules, the priest brought Vicente de Barros to the governor of Benguela, João Victor Jorge.[54]

Besides violence, another downfall of early nineteenth-century Benguela was the corruption of Portuguese officers. Despite the regulations, Portuguese authorities were willing to risk breaking the law to increase their profits. In January 1829, Francisca Joaquina Ignácia reported to the interim governor of Benguela that the captain of the Benguela militia had strangled a couple of free people and enslaved others, including her sister, Maria Joaquina Ignácia. The governor of Benguela, Joaquim Aurélio de Oliveira, supported the claim of Francisca Joaquina Ignácia and notified the governor of Angola about the behaviour of the captain. Oliveira declared his commitment to locating Ignácia's sister, although it is not clear if she was ever found. Although military officials were prohibited from profiting from the commerce which they were supposed to protect, they usually were able to avoid prosecution if they engaged in trade.[55]

Conclusion

Historians have emphasised the role of runaway resistance in West Central Africa.[56] This essay demonstrates that there were other mechanisms available to avoid enslavement. Some Africans resisted through legal means, using the Portuguese legal code to regain their freedom. The appointment of Benguela's first *juiz da liberdade* in the 1770s indicates that the enslavement of people who were supposed to be protected was common. The lack of freedom suits before the end of the eighteenth century might be related to the absence of an authority in charge of invigilating the rights of Portuguese vassals. It was only after the appointment of the interrogator and judge of freedom that claims of original freedom started to show up in the colonial documentation. The new bureaucracy and authorities heard the cases and created the written documents available. Dona Leonor took advantage of the regulation and employed the argument of being a vassal and a mulatto to contest her enslavement. Yet, the judicial apparatus of the Portuguese Empire, including the creation of the *juiz de fora* and *juiz da liberdade*, only worked in collaboration with metropolitan officers committed to respect the law. Some officials were more invested in enforcing the law than others, as the dispute between the governors of Benguela and Angola over Dona Leonor's enslavement demonstrates. Free blacks who were aware of rights engaged with colonial administration and pushed the boundaries of the colonial state. Thus, the same empire committed to the spread of violence, slavery and the slave trade created mechanisms to protect those viewed as allies. Like Dona Leonor, other vassals of the Portuguese Crown had certain knowledge of colonial legislation and the Portuguese language.

The expansion of slaving practices in regions close to the coast provoked more violence and weakened some African states. The Portuguese colonial state introduced a language of rights regarding enslavement, allowing some people to challenge their capture. However, few could pursue legal strategies. The majority did not necessarily know their rights and were not lucky enough to find honest colonial authorities who pushed their cases forward. Freedom suits allow us to rescue people from the anonymity of African history and studies on the transatlantic slave trade. Demographic analyses are important, but dispassionate, focusing more on numbers than on individual cases. Following Paul E. Lovejoy's call for a careful examination of processes and circumstances of enslavement in Africa[57], I have explored the case of a merchant woman who lived in Benguela and, when enslaved, told her story. In most cases, captives left their testimonials about enslavement in sources written by Europeans; yet these accounts are valuable in elucidating the process of enslavement in West Central Africa. It is through these colonial documents that scholars can understand how people were captured and enslaved.

Like others, Dona Leonor used a judicial system that was essentially in place to facilitate Portuguese territorial expansion and ensure its domination. Yet, by defending her freedom, Dona Leonor differentiated herself from others living outside of Portuguese-controlled regions. By requesting Portuguese arbitration, she solidified the role of the colonial agents – in this case, the governor of Angola – as responsible for her destiny. Although it can be interpreted as a challenge to the power of the governor of Benguela, inevitably Dona Leonor and others who used the Portuguese courts reinforced the power of foreign agents over African lives. Freedom suits in Benguela show how few people were immune to enslavement, and help us to explore an overlooked aspect of the process that led to the enslavement and dispersal of millions of people throughout the diaspora.

Acknowledgements

I would like to thank Sue Peabody, Paul E. Lovejoy, Wendy Belcher and Yacine Daddi Addoun for their comments. I also benefitted from José C. Curto, Olatunji Ojo and Stacey Sommerdyk's suggestions and advice on an earlier version. I am also grateful to Zack Kagan Guthrie and Brooke Fitzgerald for help in editing this article.

Notes

[1] *Sertanejos* were the agents of coastal merchants in the interior, who transported imported goods inland from the coast and brought slaves, wax and ivory from the interior. See Joseph Miller, *Way of Death: Merchant Capitalism and the Angolan Slave Trade, 1730–1830* (Madison: University of Wisconsin Press, 1988), 392; Isabel Castro Henriques, *Percursos da modernidade em Angola: dinâmicas comerciais e transformações sociais no século XIX* (Lisbon: Instituto de Investigação Científica Tropical, 1997), 767.

[2] Arquivo Histórico Nacional de Angola (AHNA), Luanda, Códice 323, ff. 28v–29, 19 August 1811; AHNA, Códice 323, ff. 30v–31, 20 August 1811.

[3] Sue Peabody, *'There Are No Slaves in France': The Political Culture of Race and Slavery in the Ancien Régime* (New York: Oxford University Press, 1996).

[4] For more on 'original freedom', see José C. Curto, 'The Story of Nbena, 1817–1820: Unlawful Enslavement and the Concept of "Original Freedom" in Angola', in *Trans-Atlantic Dimensions of Ethnicity in the African Diaspora*, ed. Paul E. Lovejoy and David V. Trotman (London: Continuum, 2003), 43–64.

[5] For other cases, see Mariana P. Candido, 'Enslaving Frontiers: Slavery, Trade and Identity in Benguela, 1780–1850' (PhD diss., York University, Toronto 2006).

[6] Arquivo Histórico Ultramarino (AHU), Angola, Códice 544, f. 9, 12 February 1676, ff. 7, 7v, Lisbon. See also Catarina Madeira Santos, 'Entre deux droits: les Lumières em Angola (1750–v. 1800)', *Annales HSSS* 60, no. 4 (2005): 817–848.

[7] Adriano A.T. Parreira, 'A primeira "conquista" de Benguela (século XVII)', *História* 28 (1990): 67.

[8] 'Benguela e seu sertão', (Lisbon: Impressa Nacionale, 1881).

[9] AHU, Códice 555, f. 52v, 25 January 1758; Ralph Delgado, *O reino de Benguela: do descobrimento à criação do governo subalterno* (Lisbon: Imprensa Beleza, 1945): 38–63; David Eltis, Paul E. Lovejoy and David Richardson, 'Slave-Trading Ports: Towards an Atlantic-Wide Perspective', in *Ports of the Slave Trade (Bights of Benin and Biafra)*, ed. Robin Law and Silke Strickrodt (Stirling: Centre of Commonwealth Studies, University of Stirling, 1999), 21.

[10] See the Trans-Atlantic Slave Trade Database at http://www.slavevoyages.org. Based on a calculation of missing voyages and incomplete data, the estimated number of slaves who embarked in Benguela is 635,160. See David Eltis and David Richardson, 'A New Assessment of the Transatlantic Slave Trade', in *Extending the Frontiers: Essays on the New Transatlantic Slave Trade Database* (New Haven, CT: Yale University Press, 2008), 1–60.

[11] Candido, 'Enslaving Frontiers', 135.

[12] Miller, *Way of Death*, 15.

[13] *Ordenações Filipinas*, Livro 4, Titulo XI, 'Que ninguém seja Constrangido a vender seu Herdamento e cousas que tiver, contra sua vontade', 790. See also Keila Grinberg, *Liberata – a lei da ambiguade: as ações de liberdade da Corte de Apelação do Rio de Janeiro no século XIX* (Rio de Janeiro: Relume Dumará, 1994), 20–32; Hebe M. Mattos, *Das cores do silêncio: os significados da liberdade no sudeste escravista, Brasil, século XIX* (Rio de Janeiro: Nova Fronteira, 1998), 173–180.

[14] Beatrix Heintze, 'Luso-African Feudalism in Angola? The Vassal Treaties of the 16th to the 18th Century', *Separata da Revista Portuguesa de História* 18 (1980): 111–131 (116).

[15] For the obligations of vassals, see Beatrix Heintze, 'The Angolan Vassal Tributes of the 17th Century', *Revista de História Económica e Social* 6 (1980): 57–78. Cruz e Silva argues that African rulers and Portuguese officials had different interpretations of vassalage and dependency. See Rosa Cruz e Silva, 'The Saga of Kakonda and Kilengues', in *Enslaving Connections: Changing Cultures of Africa and Brazil during the Era of Slavery*, ed. José C. Curto and Paul E. Lovejoy (New York: Humanity Books, 2004), 245–259.

[16] AHU, Caixa 111, doc. 1, 4 September 1804.

[17] Heintze, 'Angolan Vassal Tributes'; Heintze, 'Luso-African Feudalism in Angola?'

[18] See Linda M. Heywood and John K. Thornton, *Central Africans, Atlantic Creoles, and the Making of the Foundation of the Americas, 1585–1660* (New York: Cambridge University Press, 2007); John K. Thornton, *Africa and Africans in the Making of the Atlantic World, 1400–1800* (New York: Cambridge University Press, 1998); James H. Sweet, *Recreating Africa: Culture, Kinship, and Religion in the African-Portuguese World, 1441–1770* (Chapel Hill: University of North Carolina Press, 2003).

[19] Carlos Couto, *Os capitães-mores em Angola*, (Lisbon: Instituto de Investigação Científica e Tropical, 1972), 323–338.

[20] Carlos Couto, 'Regimento de governo subalterno de Benguela', *Studia* 45 (1981): 288–289. See AHU, Caixa 83, doc. 41, 13 April 1796.

[21] Arquivo Nacional da Torre do Tombo (ANTT), Lisbon, Conde de Linhares, mc 52, doc. 14, 11 November 1769.

[22] This was not the first time that governors clashed on issues related to slavery; see Curto, 'Story of Nbena', 54–59. For more on the use of the title *Dona*, see Maria Beatriz Nizza da Silva, *Donas e plebeias na sociedade colonial* (Lisbon: Editorial Estampa, 2002), 64–65.

[23] See AHU, Caixa 83, doc. 41, 13 April 1796; Sidney Challoub, *Visões da liberdade: uma história das últimas décadas da escravidão na Corte* (São Paulo: Cia das Letras, 1990); Grinberg, *Liberata*; Mattos, *Das cores do silêncio*; Eduardo S. Pena, *Pajens da casa imperial: jurisconsultos, escravidão e a lei de 1871* (Campinas: Unicamp, 2001); Regina Xavier, *A conquista da liberdade: libertos em campinas na segunda metade do século XIX* (Campinas: Unicamp, 1997). On West Central Africa, see José C. Curto, 'Struggling against Enslavement: The Case of José Manuel in Benguela, 1816–20', *Canadian Journal of African Studies* 39, no. 1 (2005): 96–122; José C. Curto, 'Un butin illégitime: razzias d'esclaves et relations luso-africaines dans la région des fleuves Kwanza et Kwango en 1805', in *Déraison, esclavage et droit: les fondements idéologiques et juridiques de la traite négrière et de l'esclavage*, ed. Isabel C. Henriques and Louis Sala-Molins (Paris: UNESCO, 2002), 315–327.

[24] Grinberg, *Liberata*, 25; Maria do Rosário Pimentel, *Viagem ao fundo das coinciências: a escravatura na época moderna* (Lisbon: Colibri, 1995), 195–237; Sue Peabody, '"Free upon Higher Ground": Sain-Domingue Slaves' Suits for Freedom in US Courts, 1792–1830', in *The World of the Haitian Revolution*, ed. David P. Geggus and Norman Fiering (Bloomington: Indiana University Press, 2008), 264–265.

[25] Grinberg, *Liberata*, 74.

[26] AHNA, Códice 292, ff. 214v–216, 16 September 1805; 'Instruções para o novo governador de Benguela', in *Textos para a história da África Austral (século XVIII)*, ed. Maria Emília Madeira dos Santos (Lisbon: Alfa, 1989), 39–40; Lauren Benton, 'The Legal Regime of the South Atlantic World, 1400–1750', *Journal of World History* 11, no. 1 (2000): 34; Maria Fernanda Bicalho, 'As câmaras municipais no Império Português: o exemplo do Rio de Janeiro', *Revista Brasileira da História* 18, no. 36 (1998): 251–280.

[27] AHNA, Códice 90, ff. 91–91v, 9 November 1799; 'Instruções para o novo governador', 44.

[28] José Subtil, 'Os ministros do rei no poder local, ilhas e ultramar (1772–1826)', *Penélope* 27 (2002): 52.

[29] *Ordenações Filipinas*, Livro 1 (Brasília: Senado Federal, 2004), 135.

[30] AHNA, Códice 292, f. 220, 11 November 1805. See also Manuel Nunes Gabriel, *Angola: cinco séculos de cristianismo*, (Braga: Literal, 1978), 234–235.

[31] A passage quoted in Robin Law, 'Legal and Illegal Enslavement in West Africa', in *Ghana in Africa and the World: Essays in Honor of Adu Boahen*, ed. Toyin Falola (Trenton, NJ: African World Press, 2003), 514.

[32] Lauren Benton. *Law and Colonial Cultures: Legal Regimes in World History, 1400–1900* (New York: Cambridge University Press, 2002), 49–55.

[33] Orlando Patterson, *Slavery and Social Death: A Comparative Study* (Cambridge, MA: Harvard University Press, 1982), 105. See also Paul E. Lovejoy, *Transformations in Slavery: A History of Slavery in Africa* (Cambridge: Cambridge University Press, 2000), 1–9. For cases of individuals kidnapped and seized by trusted people, see Curto, 'Story of Nbena'. For a parallel situation in West Africa, see Jennifer Lofkrantz, 'Ransoming Policies and Practices in the Western and Central Bilad al-Sudan, *c.*1800–1910' (PhD diss., York University, Toronto, 2008).

[34] Lovejoy, *Transformations in Slavery*; Claude Meillassoux, *Anthropology of Slavery: The Womb of Iron and Gold* (Chicago: University of Chicago Press, 1991); Paul E. Lovejoy, introduction to *The Ideology of Slavery in Africa*, ed. Paul E. Lovejoy (Beverly Hills: Sage, 1981); David Eltis, *The Rise of African Slavery in the Americas* (Cambridge: Cambridge University Press, 2000).

[35] For more on skin colour and social status, see C.R. Boxer, *Race Relations in the Portuguese Colonial Empire, 1415–1825* (London: Clarendon Press, 1963), 103–113; A.J.R. Russell-Wood, 'Iberian Expansion and the Issues of Black Slavery: Changing Portuguese Attitudes, 1440–1770', *American Historical Review* 83, no. 1 (1978): 16–42; Frederick Cooper and Ann Laura Stoler, *Tensions of Empire: Colonial Culture in a Bourgeois World* (Berkeley: University of California Press, 1997), 609–621.

[36] See John Thornton, *Africa and Africans in the Making of the Atlantic World* (Cambridge: Cambridge University Press, 1992), 98–125.

[37] Candido, 'Enslaving Frontiers', 42–97.

[38] Roquinaldo Amaral Ferreira. 'Transforming Atlantic Slaving: Trade, Warfare and Territorial Control in Angola, 1650–1800.' PhD diss., University of California, Los Angeles, 2003, 177–178.

[39] Luis Candido Cordeiro Pinheiro Furtado to Barão de Mossamedes (Governor of Angola), 22 September 1785, Biblioteca Nacional, Lisbon, Códice 8094. See also Claude Meillassoux, *L'esclavage en Afrique precolonial* (Paris: Maspero, 1975); Paul E. Lovejoy, 'Slavery in the Context of Ideology', in Lovejoy, *Ideology of Slavery*, 11–38; Martin Klein and Paul E. Lovejoy, 'Slave Marketing in West Africa', in *The Uncommon Market: Essays in the Economic History of the Atlantic Slave Trade*, ed. Henry A. Gemery and Jan S. Hogendorn (New York: Academic Press, 1979), 213–35; Edward Alpers, 'The Story of Swema: Female Vulnerability in Nineteenth Century East Africa', in *Women and Slavery in Africa*, ed. Claire Robertson and Martin Klein (Madison: University of Wisconsin Press, 1983), 185–219.

[40] Instituto Histórico e Geográfico Brasileiro, Rio de Janeiro, DL 45, 11, 'Proposta sobre escravaria das terras da conquista de Portugal'. For the similarities between the legal systems, see Lauren Benton, Legal Regime of the South Atlantic World, 1400–1750: Jurisdictional Complexity as Institutional Order. *Journal of World History* 11, no. 1 (2000): 3 Mariza de Carvalho Soares highlights the affinity between Christianity and legislation in Portuguese expansion. See Mariza de Carvalho Soares, 'Descobrindo a Guiné no Brasil colonial', *Revista do Instituto Histórico e Geográfico Brasileiro* 161, no. 407 (2000): 71–94.

[41] AHU, Caixa 159, doc. 55, 9 August 1828. For the purchase of slaves directly from *gentio* ('heathen'), see AHU, 'Correspondência dos governadores', Pasta 1B, 12 September 1837.

[42] Lauren Benton, Colonial Law and Difference: Jurisdictional Politics and the Formation of the Colonial State, *Comparative Studies in Society and History*, vol. 41, no. 3 (1999): 586.

[43] Curto, 'Struggling against Enslavement'. See also his Resistência á escravidão na África: o Caso dos escravos fugitivos recapturados em Angola, 1846–1876. *Afro-Ásia*, 33 (2005): 67–86, as well as Silvia Lara, *Campos da violência: escravos e senhores na capitânia de São Vicente, 1750–1808* (São Paulo: Paz e Terra, 1988).

[44] Benton, 'Colonial Law and Difference', 564.

[45] Joseph C. Miller, 'Angola central e sul por volta de 1840', *Estudos Afro-Asiáticos* 32 (1997): 7–54.

[46] See the Trans-Atlantic Slave Trade Database at http://www.slavevoyages.org/tast/database/search.faces. For the suppression of the trade, see Lovejoy, *Transformations in Slavery.*

[47] AHU, Caixa 125, doc. 42, 5 October 1812.

[48] See Couto, 'Regimento de governo subalterno', 289; AHU, 1812, Caixa 125, doc. 22.

[49] Part of the duties of the priest in charge of baptising slaves before embarkation was to brand the bodies. See AHNA, Códice 292, f. 115v, 10 July 1802.

[50] AHNA, Códice 446, ff. 112v–113v, 31 January 1817; AHNA, Códice 446, f. 136v, 12 July 1817. See also AHU, Caixa 132, doc. 30, 31 January 1817.

[51] In *Central Africans, Atlantic Creoles*, Heywood and Thornton analyse the impact of the enslavement of people exposed to Portuguese culture in the Americas. See also Linda Heywood, 'Portuguese into Africa: The Eighteenth Century Central African Background to Atlantic Creole Cultures', in *Central Africans and Cultural Transformations in the American Diaspora*, ed. Linda Heywood (Cambridge: Cambridge University Press, 2002), 91–115; Paul E. Lovejoy

and David Trotman, 'Enslaved Africans and Their Expectations of Slave Life in the Americas: Toward a Reconsideration of Models of "Creolisation"', in *Questioning Creole: Creolisation Discourses in Caribbean Culture*, ed. Verene Shepard and Glen L. Richards (Kingston, Jamaica: Ian Randle, 2002), 67–91.

[52] AHNA, Códice 508, ff. 74–74v, 4 October 1826. For a discussion on the baptism and branding of slaves in Angola, see Antônio Carreira, *Notas sobre o tráfico português de escravos* (Lisbon: Universidade Nova de Lisboa, 1978), 60. For an interesting report on this matter, see AHU, Caixa 40, doc. 25, 21 March 1755.

[53] See AHU, Caixa 83, doc. 41, 13 April 1796.

[54] AHNA, Códice 508, f. 74v, 4 October 1826.

[55] Couto, *Capitães-mores em Angola*, 69, 96.

[56] William G. Clarence-Smith, 'Runaway Slaves and Social Bandits in Southern Angola, 1875–1913', in *Out of the House of Bondage: Runaways, Resistance and Marronage in Africa and the New World*, ed. Gad Heuman (New York: Routledge, 1986), 23–33; Roquinaldo A. Ferreira, 'Escravidão e revoltas de escravos em Angola (1830–1860)', *Afro-Ásia* 21–22 (1998–1999): 9–44; Beatrix Heintze, 'Asiles toujours menacés: fuites d'esclaves en Angola au XVIIe siècle', in *Esclavages: histoire d'une diversité de l'océan Indien à l'Atlantique sud*, ed. Katia de Queiros Mattoso (Paris: L'Harmattan, 1997), 101–122; Aida Freudenthal, 'Os quilombos de Angola no século XIX: a recusa da escravidão', *Estudos Afro-Asiáticos* 32 (1997): 109–134; Curto, 'Butin illégitime'.

[57] Paul E. Lovejoy, 'Identifying Enslaved Africans in the African Diaspora', in *Identity in the Shadow of Slavery* (London: Cassell Academic, 2000), 3.

Legislation on Free Soil in Nineteenth-Century Spain: The Case of the Slave Rufino and Its Consequences (1858–1879)

Aurelia Martín Casares and Margarita García Barranco

This article aims to deepen our knowledge of legislation and social practice relating to the establishment of the principle of free soil in Spain, as considered in the case of a black African slave from the West Indies called Rufino. The court's decision in this case became a fundamental pillar of abolitionist legislation. The immediate precedent had been set by the Royal Order of 29 March 1836, whereby slaves brought to the Peninsula were declared to be free. The authors have analysed the documents arising from the case of Rufino to explore the establishment of free soil in Spain, and the wider European context.

Introduction

Although significant scholarship has been conducted on eighteenth-century iterations of the idea of free soil in the French and English contexts, the nineteenth century and, in particular, Spanish evocations of this legal idea are only beginning to be examined by scholars.[1] Unlike the French, English and Dutch nations, which, to varying degrees, admitted versions of the free soil principle in the early modern period, the kingdoms of the Iberian Peninsula regulated slavery via legal codes from Roman times through to the Middle Ages. Due to their proximity to wider Mediterranean networks, Christians and Muslims alike participated in the enslavement of enemies and the commercial trade of slaves, especially in a period of continuous tensions between the different Iberian kingdoms. Therefore, the Spanish pioneers had no problems in exporting both the practice and the legal regulation of slavery to the New World. There was no need to justify this fact; it had been fully legitimated since antiquity in Iberian territory.

Nonetheless, the supposed 'weakness' of Amerindians, together with the defence of these people by Montesinos and Las Casas and the relative ease of importing slaves from sub-Saharan Africa, turned the African continent into the principal provider of slave labour in Spanish colonies of the Americas. Few advocates challenged the enslavement of sub-Saharan Africans and, of course, the Catholic Church never played an important role in the process of abolition in the eighteenth and nineteenth centuries in Spanish territories.[2]

Spanish legal tradition was based on the idea of the establishment of rights, taken from compilations of post-classical Roman legal tradition expressed in the *Siete Partidas* of the King of Castile, Alfonso X the Wise. Later elaborations, like the *Nueva Recopilación* in 1567 and, much later, the *Novísima Recopilación* of 1805, modified these laws.[3] But it was in medieval legislation that the fundamental questions on servitude were established, principally in the fourth *Partida*. For example, this provision established the limits of owners over their slaves, holding that in cases of proven abuse, the slave should be sold to another owner;[4] this principle had remained essentially unchanged into the nineteenth century and became the justification by which the Royal Order of 1836 declared the principle of free soil in Spain. On the other hand, some medieval clauses, such as enslavement for debt, fell out of use without being directly abolished. This explains the almost total absence of general laws regulating slavery in the great peninsular codes of the Modern Age (1567, 1805) and, at the same time, the presence of specific measures and decrees regulating slavery.[5]

These compilations constitute the sources of Castilian law which, upon the incorporation of the Indies into the Crown of Castile, were exported to the new territories, augmented by specific colonial legislation – *Leyes de Indias* – that addressed the conditions of slaves. The production of unique colonial laws established a distinction between Castilian law and the law of the Indies, which ultimately gave rise to a dichotomy between the metropolitan country and its colonies (which came to be regarded largely as separate entities) over free soil.

This dichotomy became obvious around the 1830s when Spanish abolitionism emerged both as a social movement and in public opinion.[6] By then, slaves hardly existed in the metropole, and efforts were directed towards the suppression of slavery in the overseas territories that Spain still possessed in the West Indies, Cuba and Puerto Rico. The abolitionist question, however, was no triviality, since it implied a profound reform of the whole colonial system, whose wealth and prosperity in those territories had been based on the labour of its slaves.

The case of Rufino touched a raw nerve, forcing awareness of the gap between the political and social systems of the colonies and the supposed spirit of renewal in the metropolis. For these reasons, it is worth studying in detail, since it helps us understand the widespread nature of slave-owning attitudes and their persistence in nineteenth-century Spain.

Sources

The lawsuit which discusses whether the slave Rufino acquired his freedom the moment he arrived in the metropolitan country began in October 1858 and continued for almost four years.[7] Queen Isabel II resolved the case through a Royal Order dictated on 2 August 1861; her decision was published in the *Gaceta de Madrid* on 14 September 1861.

This dossier, comprising more than 300 pages, has four basic parts: (1) the file of the hearing of the case of Rufino forwarded by the Gran Capitán General ('Governor Captain General') of Puerto Rico to the Spanish authorities in 1858; (2) a report sent in 1859 by the Sala de Indias ('Court of the Indies') to Isabel II asking her for a decision with regard to the case; (3) an 1861 report, issued by the Consejo de Estado ('Council of State') in plenary session, to analyse the case of Rufino and advise the Queen on the decisions that should be taken; and (4) the resolution of Isabel II of 1861.

The various manuscripts included in these legal proceedings include an exposition of the facts and consultations to decide whether Rufino automatically became a free person the moment he arrived in the metropolitan country (specifically, on the soil of the Spanish Peninsula or its adjacent islands), or whether, on the contrary, he required a letter of emancipation authorised by his owner for his liberty to be effective – a point on which there was a divergence of opinions between the different authorities. These discrepancies were based on the various interpretations of the Royal Order of 29 March 1836[8], which declared that 'only as free persons, and in no other way' could slaves be brought to Spain, expressly warning those owners who wished to bring back slaves that they were obliged to free them as soon as they reached the Peninsula.

Historical background of Rufino's case

For Spain and its colonial empire, the nineteenth century began in a state of upheaval. The Napoleonic invasion and the exile of King Charles IV between 1810 and 1830 created confusion and a power vacuum which opened the way to independence in the colonies. While mainland Spanish America battled for its independence, the Crown attempted to retain the loyalty of the islands of Cuba and Puerto Rico. These were the last strongholds of empire and the slave system while, at the same time, in the newly independent states, slavery was being progressively abolished.[9]

From 1817, when Spain signed a treaty with England abolishing the transatlantic trade, to 1886, when slavery was definitively abolished in Cuba, both the Peninsula and the remaining colonies faced challenges to the slave system. However, the process of eliminating the slave trade was extremely difficult and can be divided into two stages: the first, between 1820 and 1845, when, despite the slave trade ban, certain authorities preferred to look the other way; and a second stage, between 1840 and 1866, when the debate shifted to the question of slavery itself.[10]

During the eighteenth century, the percentage of enslaved persons in the Peninsula declined, so that by the nineteenth century their numbers were few. But, simultaneously, slavery reached new heights in the American colonies, with the introduction of a plantation economy in the Spanish island colonies of the Caribbean. In Cuba, the sugar revolution began in the 1790s and continued during the whole of the nineteenth century. Around 1861, 25 per cent of the land was under cultivation for sugar cane and, by 1865, the production flooded the North American and Spanish markets (65 per cent of the sugar crop was exported to the United States and 38 per cent to Spain).[11] Meanwhile, in the 20 years following the treaty of 1817 abolishing the slave trade, the Cuban slave population increased by 83.9 per cent and, according to the census taken in 1841, Cuba's 1,000,524 slaves accounted for 43.6 per cent of the total population. This gives us an idea of the strength of the illegal trade in spite of the treaties, as do the official figures: between 1835 and 1864, a total of 20,094 slaves were intercepted as traders attempted to import them illegally.[12] In Puerto Rico, sugar and coffee were also the basis of agricultural exports. In 1846, the island had some 443,000 inhabitants, of which around 51,000 were slaves.[13] Corrupt governments and officials in Cuba and Puerto Rico, along with representation in Parliament of the interests of the slave-owning plantation owners, resulted in the Crown turning a blind eye, particularly as the profits from these illegal activities were vital for the public treasury. The royal family itself received part of the profits from Cuban sugar, since Queen María Cristina de Borbón participated, up until 1860, in various schemes which resulted in La Gran Azucarera ('The Great Sugar Refinery'), the biggest sweet production company in the island.[14] So, what were the factors which brought about a change of attitude in the monarchy leading to the establishment in Spain of the fundamentals of the principle of free soil?

The death of Fernando VII in 1833, leaving his three-year-old daughter Isabel as heir, opened up a troubled period in which the regency was assumed by Queen María Cristina de Borbón. Faced with internal chaos caused by the outbreak of the Carlist Wars, the Queen Regent decided to approach the liberals and foreign powers such as Great Britain and France. In 1835, María Cristina signed a second treaty with England abolishing the slave trade, a gesture which was doubtless intended to win favour with these powers and gain their support.

It is in this context that the Royal Order given by the Queen Regent María Cristina on 29 March 1836 must be understood. This order resulted from a petition for freedom made by three slaves, and it laid the foundations of free soil in Spain. Tomasa Jiménez, María Antonia García and Tomás Bayanza went to court, charging their owners with ill-treatment. According to Spanish law, dating to the medieval *Siete Partidas*, ill-treatment was one of the causes considered legally binding on the owner to sell the slave. However, due to the lack of buyers in the Peninsula, the slaves addressed their petition of liberty to the Queen, who issued the order of 1836. Perhaps the possession of slaves was already not accepted or considered socially disadvantageous by the 1830s in Spain. In fact, the actual text of the Royal Order stresses the need to 'avoid the inconveniences resulting from the presence of serfs [*siervos*] in Europe'.[15]

This order can be directly related to one authorised by Louis-Philippe of France on 29 April 1836, drawn up in similar terms: slaves must be liberated before being brought to France or they would be automatically freed from the moment they disembarked on metropolitan soil.[16] However, while the French order was concise respecting the conditions of access to freedom, the Spanish order was more ambiguous, giving rise to diverse interpretations and arguments, which we shall analyse in the documentation on Rufino.

Nevertheless, in the legal arguments later advanced in the case of Rufino, various precedents were presented which formed the bases of the order of 1836. Thus, the authors of the report of the Court of the Indies argued that slaves who arrived in Spain could not have worse treatment 'than black fugitives from foreign colonies welcomed into the dominions of His Majesty and declared free under the terms of the Royal Decree of 14 April, 1789'.[17] This regulation, dictated by Carlos IV, is based on an earlier one of 20 February 1773, in which his father, Carlos III, granted freedom to all the black African slaves who arrived on the island of Trinidad, which was under Spanish dominion.[18] The 1773 law was promulgated on account of the arrival on the island of various runaway slaves coming from Tobago, then English territory. These were declared free, but it specified that they must serve 'as mercenaries, and not as slaves' in the works and lands of Trinidad. The interests of the Spanish Crown are clear: they took away manual labour from their British competitors, and acquired hands to work for the benefit of their own dominions.

The later 1789 decree was prompted by the escape of a *morena* ('dark' female) slave called Teresa, with her six children (Rafael, León, Carlos, Reny, Yany and Carlota), from the island of Grenada, also under British rule. Teresa had another daughter, Margarita Marizo, a free mulatto living in Trinidad who, in the name of her mother, appealed against 'the inhuman and harsh punishments with which in these cases the English treated their slaves'. On this account, she pleaded that the return of her mother and siblings be suspended; in exchange, they would pay off in three years the sum considered the fair price of all seven. However, Carlos IV decreed that their freedom should be recognised by the fact of being in his dominions and that no money should be paid to their former owner for their ransom, considering them to be free persons. This rule then became applicable to all runaway slaves who went from Grenada to Trinidad.

In 1837, a legal commission on the abolition of slavery was created, whose objective was to prepare a general law reinforcing the dictates of the Royal Order of 1836.[19] However, its report was never discussed in the Spanish Parliament, for fear of the reaction of Cuba and Puerto Rico towards such a law.[20] Spain wished to keep her last colonies at any price. With the treasury exhausted by warfare, the West Indies represented a source of incalculable wealth, due to the generous remittances sent to the metropolitan country. It was preferable to accept the principle of free soil in the Peninsula as a means of prolonging slavery in the colonies and postponing the question of abolition. Moreover, to the political instability in the Peninsula throughout the nineteenth century was added the threat of independence, which the overseas territories used as a means of pressure.

Under the monarchy of Isabel II, Spain avoided the process of abolition carried out elsewhere in Europe. Furthermore, when in 1866 the Minister of Overseas created a commission to analyse the reforms needed for Cuba and Puerto Rico, the members appointed by the government were chosen from among the pro-slavery sectors, rather than among those who favoured a gradual abolition. However, the commission was dissolved without reaching any agreement on the subject.[21] The landowners in the colonies were always ready to defend their union with Spain and fight for the cause of the monarchy, if, in compensation, it was accepted that the system on which they had built their fortunes should remain.

Rufino's case

Accusation from the government of Puerto Rico

The investigation was initiated by the highest authority in Puerto Rico upon reliable and confidential word that a black child of some 10 years called Rufino had arrived in port in the summer of 1857 on the Spanish brigantine *Cid* coming from Mallorca. But we must go back a few years in order to understand Rufino's history.

The presbyter Antonio Vilella, a native of Mallorca, had been a priest for some years in the village of La Isabela, Puerto Rico. On 10 April 1854, he bought Rufino, a black Creole boy of seven, for 150 pesos. He had belonged to Eugenio Alens and was the son of one of his black female slaves. Shortly afterwards, on 19 April, Vilella and his slave left the island to return to Mallorca. Ignoring the Royal Order of 1836, Rufino was not liberated when he arrived in the Balearic Islands and remained as a slave.

Three years later, on 6 May 1857, the presbyter authorised his nephew, Antonio Vilella y Deya, to take Rufino back to Puerto Rico and sell him as a slave. This point is particularly striking since, in specifying Rufino's condition as a slave, the deed implicitly accepted the presbyter's authority to sell Rufino. Yet the notary did not appear to have raised any objections – an indication of the lenient attitude towards colonial slavery in the Peninsula.

On 7 May 1857, the Captain General of the Balearic Islands issued a passport permitting Antonio Vilella y Deya to travel to Puerto Rico accompanied by his *criado* ('servant') Rufino. It is interesting that the passport avoided the word 'slave', designating the black boy as a free servant, which was a deliberate deceit so that the authorities would issue the passport. On 23 July of the same year, the nephew of the presbyter Vilella was in Puerto Rico, where he sold the 'little slave called Rufino' to Fermín Sarabia for 400 pesos. That same day, and before the same notary, the buyer, in his turn, sold Rufino to Francisco Sancho. In both instances, Rufino was declared a slave.

On 29 July 1857, the Governor Captain General of Puerto Rico issued a passport to Francisco Sancho, enabling him to travel to Havana with his *criados* Rufino, Román, José, Inés, Luciana, Bonifacio and Trinidad. Once again, the slave status of these individuals was concealed. But once on the island, Francisco Sancho sold Rufino for 416 2/3 pesos to Joaquín Gómez, an inhabitant of Pinar del Río, together with the six other slaves. This is the action that gave rise to the investigation. By arranging for the sale, Sancho broke his promise to the Captain General of Puerto Rico when he applied for the passport for Cuba – that he would keep Rufino in his service as a free person since he had lived in Spain. Rufino had stayed in Palma de Mallorca since 1854 for more than three years, 'talking and dressing in the Mallorquín dialect and clothes'.

The Captain General of Puerto Rico conveyed the facts to the government of Cuba, and requested officials to discover the whereabouts of the slave Rufino. At the same time, Francisco Sancho was requested to make good to the Puerto Rican authorities the sum for which he had sold the youngster in order to give him a letter of freedom. Sancho, having been notified of this decision, appealed against the order, pointing out the serious damages which, according to him, would result from its enactment. In his defence, Francisco Sancho pointed out that the slave could have claimed and obtained his freedom, but did not do so. He added that a third of the slaves (in Cuba) were in the same situation as Rufino, because they or their parents had been in countries where there was no slavery and where the same situation prevailed as in the Peninsula.[22] Such a declaration would indicate that the Cubans were aware of many foreign legal contests concerning free soil – it seems likely that they would have learned of the 6 March 1857 decision regarding Dred Scott in the United States – but wilfully and explicitly sought to prevent the legal recognition of this principle when slaves returned to Cuba from jurisdictions where slavery had been abolished.

Finally, a report was passed to the advisory body of the Cuban government, which determined that it lacked the authority to decide on the case. It was then passed on to a court of law, which brought a case of *plagio* ('kidnapping') against Francisco Sancho.[23] Furthermore, the *síndico de esclavos* ('trustee for slaves') confirmed the right of this slave to manumission.[24] Clearly, the affair was initiated and pursued by the Puerto Rican authorities, aware of the importance of creating jurisprudence in relation to the law of free soil, in which Rufino himself hardly had a voice.

On this point, it needs to be said that Puerto Rico was at a disadvantage in terms of population and resources compared to Cuba. Production was concentrated on dark sugar, which was less expensive to produce than white. Thus, when the Puerto Rican sugar industry suffered a crisis in the years 1840–1850, the losses caused bankruptcies, and the landowners found it increasingly difficult to pay the high prices demanded for slaves, making it necessary to look for alternatives.[25] Also, after 1845, when illegal slave trading began to be prohibited in earnest, there was a new phenomenon, which has received little scholarly attention – the removal of Puerto Rican slaves to Cuba.[26] In 1854, slave owners complained to the Captain General of Puerto Rico as they thought this practice would ultimately damage agriculture on the island. For his part, the Captain General reminded them of the monarchy's concern to encourage Puerto Rican agriculture, expressed in different orders given in 1815[27] and 1836, which forbade the removal of slaves from Puerto Rico without a royal license. Finally, on 1 April 1854, all removal was prohibited, except for slaves in the personal service of those who took up permanent residence in Cuba and never for slaves who worked the land.

In this context, we can understand why the justices decided to pursue Francisco Sancho and not Vilella, his nephew or the previous buyers of Rufino. The root problem was not so much that Rufino had been sold while knowing that he was free, but that he had been taken from Puerto Rico to Cuba. But now it was necessary to find out under what conditions Rufino had acquired his freedom. Consequently, this first part of the document ends with the consultation with the Queen on whether the spirit of the Royal Order of 1836 was to ordain that all slaves who, like 'the black Rufino', had been on Spanish soil were free in fact and in law. The reply was crucial, since it carried important implications at a socio-political level on the permanence of slavery, the dichotomy between metropolis and colonies, as well as the advance of abolitionist feeling. This explains why pressure was put on the Crown to declare itself on the subject and cease to hold an ambivalent, distant attitude towards a pressing reality.

Report of the Court of the Indies[28]

This report was sent to Queen Isabel II on 30 June 1859. The arguments put forward in favour of Rufino's freedom, and consequently of any slave who set foot on Spanish soil, are reduced to seven points – similar to those put forward by the authorities in Puerto Rico – which are lightly sketched in, with little attempt to explore them in depth. These points are strongly refuted by a lengthy exposition on the relevant legislation and its interpretation. From this it is clear that the magistrates and the public prosecutor of the Court of the Indies accepted the institution of slavery and rejected the principle of free soil in Spain.

The arguments in favour are very poorly developed and constitute a minimal part of the reasoning followed by the Court of the Indies, which was obviously under pressure from planters in Cuba and the need to maintain the status quo of the Cuban–Spanish slave traders. The profits that a plantation-based economy brought to the national treasury doubtless came before humanist ideals, freedom and civilisation. However, it is true that appeal was made to certain regulations and royal warrants which constitute the germ of free soil, or at least could be considered its forerunners. Although Spanish liberals and republicans were committed to the abolitionist cause, until the overthrow of Isabel II in 1868 the question of abolition could not be introduced into state institutions.

The first argument in favour of immediate freedom for Rufino was based on the spirit of the Royal Order of 1836. It specifies that the order obliges the owner to release the slave when he or she goes to a country where slavery is punishable. In addition, it makes clear that once freedom is obtained, this can never be lost or renounced by the person who obtains it. This more extensive interpretation, which goes to the substance of the law, would finally be adopted at a later date, in 1862.

Based on this first argument, the report concludes that in order to acquire freedom by this procedure, a letter of manumission from the owner is not necessary. The absence of such a letter should not be held against the slave. Indeed, citing medieval law, the report asserts that slaves arriving in Spain should not suffer worse conditions 'than fugitives to Moorish lands'.[29] In other words, medieval slave owners lost their rights over any slave who returned to the land where he or she was once free. In the same vein, the authors of the report make reference to the aforementioned Royal Decrees of 20 February 1773 and 14 April 1789.

Another argument in favour of Rufino's case points out that the loss of wealth caused to the owner, having bought the slave in good faith, did not justify denying him freedom because that infringed the law. Lastly, the report emphasises that there were not many slaves in these particular circumstances, and thus the number of manumissions on account of free soil would not be great.

On the other hand, the report's arguments against the liberation of Rufino – some 20 in all – not only call for the exoneration of Francisco Sancho, the dealer who took him to Cuba to sell him, but also offer a substantial justification for the institution of slavery, particularly in the Spanish colonies of the Caribbean. In the first place, the report notes that the Royal Order of 1836 'explicitly' required the manumission of the slave by the owner, a necessary first step which did not occur with Rufino. Therefore, the Court declared that it would be necessary to abolish, amplify or restrict the order of 29 March 1836. Similarly, the report notes that the owner should have been informed of his duty to apply for Rufino's passport, but also excuses this as a bureaucratic oversight (one wonders whether involuntary or calculated). It is also emphasised that the Governor Captain General of Puerto Rico was required by the order of 1836 'to endeavour not to frank passports for slaves for the Peninsula, adding that it was the royal will that those who wished to bring slaves on-board would be obliged to emancipate them later when they reached the Peninsula'. For these reasons, doubts are expressed as to whether Rufino's precise situation is anticipated in the law, and what implications would result from a failure to grant freedom in explicit form. The report notes, with opprobrium, that the freeing of Rufino could lead to abuses and harm, since many slaves would follow his example and claim their freedom.

But perhaps one of the most malicious arguments against Rufino's freedom lies in the assertion that slaves had the right to renounce their freedom 'tacitly and spontaneously' if they preferred to maintain their original condition on returning to the West Indies. Rufino did not claim his freedom and therefore 'renounced' this right – which is all based on the idea that he who obtains a right may renounce it. In consequence, they point out that the provisions of the law should be stricter and more explicit. This argument had been put forward in Francisco Sancho's appeal against his indictment for the sale of Rufino.

The report notes that slave owners in Cuba frequently travelled to countries where slavery did not exist, and even lived there for some time, but when they returned with their slaves, the slaves kept their condition – an argument which was also used by Sancho. Similarly, though laws and abolitionist treaties prohibited the enslavement of free Africans, they did not prevent the slave owner in Puerto Rico from taking them to Cuba or other places, or from selling them. On this point, the Court of the Indies appears to have forgotten the provisions of the Governor Captain General of Puerto Rico in 1854 regarding the movement of slaves from that island to Cuba.

Among the arguments against the manumission of Rufino was that giving him his freedom would upset respectable interests invested in good faith in the buying of slaves. This was followed by arguing for the legitimacy of slavery, emphasising that the rights of slave owners should not be damaged, since the latter constitute 'the principal element of the wealth of the Antilles'. Thus, 'considerations of high interest and policy' advise proceeding with prudence, lest 'excessive philanthropic zeal, however noble and laudable its origin', introduce alarm and distrust by restricting the right to property.

Along the same lines, the report maintains that slavery existed in fact and in law in Puerto Rico and Cuba, hence it is claimed that private property should be respected and sacred, 'as it is with all civilised peoples whatever may constitute possessions'. Clearly, the argument regarding the wealth produced by slavery and the fear of losing economic power was, in fact, at the basis of all the reasoning.

In addition, the opponents of Rufino's freedom referred to a gap in the regulations, since the Royal Order of 1836 had only been conveyed to the Captain General of Puerto Rico, but not to Cuba. This would imply that slaves brought from Cuba to the Peninsula would not have the right to regain their liberty, while those from Puerto Rico would have it as long as their owners authorised their emancipation. Thus, the pro-slavery authors of the report made the most of procedural discrepancies to minimise the enforcement of the 1836 order. The discrepancies between Puerto Rican and Cuban registration of the order reflect distinctive political relationships to slavery in each colony: while in Puerto Rico peaceful progress was being made towards abolition, in Cuba ideas on slavery were much more deeply rooted. Doubtless the socio-economic and demographic differences between Puerto Rico and Cuba played an important role in the way they tackled the question of abolition. From 1840 onwards, the Puerto Ricans were looking for alternatives to slave labour. In addition, between 1830 and 1840, the elite of Puerto Rico went to be educated in Spain, Europe and the United States, where they soaked up political ideas associated with liberalism. And in many cases, on their return, they committed themselves to the struggle for civil liberties and the abolition of slavery.

A second line of argument against the freeing of Rufino was based on the paternalism and goodness with which the Spanish treated their slaves, especially in comparison with slave owners of other European nationalities. The report celebrates the 'kindly nature' of the Spanish colonists, citing the Royal Warrant of 31 May 1789, which gave instructions for the education, treatment and occupations of slaves.[30] If these obligations were not observed, the slave could present a complaint to the trustee for slaves and, upon verification, the owner could be made to sell the slave to another owner. Furthermore, as though this were something extraordinarily humane, it specifies that slaves had rights to property (pointing out that this did not occur in Rome), and that the trustee would restore their goods if their owner took them away. It also says that they could own birds, animals and the vegetables which they grew on their *conuco* (land which the owner conceded close to their *bohio* or 'hut'), on which they could work on Sundays and in the evening 'after finishing their tasks'. It is also pointed out that through these 'paternal customs', they had the 'precious' right of *coartación*, a form of restricted liberty. This was an old Spanish custom, of which we can already find evidence in seventeenth-century Spain[31], but which became consolidated in the Caribbean colonies.[32] The *coartados* could live by their own means as long as they paid their owner an agreed salary proportional to their price. In fact, it was simply another form of making profit from slaves, although it is true that it was understood by some authorities as a step towards freedom.

Furthermore, the Court of the Indies maintained that other European countries, on their preparatory path towards the abolition of slavery, copied benevolent Spanish legislation, which was qualified – with a massive charge of hypocrisy – as 'favourable to the extinction of slavery'. Denmark, England and France were cited among such countries. To all this must be added a final argument on ways to make up for slave labour should abolition definitely come about, since it was considered proven that 'imported' free Chinese were incapable of offering such high yields as slave labour. The authors also claimed that Asians lived marginalised and in isolation, since only males came and neither white nor black women wished to marry them.[33]

Finally, the Court of the Indies agreed to present the consultation before the Queen, to be resolved by her in the fairest and most advisable manner, but clearly showed itself to be against Rufino's liberation and in support of the continuation of slavery in the Spanish West Indies, especially in Cuba. This was undoubtedly because of the profitable economic returns that sub-Saharan slaves represented in the economy of the islands and, in consequence, the vested interests of the metropolitan country.

Report of the Council of State

In the nineteenth century, the Council of State was a consultative body, but it influenced executive power since it reported on certain affairs which the monarchy found perplexing. It was also qualified to participate in matters of legislation – for example, preparing reports for the king or queen if it had been consulted on certain bills.[34] In addition, although the overseas provinces were excluded from representation in Parliament, this only applied to *diputados* ('elected members') and not to the life senators appointed by royalty, allowing some Cuban landowners direct access to peninsular politics. During the reign of Isabel II, there were individuals close to the Queen's intimate circle who defended the interests of these landowners, some of whom became councillors of state.[35]

By the Royal Order of 6 June 1860 sent by the Ministerio de Guerra y de Ultramar ('Ministry of War and Overseas'), the Council of State was asked to report on the case of Rufino and whether the law of 1836 with regard to free soil had been carried out. In contrast to the Court of the Indies, the Council of State in plenary session declared clearly and categorically in favour of Rufino's liberation on 2 July 1861. At that time, the Council of State, like the Court of the Indies, was composed mainly of moderates who were favourable to introducing changes in the Peninsula, emphasising the dichotomy with the colonies in order to maintain, or at least extend as long as possible, the slave system in the West Indies and, incidentally, to try and please other European powers.

The Council explained that the issue which gave rise to the Royal Order of 1836 was the freedom of slaves, from which it must follow that such freedom was acquired from the moment the slaves arrived in the territory of the Peninsula, without need of explicit manumission by the owners. In addition, the Council emphasised that this order aimed to avoid the problems of the presence of slaves in the metropolitan country, bearing in mind that their position in Spain was even more unfavourable than in the United States, and that slavery 'disgusts and harms the social customs of Europe'. On this subject, the Council argued that it was a matter of satisfying public convention and improving the condition of slaves, and thus could not depend on whether owners did or did not fulfil the requirement of manumission, or on whether those affected explicitly claimed their rights, since freedom was not a right that could be renounced.

Here, the Council of State showed its complete agreement with the interpretations of the court of Puerto Rico. It affirmed that freedom was acquired merely by staying in the metropolitan country, whether or not another confirming act existed. By the same token, the Council held that freed persons retained their status even when they returned to a place where slavery was legally authorised. It specified that this applied not only to slaves from Puerto Rico, but also those from Cuba. The Council recommended against opening a new enquiry for Cuba, but ordered the respective authorities of both colonies to publicise the 1836 Royal Order in their official newspapers so that it might be known by all interested persons. Subsequently, on 2 August 1861, a month after the announcement by the Council of State, Queen Isabel II dispatched a resolution to the Governor Captain General of Puerto Rico. A copy of the document was also sent to the Governor General of Cuba in order to put this regulation into practice. It was published in the *Gaceta de Madrid* on 14 September 1861 under the title 'Royal Order Resolves That Slaves from Puerto Rico and Cuba Who Come to Spain with Their Owners Must Be Considered Emancipated'.

Subsequent laws relating to free soil (1862–1879)

The Royal Order of 1861 was amplified by another order, promulgated on 12 December 1862, in which the freedom of the slaves of the Spanish West Indies was extended not only to the case of treading on metropolitan soil, but also to the North of the United States[36] or to countries where slavery did not exist. This law, then, definitively and expansively established the principle of free soil in Spain and its remaining colonies. While the law came very late in relation to other European nations, due to the pressures and unwillingness shown especially by Cuban slave traders, it also innovated liberally in an important way on the English free soil tradition, which applied only to slaves who remained in the metropole.[37]

Subsequently, on 29 September 1866, a Royal Decree was issued which reiterated all of the previous orders.[38] This was most certainly due to the pervasive failure by slaveholders and colonial officials to respect them, which, together with the absence of a general regulatory law, made it necessary to refer to the regulation first applied in 1836.[39]

The Spanish position on free soil in the European context

The debate over free soil in Spain came relatively late compared to other European countries, but paralleled a similar judicial struggle in the United States. In the Spanish case, the weight of economic factors was decisive in slowing down the process of abolition, due to the pressure from the West Indies, where the wealth produced by sugar and coffee was directly linked to slave labour. There was a tacit agreement to keep quiet about the cruel reality of Spanish colonial slavery, balanced with an awareness of anti-slavery liberalism adopted by European neighbours. The signing of treaties in 1817 and 1835 with Great Britain for the abolition of the slave trade was influenced more by material reasons than moral or humanitarian considerations, given the threat of an economic blockade and the possibility of an eventual military attack. This is the context in which the regulation on free soil in the Peninsula can be placed.

As can be inferred from an analysis of Rufino's case, it was better to make concessions on metropolitan soil in order to continue with the subjection of slaves in the West Indies. This would convey an impression of change without, in fact, changing anything, although by 1865, with the abolition of slavery in the United States, all the institutions of power were aware that the abolition of slavery was inevitable. The Glorious Revolution of 1868 speeded up the process of abolition with the drawing up of the *Ley Moret* in 1879, which decreed the *libertad de vientres* ('freedom of the womb'). The government of liberals and republicans brought about the definitive abolition of slavery in Puerto Rico. This revolutionary period also had as a consequence the Ten Years' War in Cuba (1868–1878), the series of later revolts and, in 1886, the final abolition in Cuba, the last bastion of slavery.

Notes

[1] For the case of France, the following can be consulted: Sue Peabody, *'There Are No Slaves in France': The Political Culture of Race and Slavery in the Ancien Régime* (New York: Oxford University Press, 1996); Koufinkana, 'Esclaves et esclavage dans la France d'Ancien Régime' (PhD diss., Université de Toulouse-Le Mirail, 1989); Erick Nöel, *Être noir en France au XVIIIe siècle* (Paris: Tallandier, 2006); Pierre H. Boulle, *Race et esclavage dans la France de l'Ancien Régime* (Paris: Perrin, 2007). For England, see Jerome Nadelhaft, 'The Somersett Case and Slavery: Myth, Reality, and Repercussions', *Journal of Negro History* 51, no. 3 (1966): 199–201; William M. Wiecek, '*Somerset*: Lord Mansfield and the Legitimacy of Slavery in the Anglo-American World', *University of Chicago Law Review* 42, no. 1 (1974): 141–146; Peter Fryer, *Staying Power: The History of Black People in Britain* (London: Pluto Press, 1984); James Oldham, 'New Light on Mansfield and Slavery', *Journal of British Studies* 27, no. 1 (1988): 45–68; William R. Cotter, 'The Somerset Case and the Abolition of Slavery in England', *History* 79, no. 255 (1994): 31–56; Ruth Paley, 'After *Somerset*: Mansfield, Slavery and the Law in England, 1772–1830', in *Law, Crime and English Society, 1660–1830*, ed. Norma Landau (Cambridge: Cambridge University Press, 2002), 165–184; Eliga H. Gould, 'Zones of Violence: The Legal Geography of the British Atlantic, circa 1772', *William and Mary Quarterly* 60, no. 3 (2003): 471–510; Steven M. Wise, *Though the Heavens May Fall: The Landmark Trial That Led to the End of Human Slavery* (London: Pimlico, 2006); George van Cleve, '*Somerset's Case* and Its Antecedents in Imperial Perspective', *Law and History Review* 24, no. 3 (2006): 601–646; Seymour Drescher, *Abolition: A History of Slavery and Antislavery* (Cambridge: Cambridge University Press, 2009). The legislation regarding slavery and its abolition in Spain has been studied in depth by Manuel Lucena Salmoral, 'Leyes para esclavos: el ordenamiento jurídico sobre la condición, tratamiento, defensa y represión de los esclavos en las colonias de la América española', in *Tres grandes cuestiones de la historia de Iberoamérica*, ed. José Andrés-Gállego (Madrid: Fundación Ignacio Larramendi-Mapfre, 2005),; *Los códigos negros de la América española* (Madrid: Universidad de Alcalá de Henares, 1996); *Regulación*

de la esclavitud negra en las colonias de América española (1503–1886): documentos para su estudio (Madrid: Universidad de Alcalá-Universidad de Murcia, 2005). See also Navarro Azcúe, Concepción, *La abolición de la esclavitud negra en la legislación española, 1870–1886* (Madrid: Cultura Hispánica, 1987).

[2] The Church's silence and ambiguous position with respect to slavery and the slave trade are clearly seen in the declaration made by Pope Gregory XVI in 1840. At the height of international pressure to abolish the slave trade, the papacy felt obliged to condemn this practice categorically, although this did not imply greater involvement in the struggle for abolition, slavery continuing to be seen as a means of converting other peoples to Christianity. 'Letras apostólicas del Papa Gregorio XVI contra el tráfico de esclavos', *Gaceta de Madrid*, no. 1879, 1 January 1840.

[3] Alejandro Guzmán, 'Historia de la codificación civil en Iberoamérica', in Andrés-Gallego, *Tres grandes cuestiones*,.

[4] *Partida 4ª*, Law 6, Title 21.

[5] Aurelia Martín-Casares, 'Domestic Service in Spain: Legislation, Gender and Social Practice', in *Domestic Service and the Formation of European Identity: Understanding the Globalization of Domestic Work, 16th–21st Centuries*, ed. Antoinette Fauve-Chamoux (Bern: Peter Lang, 2004),.

[6] Belén Pozuelo Mascaraque, 'Sociedad española y abolicionismo en la segunda mitad del siglo XIX', *Cuadernos de Historia Moderna y Contemporánea* 10 (1988): 71–92.

[7] Archivo Histórico Nacional (Madrid), Ministerio de Ultramar, Legajo 5086, Expediente 16.

[8] 'Real Orden declarando libres los esclavos conducidos a la Península. Madrid, 29 de marzo de 1836', in *Legislación Ultramarina*, ed. Joaquín Rodríguez San Pedro, vol. 2 (Madrid: Imprenta de los Señores Viote, Cubas y Vicente, 1865), 597.

[9] An overall view of this period can be found in the work of Manuel Lucena Salmoral, ed., *Historia de Iberoamérica*, vol. 3, *Historia contemporánea* (Madrid: Cátedra, 1992).

[10] Salmoral, *Regulación de la esclavitud.*

[11] Brian R. Hamnett, 'La regeneración, 1875–1900', in Salmoral, *Historia de Iberoamérica*, 394–401.

[12] A development of the figures, according to different sources and authors, can be found in Salmoral, *Regulación de la esclavitud*, 227–230.

[13] José Manuel García Leduc, *Apuntes para una historia breve de Puerto Rico* (San Juan: Isla Negra, 2002).

[14] José Antonio Piqueras, 'La reina, los esclavos y Cuba', in *Isabel II: los espejos de la reina*, ed. Juan Sinisio Pérez Garzón (Madrid: Marcial Pons, 2004), 91–110.

[15] 'Real Orden declarando libres los esclavos', 597. In Spain, there is a confusion of terms in medieval legislation between *siervo* ('serf') and *esclavo* ('slave'), which, together with the lack of more extensive rulings in the Modern Age, has made for confusion in the actual definitions of slavery and servitude. In the reference manuals to the history of Spanish law most commonly used (*Nueva enciclopedia jurídica española* [1910] and *Nueva enciclopedia jurídica* [1956]), reference is made to the idea of slave, exchanging it with that of serf. And even in dictionaries (for example, Sebastián de Covarrubias, *Tesoro de la lengua castellana o española* [1611]), they are interchangeable terms, a serf being defined as a slave and a slave as a serf or captive.

[16] Sue Peabody, 'La question raciale et le "sol libre de France": l'affaire Furcy', *Annales. Histoire, Sciences Sociales* 64, no. 6 (2009): 1330.

[17] 'Real Cédula ratificando la libertad de los esclavos fugitivos procedentes de otros dominios extranjeros. Madrid, 14 de abril de 1789', in *Cedulario de Buenos Aires*, ed. Ricardo Levene, vol. 1 (La Plata, 1929), 275–278.

[18] 'Real Cédula concediendo la libertad a los esclavos llegados a Trinidad desde colonias extranjeras. El Pardo, 20 de febrero de 1773', in Levene, *Cedulario de Buenos Aires*, 275–276.

[19] 'Dictamen de la comisión de Legislación sobre abolición de la esclavitud', *Gaceta de Madrid*, no. 824, 8 March 1837.

[20] Candelaria Saiz Pastor, 'La esclavitud como problema político en la España del siglo XIX (1833–1868)', in *Esclavitud y derechos humanos: la lucha por la libertad del negro en el siglo XIX*, ed. Francisco de Solano and Agustín Guimerá (Madrid: Consejo Superior de Investigaciones Científicas, 1990), 83–84.

[21] Piqueras, 'La reina', 108.

[22] 'Causa de plagio seguida contra Francisco Sancho', Archivo Histórico Nacional (Madrid), Ministerio de Ultramar, Legajo 5086, Expediente 16.

[23] The offence of *plagio* consisted, among the ancient Romans, of buying a free person and keeping them in slavery. In the Spanish American colonies, it also meant kidnapping someone in order to obtain the ransom for their freedom.

[24] The *síndico de esclavos* was the person chosen by the authorities of the islands of Cuba and Puerto Rico to watch over the interests of slaves.

[25] García Leduc, *Historia breve de Puerto Rico*, 195.

[26] Salmoral, *Regulación de la esclavitud*, 235–236.

[27] The royal warrant of Gracias of 10 August 1815 granted facilities for the development of Puerto Rico, such as the abolition of taxes, authorisation to import agricultural machinery, work tools and slaves, as well as the right to trade with other foreign nations and the immigration of white colonists with slaves. Guillermo A. Baralt, 'Un capítulo de la historia social y económica puertorriqueña, 1800–1880', in *Temas de la historia de Puerto Rico*, ed. Ricardo E. Alegría (San Juan: Centro de Estudios Avanzados de Puerto Rico y el Caribe, 1988), 137–139.

[28] It should be pointed out that between 1834 and 1836 the Crown abolished the old Consejos de España y de Indias ('Council of Spain and the Indies') and established a single Tribunal Supremo de Justicia ('High Court of Justice') composed of various courts, among which was that of the Indies, dedicated to overseas affairs. This reorganisation was designed to reduce abusive arbitrary justice, but up to 1858 not a year went by without the announcement of some regulation on the organisation of the court, which extended the length of time taken to resolve court cases. The report on the case of Rufino was delivered by the magistrates Ramón López Vázquez, José Gamarra y Cambronero, Manuel García de la Botera, Vicente Valor, José Portilla y Gutiérrez and Gabriel Ceruelo de Velasco. The Court of the Indies at that time was politically mainly moderate (though Vicente Valor was a progressive). Braulio Díaz Sampedro, *La politización de la justicia: la designación de los magistrados del Tribunal Supremo (1836–1881)* (Madrid: Dykinson, 2005).

[29] *Partida 7ª*, Law 23, Title 14. This law refers to escaped Muslim slaves during the reign of Alfonso X, and states that if these fled to the north of Africa and later returned of their own will to Christian lands, they would be treated as *moros de paz* ('peaceful Moors') – that is, as free Moors resident in Spain.

[30] *Real Cédula de Su Majestad sobre la educación, trato y ocupaciones de los esclavos en todos sus dominios de Indias e islas Filipinas, bajo las reglas que se expresan* (Madrid: Imprenta de la Viuda de Ibarra, 1789).

[31] Aurelia Martín Casares, *La esclavitud en la Granada del siglo XVI: género, raza y religión* (Granada: Universidad de Granada, 2000), 464–465.

[32] Manuel Lucena Salmoral, 'El derecho de coartación del esclavo en la América española', *Revista de Indias* 59, no. 216 (1999): 357–374; Alejandro de la Fuente, 'Slave Law and Claims-Making in Cuba: The Tannenbaum Debate Revisited', *Law and History Review* 22, no. 2 (2004): 339–369.

[33] The Court of the Indies did not spare its insults and defamatory remarks towards the Chinese, describing them as 'veritable idiots', criminals, alcoholics and opium smokers. The deep-rooted racist thinking towards the Asiatic world is clearly revealed.

[34] María Isabel Cabrera, 'Algunas consideraciones en torno al Consejo de Estado en la Constitución de 1812', *Revista de Estudios Políticos* 93 (1996): 233–241.

[35] Piqueras, 'La reina',.

[36] This is very significant since the American Civil War had recently broken out; this signalled Spanish royal support of the northern unionists and against the secessionist South.

[37] By the time of the 1827 English Admiralty Court decision regarding the slave Grace, any slave who achieved their freedom while resident in England forfeited that free status upon voluntarily returning to a slave colony. Of course, English slavery was entirely abolished by 1838, so the salience of the Grace decision was not significant thereafter.

[38] 'Real Decreto declarando libre al esclavo de Cuba o Puerto Rico al pisar el territorio de la Península o llegar a su zona marítima', *Gaceta de Madrid*, no. 275, 2 October 1866.

[39] That Cuban slaveholders continued to ignore Spanish free soil is evident in a case from 1879 (Puerto Rico had abolished slavery in 1873). The slave Catalina claimed her liberty, and that of her sons José and Federico, before the trustee of slaves in Havana on 25 November 1875. She argued that, in 1841, she embarked for the Peninsula where she lived for 18 months in Málaga, in the service of a lady who failed to keep her promise to free her on her return to Cuba. On the contrary, she was subsequently sold; on her return from the Peninsula she gave birth to her two sons, who were also sold as slaves, one in Havana and the other in Matanzas. But in addition, since 1871 she had become a slave *coartada*, paying the price fixed by her owner for her freedom, which further complicated the case, although it provided multiple arguments for her freedom. Once her case had been examined, King Alfonso XII, in accordance with the report issued by the overseas section of the Council of State, and bearing in mind the orders and decrees issued earlier over the question of free soil, decided that Catalina and her sons should be freed. Similarly, he ordered that the sums paid on account of her *coartación* should be returned to her, and declared that the same principles should be applied to all individuals in a similar situation. 'Real Orden disponiendo que se declare en estado de libertad a la esclava Catalina y sus hijos José y Federico', *Gaceta de Madrid*, no. 108, 18 April 1879.

Index

Note: Page numbers followed by 'n' refer to notes

Abolition (Drescher) 2
abolition (slavery) 56–7, 59, 140; Pennsylvania 83, 84, 91–5
abolitionists: white 89
Académie Française 73
Africa: diverse legal systems 122; freedom suits 117–25; North 69, 79n; violent capture of slaves 122; West Central 117–18, *see also* Angola
African Americans 85; cultural freedom 96; liberty 91; white rioters 96
aid networks 90
Akte van Verlatinge (1581) 53, 63n
Alens, E. 136
Alfandega Grande do Açúcar 106
Algarve, Kingdom of 114n
Allen, R. 94; and Jones, A. 92
Almeida, Captain Manoel Pinto de 124
Alsford, S. 3, 33–43
Alveos Leiria, J. de 123
Amsterdam (Netherlands) 50; freedom 51–2
Anglo-Luso treaties 123
Angola: Christianity 120; enslavement in 117–25; *inquiridor das liberdades* 121; *sertanejos* 125n; slaves' freedom 123–4, *see also* Benguela
Anjou, L. d' 22
Aragon: and France borderland conflicts 21–5
Aranda, E. d' 69–70
Araújo, M.J. de 105
Arnoul, P. 75

Baker, N. 38
Balearic Islands 136
Bankton, Lord Andrew MacDowell 53, 62n
Barclay, D. 95
Barranco, M.G.: and Casares, A.M. 131–43
Barros, V. de 124
Bateson, M. 35
Beceto, P. de 28n
Benguela (Angola): *juizes de fora* 121; law 119–20; legal mechanisms for fighting enslavement (1800–30) 117–25; transatlantic slave trade 119–20
Bishop, J. 42
Black Death (1349) 40
black freedom-seekers 87, 89
black leaders 89
Blackmore, S. 93–4
blacks: West Central Africa 118
Bloch, M.: *Slavery and Serfdom* 29n
Bodin, J.: *Les Six Livres de la République* 26; Parlement of Toulouse 26
Borbón, Queen Maria Cristina de 134
borderland: Aragon and France conflicts 21–5; Pennsylvania anti-slavery 83–98
Bosch, J. van den 57
Bourjon, F.: *Le Droit commun de la France* 75
Bracton 37
Brazil 102–3; independence 106; Recife 51
British Canada 86
Brotherhood of São Benedito 106
Brown, E.B. 89
Burgos, E. 51

Cairns, J. 62n
Canada 88; British 86
Candia: French merchant community 80n
Candido, M. 4, 117–25
Canterbury (England) 40
Cape Verde Islands 108
Caribbean: slave travel 56; Spanish colonies 139
Carlos III, King of Spain 135
Carlos IV, King of Spain 135
Carvalho e Mello, S. de 101
Carvalho Fonseca, D.L. de 117–18
Casares, A.M.: and Barranco, M.G. 131–43
Casas, B. de las 63n
Castle, C. 83, 84
Catalonia 22
Charles IV, King 133
Charles V, Emperor 26

Charles VII, King of France 24
Chester (England) 38
Christianity 120
citizenship rights 58
City, The (Weber) 3
civil rights 62n
Cleve, G. van: *A Slaveholder's Union* 7
Coachman, B. 89
Cobb, T.R.R. 7
Code Noir (1685) 2, 52
coffee 134; *turcs* sale of 78n
Coke, Sir Edward 33
Colbert, J-B. 69
colonies: Roman law 63n
conflicts: borderland 21–5
Congrégation de la Mission 74
Consejos de España de Indias 145n
Cornwall, Earl of 40
Costa, J.J. da 106
Council of State (Spain) 141–2
Court of Conscience (Sorbonne) 73
Court of the Indies (*Sala de Indias*) report (1859) 133, 135, 138–41, 145n
Cuba: abolition 140; landowners 141; slave owners 139; slavery 133–4; and Spanish free soil 146n; sugar revolution 134
cultural spaces 95–7

de Colton, W. 39, 41
DePonceau, P. 95
diaspora: Sephardic 50
Dictionnaire de l'Académie française: *esclace* definition 81n
Domesday Book 41
Douglass, F. 96
Drescher, S. 49; *Abolition* 2
Dunmore, Lord: Proclamation (1775) 87
Dunwich (England) 38
Dutch West Indian colonies 54, 58
Dutch West Indies Trade Company 54

Egerton, D. 98
Ely, Bishop of 41
Emancipation Act (1780) 88
Encyclopédie 75
England 37, 38, 39, 40; Admiralty Court 5, 146n; Domesday Book 41; Earl of Cornwall 40; free air privilege 36; free air tradition 3; free soil 142; freeholdings 35; fugitives 39; *Glanvill* (1188) 33; Lynn ordinance 40; medieval 33–43; Municipal Corporation Act (1835) 33; Peasants' Revolt (1381) 41; ruling class 35; slavery 1; Somerset freedom suit (1772) 52
enslavement: in Angola 117–25; legal mechanisms for fighting in Benguela (1800–30) 117–25; unlawful 120–1

Epstein, S.A. 49
Europe: crises in 21; free soil 142–3; freedom 48; languages 48; multiracial 47–8

Ferreira, R. 122
Fitz-Osbern, W. 36
Fonseca Coutinho, Colonel Anselmo de 105
Forten, F. 85
France 143–4n; *Académie Française* 73; and Aragon borderland conflicts 21–5; asylum 72; *Code Noir* (1685) 2, 52; *Encyclopédie* 75; free soil tradition 12, 25–7; *Golden Crescent* landing 71; juridical suppositions 75–6; Marine Louis Phélypeaux 73; Muslims 71; naval ambitions 69–71; Protestantism 74; slavery 5; spatial judgements 71–2; strategic deference 72–3; theological distinctions 73–5; trans-Mediterranean communities 74, *see also* Marseille; Toulouse
Franco-Tunisian treaty (1604) 68
Frederickson, G. 56
free air 3, 36
free birth law 104
freedom suits: Africa 117–25
freeholdings 35
fugitives 39

Gilles, H. 20
Glanvill 37
Gloucester, Duke of 42
Gloucester (England) 38
Gómez, J. 136
Gonçalves, M. 120
Gorsuch, E. 92
Green, M. 93–4
Gregory XVI, Pope 144n
Grenada 135
Grinberg, K.: and da Silva, C.N. 4, 101–12

Hahn, S. 85
Haiti 5
Henry I, King of England 34
Henry III, King of France 67
Hereford (England) 38
Hondius, D. 3–4, 47–60
Hulsebosch, D. 53, 62n
Hundred Years War (1337–1453) 21

Ignácua, F.J. 124
immigration restrictions: Dutch 54–5
Imposta 52
Institutes coutumières (Loisel) 27
Ipswich (England) 38
Isabel II, Queen of Spain 133, 135
Izarn, A.: and Guillaume/Pierre case study (1203) 15–18

Johnston, W. 92
Jones, A.: and Allen, R. 92
José, D. 110

Kardux, J. 53, 63n
Kingdom of Algarve 114n
Kitty v Chittier (1815) 94

La Faille, G. de 12–13
Lahon, D. 112–13n
languages: Europe 48
law: colonies 63n; development 44n; multiple systems 122; Roman 63n, 121
Law of Good Reason 103
Le Droit commun de la France (Bourjon) 75
Le Hutin, L. 21
legal and social historical practices: in 16th–19th centuries 47–60
Legêne, S. 57
Leges Henrici Primi 34
legislation: on free soil in 19th century Spain 131–43
Leicester (England) 38
Les Six Livres de la République (Bodin) 26
Lisbon (Portugal) 103; confraternities 104; Customs Service 103; slave sailors 106
Liz Teixeira, A.R. de 108
Loisel, A.: *Institutes coutumières* 27
London (England) 37
Louis X, King of France 21
Louis XIV, King of France 69
Lovejoy, P. 125
Lynn ordinance 40

MacDowell, Andrew (Lord Bankton) 53, 62n
Maduro, E. 54
Manique, P. 105
manumissions 114n
Marseille (France): Chamber of Commerce 72; transformation 81n
Marteilhe, J. 74
Martin, L. 90
masters: slavery 90
medieval England 33–43
medieval Tououse 11–27
Mediterranean: exception to France's Free Soil Principle 67–76
Mello e Castro, M. de 105
Mello e Freire, P. de 108, 110
Ministerio de Guerra y de Ultramar 141
Mississippi Territory 88
Montesquieu 103
Montgomery, R. de 36, 38
multiracial Europe 47–8
Mundy, J.H. 13
Municipal Corporation Act (1835) 33
Muslims 67–76

Netherlands: abolition 56–7, 59; Amsterdam 50, 51–2; black Africans 48; Dutch West Indian colonies 54; Dutch West Indies Trade Company 54; freedom in 51; immigration restrictions for slaves 54–5; patronage system 59; Royal Decree 65n; slaves 49–50; slaves' citizenship rights 58; slaves' permission to travel 58
Netherlands, King of 57
New York (US): Vigilance Committee 97
Newman, R. 4, 83–98
North Africa: French slaves in 69, 79n
North America: sugar cane 134, *see also* Canada; United States of America (USA)
Norwich (England) 38, 39
Nueva Recopilación (1567) 132

Oliveira Barbosa, J.A. de 118
Oliveira, J.A. de 124
Ordenações Filipanas 119
Oxford (England) 38

Painter, N.I. 49
Paiva, V.F.N. 108
Paris, S. de 39, 41
Parker, W. 86
patronage 58–9
Patterson, O. 48, 60n
Peabody, S. 3, 11–27; and Grinberg, K. 1–6
Peasants' Revolt (1381) 41
Pennsylvania (US): Abolition Act (1780) 83; abolition policy 84; Abolition Society 84; abolitionist mediators 91–5; African Americans 85; aid networks 90; anti-slavery borderland 83–98; black freedom-seekers 87; borderland 83–98; contested soil 86; freedom 84
Pétion, A. 5
Phélypeaux, Louis (Comte de Pontchartrain) 73
Phillippe III, King of France 20
Phillipsburg Proclamation (1779) 87
Pombal period 107
Portugal: *Alfandega Grande do Açúar* 106; Baía das Vacas 119; Brazilian independence 106; Brotherhood of São Benedito 106; Civil Code (1867) 108; decree (1761) 102–12; eighteenth-century doctrine 107–12; free birth law 104, 107; free soil 104; *inquisidor da liberdade* 120; judicial system 118; language of rights 125; Law of Good Reason 103; legal scholars 109; Order of 12 April (1761) 111; Order of 16 January (1773) 111; Order of March (1810) 110; overseas territories 107; Pombal period legislation 107; Porto 105; Recife conquest 51; *sertanejos* 125n; slave law in late 18th- and early 19th-century 101–12; slavery 101–12; transatlantic slave trade 102;

unlawful enslavement 120–1; vassal status 117–25; vassals 120–1, *see also* Lisbon
post-city slavery 68–9
procurement modes 79n
Protestantism 74
Puerto Rico: abolition 140; accusation against Rufino 136–42; agriculture 137; Captain General 136–7; coffee 134; sugar 134; sugar industry crisis (1840–50) 137
Purvis, R. 96–7

Recife (Brazil): Portuguese conquest 51
Reppes, L. de 42
Reynolds, S. 17
rioters: white 96
Rocha, M.A.C. da 109
Romans: law 63n, 121; slavery 110
Royal Decree 65n
Rufino *see* slave Rufino
Ruggles, D. 97

safe havens: urban medieval England 33–43
sailors: slave 106
Saint Pierre, J-H.B. de 76
Saint-Domingue (Hispaniola) 98
Sancho, F. 136, 137
Sande Magalhães Salema, J. de 110
scholars: twentieth-century 77n
Scotland: civil rights 62n
Scott, D. 137
Scudéry, M. de 70
Sephardic diaspora 50
sertanejos 125n
Sharp, G. 1
Shrewsbury (England) 38
Silva Bruschy, M.M. da 108
Silva, C.N. da: and Grinberg, K. 4, 101–12
Slave and Citizen (Tannenbaum) 2
slave law: in late 18th- and early 19th-century Portugal 101–12
slave Rufino 131–43; arguments against manumission 139; freedom 138; historical background 133–6; Puerto Rico accusation 136–42
slave trade: West Central Africa 117–18
Slaveholder's Union, A (Van Cleve) 7
slavery 5, 49; African Americans 91; black freedom-seekers 89; black leaders 89; citizenship rights 58; Cuba 133–4, 139, 140; eighteenth-century challenges 52–4; manumission 58–9; masters 90; patronage 58–9; Portugal 101–12; post-city 68–9; Romans 110; travel permission 58; vagrancy 58–9; violent capture 122; white abolitionists 89, *see also* abolition (slavery)
Slavery and Serfdom (Bloch) 29n
slaves: freedom through legal means 123–4; humanity of 57; Netherlands 49–50, 58; sailor 106; sub-Saharan origins 77n
Sociéteit van Suriname 55
Solacii, J. 24
Soldani, A. 22
Somerset freedom suit (1772) 52
Soulreys, M. 72
Souza, J.N. de 124
Spain: abolition 135; Caribbean colonies 139; Catalonia 22; *Consejos de España de Indias* 145n; Council of State 141–2; *esclavo* 144n; free soil in Europe 142–3; free soil legislation (19th century) 131–43; legal tradition 132; medieval law 138; Minister of Overseas 135–6; *Ministerio de Guerra y de Ultramar* 141; *Novísma Recopilacón* (1805) 132; *Nueva Recopilación* (1567) 132; Royal Order (1836) 132; Royal Order (1860) 141; Royal Order (1861) 134; Royal Warrant (1789) 140; Royal Warrant of Gracias (1815) 145n; *siervo* 144n; sugar cane 134; *Tribunal Supremo de Justicia* 145n, *see also* Slave Rufino
Spynk, R. 41
Stephens, G. 97
Stewart, M. 96
Still, W. 88
Studia Rosenthaliana 61n
sugar cane 134, 137; Cuba revolution 134
Suriname 55, 57

Tannenbaum, F.: *Slave and Citizen* 2
Toulouse (France): consular court 14; expansion 13; free soil case study 15–18; French crown 19–21; medieval 11–27
transatlantic slave trade: Benguela 119–20; Portugal 102
Treaty of Meaux (1229) 19
Tribunal Supremo de Justicia 145n
turcs: sale of coffee 78n
Turner, N. 98

United States of America (USA): black uses of law in 99n; Civil War 85; inaugural free soil territory 94; New York Vigilance Committee 97; slavery borders 94, *see also* African Americans; Pennsylvania
urban safe havens: for unfree in medieval England 33–43

vagrancy 58–9
vassal status: Portugal 117–25
Veinstein, G. 77n

Vigilance Committee: New York 97
Vilella y Deya, A. 136

Washington, G. 91
Weber, M.: *The City* 3
Weiss, G. 3, 67–76
Welsh Marches 36
West Central Africa: free blacks 118; slave trade 117–18
Wheeler, J. 97
white abolitionists 89
white rioters 96
Whithorne, J. 42
William of Amesbury 38
William I (the Conqueror), King of England 34, 37
Winchester (England) 38
Wycombe (England) 38

Zeeland 53

For Product Safety Concerns and Information please contact our EU representative GPSR@taylorandfrancis.com Taylor & Francis Verlag GmbH, Kaufingerstraße 24, 80331 München, Germany

Batch number: 10726294

Printed by Printforce, the Netherlands